Sexuality and the Erotic in the Fiction of Joseph Conrad

CONTINUUM LITERARY STUDIES SERIES

Also available in the series

Sexuality and the Erotic in the Fiction of Joseph Conrad

Jeremy Hawthorn

continuum

Continuum

The Tower Building
11 York Road
London
SE1 7NX

80 Maiden Lane
Suite 704
New York
NY 10038

British Library Cataloguing-in-Publication Data
A catalogue record for this book is available from the British Library.

ISBN: HB: 0-8264-9527-3
9780826495273

Library of Congress Cataloging-in-Publication Data
A catalog record for this book is available from the Library of Congress

Typeset by the author
Printed and bound in Great Britain by Biddles Ltd, King's Lynn, Norfolk

Contents

Acknowledgements

The author and publisher thank the following for permission to reproduce copyright material.

1. The Trustees of the Joseph Conrad Estate for permission to reproduce extracts from Joseph Conrad's manuscript of *Under Western Eyes* (p. 147) and *The Shadow-Line* (p. 132).

2. Editions Rodopi BV, Amsterdam, for permission to reproduce in amended form the article 'Conrad and the Erotic: "A Smile of Fortune" and "The Planter of Malata"', published in Daphna Erdinast-Vulcan, Allan H. Simmons and J.H. Stape (eds), *Joseph Conrad: The Short Fiction*. Amsterdam: Rodopi, 2004, pp 111–41. This material forms part of Chapter 3.

3. Cambridge University Press, Professor S.W. Reid and Mrs Barbara M. Harkness, for permission to reproduce a number of extracts from Joseph Conrad, *The Secret Agent*, Bruce Harkness and S.W. Reid (eds), The Cambridge Edition of the Works of Joseph Conrad, 1990.

Chapter 2 is an expanded and amended version of 'Reading and writhing: the exotic and the erotic in Joseph Conrad's *An Outcast of the Islands*', published in Charles Armstrong and Øyunn Hestetunn (eds), *Postcolonial Dislocations: Travel, History, and the Ironies of Narrative*. Oslo: Novus Forlag, 2006.

I owe warm thanks to John Stape, Jakob Lothe, Gordon Williams, Stephen Donovan, Allan Simmons, Daphna Erdinast-Vulcan, Paul Goring, Ruth Sherry, Domhnall Mitchell, Gail Fincham and many others for comments, conversations, and constructive criticisms. All errors and inadequacies in the book are of course my responsibility alone.

This book was started during a period of research leave granted by my employer, the Faculty of Arts of the Norwegian University of Science and Technology, Trondheim. I acknowledge with gratitude the generous provision of research leave offered by the faculty. The book was completed while I was working as a member of the 'Narrative Theory and Analysis' team led by Professor Jakob Lothe at the Centre for Advanced Studies, Oslo, in the academic year 2005–6. I would like to thank Professor Lothe, my fellow team members, the staff at the Centre, and the Centre's leader Professor Willy Østreng, for their friendly, efficient, and collegial support and encouragement during a most productive year.

My especial thanks go to my wife, Bjørg. The questions she has asked me during her work translating three of Conrad's novels have reminded me that however much critics talk about close reading, no-one reads more carefully than a good translator. I thank her for her unfailing support and good humour, and a shared dislike of housework that has left space for more pleasurable and useful occupations for both of us.

A Note on Presentation

Conrad is very fond of ellipses. In order to distinguish between Conrad's ellipses and ellipses indicating that I have omitted a section from a quotation, all such omissions are marked by ellipses enclosed in square brackets – thus [...]. However where I quote from critics who have marked their own omissions from quotations by means of a standard ellipsis, I have reproduced their own presentation without alteration.

In works such as *Heart of Darkness* where the bulk of the narrative is ostensibly delivered orally by a personified narrator to a group of listeners, standard editions indicate this by placing a quotation mark at the start of each narrated paragraph. I have retained such quotation marks when citing from these editions, although this may sometimes appear odd as a citation will include an opening, but not a closing, quotation mark.

References to letters included in volumes of *The Collected Letters of Joseph Conrad* (Cambridge University Press, 1983–) are indicated thus: (CL2), (CL3), etc. Full bibliographic details are provided in the bibliography at the end of the book. This bibliography also contains information about all sources from which quotations are taken.

For my wife, Bjørg
– who will dust

Introduction

Conrad and sexuality

'Wouldn't it be easier to write about Henry James and water-skiing?' The response of friends and colleagues to the news that I have been writing a book about the sexual and the erotic in Joseph Conrad's fiction has not generally been that this is a subject crying out to be tackled. Such a view of Conrad's fiction is, I have come to believe, part of a self-confirming circle of assumptions and non-discoveries. The surest way to fail to discover something in a writer's work is to start off with the conviction that it is not there – or alternatively, that if it is there, it is not worth investigating.

In more serious responses, a general attitude of scepticism towards the project can be sub-divided into three related contentions. First there is the claim that Conrad the man was about as uninterested in sexuality and the erotic as it is possible for any mature male not technically a eunuch to be, and that this biographical truth is reflected or refracted in various ways in his fiction. Second, while it may be conceded that Conrad did indeed attempt to write about sexuality and the erotic, the concession is followed by an insistence that the attempt had an invariably negative effect upon his art. And third there is the counter-assertion that Conrad is essentially a political novelist whose art is important only when it engages with the public and the impersonal, and that it becomes trivial and embarrassing when it investigates the complexity of individual feelings and relationships, especially those concerned with the passionate and the erotic.

So far as the first of these views is concerned, Zdzisław Najder's justly admired and authoritative biography of Conrad offers a useful starting point. Discussing the evidence that Conrad had an affair with the much younger American Jane Anderson in the early years of the First World War, Najder reports on his discussion of the sexual side of Conrad's life with the author's fellow countryman Jósef Retinger – who on his own account saw Conrad as a rival for the affections of Jane Anderson.

Retinger, who knew quite a lot about the whole affair, denied that there was a romance between Conrad and Jane. But he denied it in a way that prompts us to ask what Conrad's sex life was like. Retinger said that Conrad had not previously known women like Jane but that he had had various 'affaires louches' [suspect, shady affairs]; he refused to comment further, taking refuge behind the statement that 'gentlemen are discreet.' And Conrad himself on the subject of sex was so exceptionally discreet in an old-world way that his reticence has occasionally provoked suspicion: was the erotic side of life closed to him entirely? Did he suffer from some abnormality or deeply rooted inhibition? Borys, when asked, burst out laughing. 'What a nonsense,' he said, and made a promising start: 'My father and I – we were always quite frank to each other about our relations with women.' But he did not want to say anything more.

In spite of the reaction of Borys (Conrad's older son), Najder pursues the suspicion provoked by Retinger's denial.

Perhaps Conrad was simply and consistently a faithful husband, which in view of Jessie's health would have condemned him to long years of celibacy or semicelibacy. However, not only Retinger's and Borys's veiled hints and Ford's romanticized gossip counsel skepticism. [...] Along with the fact that Conrad felt very much at ease in cabarets and nightclubs – all this is in keeping with the stereotype of the husband who now and again amuses himself on the side; but we lack clear evidence. At any rate it seems that Eros did not play an important part in Conrad's spiritual life. It is impossible to tell why; we know too little of that aspect of his life even to attempt to answer the question whether this resulted from some traits of Conrad's personality or was due to some enforced separation of his emotional and sexual life, or was simply a consequence of depression, which usually lowers sexual potency and desire. (1983, 420)

These comments, though limited, are not without their own internal contradictions. If it is indeed the case that we know little or nothing about the erotic side of Conrad's life then it is hard to justify the view that it did not exist and that Eros did not play an important part in the novelist's spiritual life. And if Conrad did have various 'affaires louches' then this does not suggest that he suffered from a radically lowered sexual potency or sexual desire. Retinger, incidentally, used a similar formulation when asked by Ian Watt whether Conrad had had any extramarital affairs. In an article written jointly with John Halvorson Watt reports that 'Retinger, though unwillingly, did finally concede that there were some, but described them contemptuously, in French, as "*de louches passes*"' (Halvorson and Watt 1991, 69). The tendency to slip into French when dealing with embarrassing and especially sexual topics should be noted: it is one that, as we will see, was shared by Conrad himself.

While many commentators have been rather too hasty in drawing the conclusion that 'the erotic side of life', as Najder terms it, was entirely closed to Conrad, sometimes the haste goes in the opposite direction. In the same article by John Halvorson and Ian Watt (one also concerned with Conrad's relationship with Jane Anderson), the two authors note in passing that there 'is one other minor piece of evidence. Graham Greene wrote in a review of Jessie's memoirs that Conrad was "unfaithful to her [Jessie] in his old age"' (71). However Greene's review does not offer any independent evidence for such unfaithfulness; it merely asserts that Jessie Conrad's second memoir of her husband reports such infidelity (Greene 1969, 186). And in spite of Greene's dogmatic statement, Jessie's account, while confirming that Conrad had something to hide with regard to his relationship with Jane Anderson, does not specify whether this was a fully consummated sexual liaison or merely a little indiscreet flirting. Greene's review is utterly unsympathetic to Jessie, and indulges its author's misogyny to excess.

It is true that there is evidence that Conrad's sexual life had its peculiarities – but then who, nowadays, would claim that theirs did not? There is for example the much-quoted evidence of Conrad's proposal to his wife-to-be Jessie, and of the oddities of his honeymoon, reported by Jessie herself. In the first of two books she published about her husband after his death, Jessie refers to Conrad's 'strange proposal of marriage', noting that he 'had begun by announcing that he had not very long to live and no intention of having children; but such as his life was (his shrug was very characteristic), he thought we might spend a few happy years together' (1926, 105).

Martin Bock reports that all of Conrad's important psychoanalytical biographers 'concur with [Bernard C.] Meyer's influential assumption that Conrad may have been "disturbed by the sexual aspects of marriage"' (2002, 81), and Jessie's report that on their wedding night her husband insisted on writing and posting their wedding announcements up to two o'clock in the morning (1935, 20) does nothing to dispel this view. But what a man thinks before his wedding and on his wedding night does not necessarily fix his attitudes towards sexuality for life. After all, Conrad announced to Jessie that he did not expect to live long and that they would have no children, but he lived a reasonably long life and had two sons.

There is, moreover, very ample evidence to substantiate the claim made by Conrad's friend and protégé Richard Curle in his Introduction to Jessie Conrad's first memoir of her husband.

Between them there was a deep bond of affection, and Conrad's anxiety as to his wife's health and as to her future when he should be gone was touching to witness. Often and often he had discussed these things with me into the small hours of the morning, and I know that they weighed heavily upon him. But if both of them worried over one another in secret, when they were together they would often talk in a vein of humorous and tender chaff, which was, in its own way, as sure a sign of their mutual devotion. (Jessie Conrad 1926, vii)

The evidence is to be found both in Conrad's letters to Jessie and also in the accounts of their relationship provided by others. Jósef Retinger, writing unlike Curle after the death of Jessie Conrad, provides a summarizing view of the Conrads' marriage that, for all that he is not the most reliable of reporters, bears a strong ring of truth.

> Conrad, although at time unmanageable in his behaviour towards her, was nevertheless devotedly attached to his wife. He rarely left her alone; she was his companion on all his travels, even on most of his short trips to London, and when once during the War he was absent for a fortnight or so inspecting 'Q' ships at the invitation of the Admiralty, he wrote to her every day. In moments of tenderness he used to call her '*Chica*,' which in Spanish means 'little girl,' probably recalling his adventurous youth in Spain and Mexico. (1941, 61)

In both of her published memoirs Jessie repeats the claim that her husband was 'a son as well as a husband' (1926, 14) to her, and in her first memoir she writes:

> There was one thing I felt certain of, and that was that we were starting on our joint adventure with a very real and profound affection between us, and with trust in each other. And I may say that already on my part there was, even then, a great deal of maternal feeling for that lonely man who had hardly known anything of a mother's care, and had no experience of any sort of home life. (1926, 24–5)

In her second memoir, Jessie adds a comment that invites interpretation but that provides no help in setting bounds to that activity – although the comment on Conrad's fidelity should be noted.

> I entered into that compact [her marriage, J.H.] with the full determination that I would leave my husband virtually as free as if no symbol of a wedding-ring had passed between us. It came as a kind of intuition that this man would find any demand upon his liberty both irksome and galling, and because of my understanding I was able to hold his interest and fidelity to the end. (1935, 17)

Jessie Conrad's accounts do however confirm that the Conrad household was never a place of prudishness – consider the following anecdote from her second memoir.

> Joseph Conrad told me of a rather amusing incident that happened during one voyage. In this case two elderly and modest spinsters had carelessly hung a bag of soiled linen too near the cabin lamp, with the result that it caught

fire. They were greatly incensed when too [? = two] smooth-faced middies were ordered into the privacy of their cabin to extinguish the flames. The two ladies reproached the officer of the watch bitterly. If he had been unable himself to be the intruder, in deference to their sex an older person should have been sent instead of these beardless youths. My husband was very fond of telling this story against the mock-modesty of my sex. I always laughed because he invariably concluded with one about the tactful plumber who, finding himself in a bathroom in which a lady was taking her bath, had the presence of mind to retire with a 'I beg your pardon, *sir*.' (1935, 17)

Anecdotes such as this suggest that the picture of the author as a repressed Victorian unable to be open about sexuality and the erotic does not square with the evidence.

In the light of the evidence from Jessie's two memoirs of her husband, from Conrad's letters to her, and from the reports of third parties who observed them together, Robert Lange's assertion that the 'special kind of affection' that Conrad 'sought and could use was not supplied by his wife or children, but primarily from four young male writers: Ford Madox Ford, Richard Curle, Stephen Crane, and R. B. Cunninghame Graham' (1992, 59) just does not hold water. Lange further claims that '[w]hat is abundantly clear ... is that Conrad invested his passion in his work and his younger, literary friends, giving, respectively, to his wife and young Boris [sic] the interest more appropriately given to a faithful servant, or a frisky puppy' (60). Well, I have to say that this is far from abundantly clear to me.

Martin Bock's very impressive study *Joseph Conrad and Psychological Medicine* (2002) provides detailed information about Conrad's history of neurasthenia and mental breakdowns, and of the ways in which then-current theories concerning mental illness interpenetrated with theories of such matters as racial difference and 'degeneration' – and with a belief that the mentally ill should not reproduce. However Bock too proceeds to draw some conclusions that surely go beyond the evidence when he claims that because 'Conrad did not wish to pass on his nervousness or to accelerate the process of his own possible degeneration', 'he married a healthy typist, planned no children, and left England with its apparently rising number of lunatics' (2002, 82).

Although the comments quoted above from Zdzisław Najder's biography of Conrad were made in a book published in 1983, they can be said to represent an attitude that predates them by many years, an attitude, moreover, that in many cases fails to distinguish Conrad's life from his fiction. Writing about Conrad in 1923, the year before his death, his fellow novelist Virginia Woolf – who was herself a great admirer of Conrad's fiction – famously had 'Penelope' (one of the two fictional discutants in her 'Mr Conrad: a conversation'), claim that '[Conrad] is composed of two people who have nothing whatever in common. He is your sea captain, simple, faithful, obscure; and he is Marlow, subtle, psychological, loquacious'. She goes on to make an interesting comparison.

> The men he loves are reserved for death in the bosom of the sea. Their elegy is Milton's 'Nothing is here to wail ... nothing but what may quiet us in a death so noble' – an elegy which you could never possibly speak over the body of any of Henry James's characters, whose intimacies have been personal – with each other. (Woolf 1966, 311)

The syntax of the final sentence is not easy to trace, but one senses immediately an aura of (among other things) sexual suggestiveness as soon as the name of James is mentioned, an aura that is lacking when the characters of the two people who compose Mr Conrad are sketched in. It is striking that a passage that begins with the words 'The men he loves' can be so lacking in any sexual implications. Even such an acute observer of sexual *frissons* as Woolf seems to see Conrad's fictional (and, doubtless, biographical) world as one devoid of sexual secrets and complex sexualities. Although Conrad is composed of two men, they seem equally lacking so far as a sexual life is concerned. It is as if we are being presented with a form of pseudo-logical reasoning along the following lines:

- Conrad's fiction is, essentially, about men and the world of men;
- Conrad is not homosexual and he does not write about homosexual desire;
- therefore sexuality does not play a significant rôle in his fiction.

   The second of the three views that I mention at the start of this Introduction was stated in its clearest – and most widely influential – form by Thomas C. Moser in his 1957 study *Joseph Conrad: Achievement and Decline*. Moser's diagnosis of what he considers a debilitating sickness in Conrad's fiction also involves a clear thesis: 'love' is 'the lowest common denominator of the apprentice work [...] of the inferior short novels [...] of the weak portions of "Heart of Darkness," *Lord Jim*, and *Nostromo*'. It also 'dominates the later period, where it is central to six of the seven novels' (3–4). Moser concludes that the 'sympathetic treatment of love between a white man and a woman is not congenial to the early Conrad's creativity' (65).
   Moser also blames Conrad's attempt to write about love (not sexuality), for inadequacies in the better work and for the period of his artistic 'decline'. But his account of the relationship between love and sexuality in Conrad – between, say, the romantic and the erotic – is not always as clear as one might wish. Discussing 'The Return' (1898), for example, which he characterizes as 'a bad piece of writing', he writes that it provides a *'locus classicus* for the near paralysis of Conrad's creativity when dealing with a sexual subject', and he concludes that 'it is significant that Conrad's one extended study of a sexual

subject should center in an inadequate male who sees female sexuality as an inescapable menace' (1957, 77). In contrast, however, and somewhat confusingly, he enthusiastically describes 'A Smile of Fortune' (1911) as 'a first-rate story of female sexuality and male impotence' (98). Once again we can note the revealing presence of a central contradiction in the case being made.

That critics still engage with Moser's thesis says something about its importance, but it has had unfortunate after-effects. Susan Jones's complaint that 'the neglect of Conrad's interest in writing for and about women has been perpetuated by a bifurcation of his work into eras of decline and achievement' (1999, 222) is representative of the misgivings many recent critics have expressed about the legacy of Moser's argument. Moser's book has also contributed to the unfortunate view that Conrad could not write well about sexuality or the erotic. At one point Moser states baldly that 'Conrad differs radically from other great modern novelists in his lack of understanding, in his almost belligerent lack of genuine, dramatic interest in sexual problems' (1957, 128). One might wonder how someone with such a 'belligerent' lack of interest in sexual problems, and whose creativity suffered near paralysis when dealing with sexuality, could have written a first-rate story of female sexuality and male impotence – just when his decline was supposedly imminent.

Conrad and the erotic

Conrad's work is not naturally associated with the 'erotic'. As far as I can ascertain the word itself occurs only once in his writings, in Part Two, Chapter 3 of *Chance* (1913): Captain Anthony is the son of 'a delicate erotic poet of a markedly refined and autocratic temperament' (309). The mention is not without interest, given the link that it suggests between the erotic and the exercise of patriarchal power. A concern with the erotic does not, of course, depend on use of the word.

Both in his lifetime and after his death, Conrad, as Susan Jones points out in her *Conrad and Women*, has often been thought of as a writer whose male characters perform centre-stage while his female ones are present on the periphery or in the wings. There is a widespread view that his romantic and potentially erotic scenes too often slide into the melodramatic, and for modern readers few things are less erotic than melodrama. We can summarize another commonly held view of Conrad's fiction as follows. In it, moments of passion or sexual excitement are rare, and are often presented in such a way as to minimize or remove any evocation of the erotic in the reader. Sometimes they are combined with conventionalized or clichéd depictions of the 'exotic' as in *An Outcast of the Islands* or 'The Lagoon'. At other times they occur 'offstage', recalled only through signs and tokens as in the glimpse of Hollis's mementoes in 'Karain'. Alternatively they may be presented in distanced, even darkly humorous ways, as in the mutual attraction between Falk and Hermann's niece in 'Falk'. And where another writer might have evoked a sense of sexual attraction between male and female characters (such as Jim and Jewel in *Lord Jim*), Conrad displays no such interest.

It is, doubtless, partly because it has been assumed that 'the erotic side of life', as Najder puts it, was closed to Conrad the man, that his fiction has been read with the assumption and – importantly – the expectation, that it will have little to do with sex and the erotic. Such an approach to the fiction generates readings that either exclude or omit any reference to sex and the erotic, or alternatively readings that conclude that Conrad could not write well about sex and the erotic. These readings can then be used to close a circular argument and to underwrite the initial assumption that the erotic side of life was closed to the author. The history of the reception of Conrad's fiction – both its critical reception and too its reception by 'common readers' – is thus quite unlike that of other major modernist novelists. This is not the way in which the fiction of James, Forster, Joyce, Lawrence and Woolf has been read. Nor is it the way in which the fiction of modernists writing in languages other than English – such as Knut Hamsun and Franz Kafka – has been read.

I mentioned above a 'third view' of Conrad – that he is essentially a political novelist whose art is important only when it engages with the public and the impersonal, and not when it investigates the complexity of individual feelings and relationships, especially those concerned with the passionate and the erotic. This is a view that defines politics in a manner reminiscent of a pre-feminist, pre-sexual politics era in which 'politics' excludes the private, the emotional, and to a large extent too the female. From such a perspective the short story 'The Informer' is a political work, whereas the rather longer work 'The Return' is not. The former details the infiltration of a group of anarchists by a police spy, while the latter depicts the breakup of a middle-class marriage that occurs when a wife who leaves her husband but then changes her mind and returns home is unable to prevent him from reading the letter she has left him. And yet both tales trace the complexities of a heterosexual relationship not just through the private emotions of characters but also by tracing these characters' ideological and political commitments, commitments that belong as much to the public sphere as to the private or domestic world. The truth is that it is very difficult to find in Conrad's fiction *any* investigation into the intricacies of a human relationship that does not involve a parallel concern with the complexities of the public world of politics in its most comprehensive sense. In like manner it is very hard to find in the fiction any investigation of such matters as imperialism and colonialism, terrorism, international relations and the suffrage movement that does not explore the ways in which such matters are both constructed from, and impact back on, the emotional and even erotic lives of individual human beings. Chapter Three of Conrad's first novel *Almayer's Folly* (1895) opens with the following sentence: 'The deliberations conducted in London have a far reaching importance; and so, the decision issued from the fog-veiled offices of the Borneo Co. darkened for Almayer the brilliant sunshine of the Tropics and added another drop of bitterness to the cup of his disenchantments' (28). Here, in miniature and right at the start of Conrad's writing career, is evidence of his constant need to see the human world as a single system, a system composed it is true of innumerable links, transitions and transformations, but one in which there is no hermetically sealed domain of the private or the individual. An Englishman at this time might believe that his home was his castle, but Conrad the Pole knew from bitter cultural experience that homes and castles could be occupied by others.

***

It is time that this circle of self-confirming but essentially incomplete or wrong attitudes and assumptions is broken. Even in terms of a crude and unsatisfactory conception of 'content', Conrad's fiction engages fully with the sexual and the erotic. His fiction makes unambiguous reference to such matters as passion and lust, sadism and masochism, homosexuality, prostitution and contraception. In his short fiction 'Falk' explicit parallels are repeatedly drawn between the need for food and the need to mate. 'He [Falk] was hungry for the girl, terribly hungry, as he had been terribly hungry for food'. The narrator pursues this similarity. 'Don't be shocked if I declare that in my belief it was the same need, the same pain, the same torture' (224). Just as the starving Falk has eaten human flesh rather than die, so too his desire for Hermann's niece imposes itself on him and will not be restrained by social taboo or cultural convention. But Conrad is careful to make it clear that what Falk experiences for the girl is not mere sexual desire, not just lust.

> He wanted that girl, and the utmost that can be said for him was that he wanted that particular girl alone. I think I saw then the obscure beginning, the seed germinating in the soil of an unconscious need, the first shoot of that tree bearing now for a mature mankind the flower and the fruit, the infinite gradation in shades and in flavour of our discriminating love. (224)

'Falk' makes continued reference to the survival of the primitive in modern humankind, suggesting that primitive desires for food and for a mate exist in more 'mature' and 'discriminating' forms in ourselves. In his own fiction Conrad repeatedly traces examples taken from this infinite gradation in the shades and flavour of our discriminating love, and reveals not just their biological sources but also their social and cultural particularities. And this is, surely, precisely what the erotic consists in: the biological sexual drive expressed in and mediated through the socially and culturally specific.

It is also time to reject the view that Conrad was so unsympathetic to, and ignorant about, women, that his fiction is incapable of portraying relations between the sexes in a satisfactory manner. In an important article, entitled 'Beyond gender: deconstructions of masculinity and femininity from "Karain" to *Under Western Eyes*' (2005), Carola M. Kaplan asserts a powerful and convincing counter-case to the prevailing orthodoxy. Arguing that '[t]he time has come to counter the myth of Conrad's misogyny' she rejects the notion that 'Conrad knew women little and liked them less' and insists that 'from his earliest fiction, Conrad was centrally concerned with issues of gender and sexuality and that his treatment of these issues grew more unconventional and more iconoclastic over time' (267).

It is perhaps even more important to insist that sexuality is not just part of the 'background' of Conrad's fictions, but is typically woven in to the thematic centres of his narratives. Like Kaplan, a few of Conrad's most perceptive recent critics have recognized that Conrad's fictions engage with the sexual and the erotic not as areas of human life that are hermetically sealed off from wider, public concerns, but as parts of human experience that impinge upon – and that are influenced by – these same public concerns. Let me give just one representative example at this stage of my argument. It has long been recognized that there are oblique but unambiguous references to contraception in *The Secret Agent*. Contraception was an 'issue' about which Conrad had opinions: Jósef Retinger reports that the novelist 'never ceased to repeat that the easiest solution [to "social problems"] could be found in what he called the French system of two children per family and in birth control' (1941, 65) – a view that, given Conrad's Catholic upbringing, certainly testifies to his open-mindedness about matters concerning socio-sexual matters.

In his fiction, however, Conrad typically uses issues from contemporary life not just for the purpose of social verisimilitude but as elements integrated into a more comprehensive and more probing artistic vision, and this is also true of the way in which allusions to contraception work in *The Secret Agent*. In a carefully argued article, Thomas Jackson Rice claims that the motif of 'protection' and contraception is much more deeply embedded in Conrad's novel than as a mere piece of background detail. He contends that Conrad effectively depicts his secret agent Adolf Verloc 'as a kind of human condom, a "mortal envelope" for protection who "exercise[s] his vocation as a protector of society" by acting as a spy amongst revolutionaries, a man who has prophylactically "prevented" terrorist plots from reaching their fulfillment and thus thwarted the contagion of the pestilential anarchists' (2004, 222). Not only is this a shrewd and convincing comment on *The Secret Agent*, it also serves to show how Conrad takes a pattern from the realm of the private ('protection' leading to sterility, non-communication, and death) and traces its outlines in the public sphere. This is not, I insist, merely the development of a literary metaphor: it involves tracing the interpenetration of patterns of private and public life in the extra-literary world.

Although he did not and probably could not have used terms such as sadism and masochism, Conrad's fiction makes it abundantly clear that he understood the conditions, drives, and experiences that these words signify. In like manner, although he would doubtless not have been familiar with the present-day, post-Freudian meaning of terms such as 'sublimation' and 'displacement', Conrad's depiction of, for example, Charles Gould's marital unfaithfulness with his mistress the silver mine, makes it palpable that he was familiar with the conditions that these terms describe.

Conrad's novels and short stories also provide ample evidence that he understood what sexual passion was, and what it felt like to the man or woman in its grip, although Conrad the man seems to have been unwilling to talk about this. Jósef Retinger, in his 1941 memoir *Conrad and his Contemporaries*, reports that 'Once I questioned him about the love affairs of his youth, which he must have had, and pointed out that in his writings the love motif played no fundamental part. Conrad assented with a sharp nod – and thus the conversation ended' (1941, 65). And yet Retinger's claim regarding the part played by the 'love motif' in Conrad's work – and Conrad's claimed assent – should not go uncontested. There is, indeed, hardly a work of Conrad's in which sexual desire does not play a key rôle in the development of its plot, whether this desire is overt and recognized by the person who experiences it, as for example with the triangle of Taminah, Nina and Dain Maroola in *Almayer's Folly*, Willems and Aïssa in *An Outcast of the Islands*, and Renouard in 'The Planter of Malata', or merely hinted at by the narrative and only half-recognized by the character as for example with the Marlow of *Lord Jim*, the captain-narrator of 'The Secret Sharer', and the teacher of languages in *Under Western Eyes*. One of the simpler tasks that I have set myself in the pages that follow is just that of establishing how pervasive – how near-universal – the sexual and the erotic are in the pages of Conrad's fiction.

There is what one can term a minority tradition within Conrad studies that has, in different ways, recognized the importance of the sexual and the erotic to an understanding of Conrad and his work. Along with the article by Carola M. Kaplan that I mention above, studies such as Bernard C. Meyer's *Joseph Conrad: A Psychoanalytic Biography* (1967), Geoffrey Galt Harpham's *One of Us: The Mastery of Joseph Conrad* (1996), and Martin Bock's *Joseph Conrad and Psychological Medicine* (2002), contain material that is particularly relevant to my concerns. Along with Thomas C. Moser, all of these writers except Kaplan have tended to focus particular attention on to recurrent elements in Conrad's fiction rather than on to details that are specific to individual texts. Thus for example Bernard C. Meyer claims that there is a 'basic and consistent formula underlying the biography of most of Conrad's invented characters', one which involves a hero who is an only child and who has lost his mother at an early age.

In this world the father nearly always outlives the mother, but whereas the fathers of sons depart at the onset of their sons' adolescence, the fathers of daughters remain alive for the duration of the story and are often in the grip of an obsession that involves the daughter (267). Meyer presents us with some telling mathematics: out of '31 stories [...] the protagonist is emotionally involved with a woman in 25; in 17 of these he loses his life, in all but two instances directly or indirectly because of a woman' (273–4). Meyer perceives a recurrent pattern of implied incest in the fiction, but cautions:

> It is noteworthy, however, that despite the several patterns in which Conrad presented the theme of incest, one is conspicuously absent – mother and son. Indeed, Conrad saw to it that such a relationship could virtually never exist in his stories, for there is scarcely a major male character in all his fiction who has a living mother, and there is but one important female character who has a living male child, namely, Amy Foster. (114)

There are, indeed, very few children in Conrad's fictional world, but there is no shortage of childless couples. Even where children could easily have been introduced as part of a fiction's setting they are typically absent from Conrad's work. One of the first things one notices when watching old film of the places in which Conrad's novels or stories are set – the Congo, the Malay Archipelago, Mauritius, South America – is how many children are picked up by the photographer. Conrad seems to have used a powerful age-filter on his own mental camera.

Meyer also argues for the existence of a recurrent pattern in the fiction that involves – at its simplest level – strong women and weak men. It is possible to go further and to suggest that although he would not have used the terms of modern theory, Conrad was very well aware of the distinction between sex and gender. In *Nostromo*, Martin Decoud writes to his sister that '[t]he women of our country are worth looking at during a revolution. The rouge and pearl powder fall off, together with that passive attitude towards the outer world which education, tradition, custom impose upon them from the earliest infancy' (234). There is also very clear evidence in the fiction that Conrad understood that a person's gender qualities could not be mechanically read off from their (biological) sexual identity. In a revealing passage in *Chance*, the character-narrator Marlow comments of Mrs Fyne that

> The good woman was making up to her husband's chess-player simply because she had scented in him that small portion of 'femininity,' that drop of superior essence of which I am myself aware; which, I gratefully acknowledge, has saved me from one or two misadventures in my life either ridiculous or lamentable, I am not very certain which. It matters very little.

> Anyhow misadventures. Observe that I say 'femininity,' a privilege – not 'feminism,' an attitude. I am not a feminist. (145–6)

Many of the strong women of Conrad's fiction (Mrs Fyne is a good example) are explicitly described as being possessed of masculine qualities, while a number of his male characters are prone to 'blush like a girl' – and especially in moments of strong emotional contact with other men. In some of Conrad's male characters a weakness and lack of masculinity are expressed in and through an impotent voyeurism. Picking up on a comment of Moser's that 'peeping is virtually a standard attribute of Conrad's "bad" characters', Meyer remarks that 'both voyeurism and exhibitionism are exceedingly common among Conrad's fictional people' (300).

In his study *One of Us: The Mastery of Joseph Conrad*, Geoffrey Galt Harpham concedes that Conrad's fictional world is not one from which sexuality and the erotic have been excluded. But for Harpham sexuality exists in concealed form in the pages of Conrad's fictional works, disguised or exiled to the margins of the text.

> Banished as uncongenial, sexuality remains as a foreign element in Conrad, one that never really finds a home in his work and yet, in involuted forms, is never truly out of it either, as currents of an indeterminate desire flash intermittently along wires designed primarily to carry other messages. The unmentioned subject, sexual desire, and especially homosexual desire, escapes the vigilance of the artist searching after the elusive *mot juste*, concentrating on one kind of exactitude while leaving the chaotic domain of secondary meanings to itself.
>
> What seems to be happening is that – especially in the period of his concentrated greatness, 1897–1900, from *The Nigger* to *Lord Jim* – Conrad makes 'mistakes' by failing to perform the kind of 'screening' that is performed more or less effortlessly by native speakers. (176)

From Harpham's perspective, then, sexuality emerges in Conrad's fiction in spite of the efforts of its author to exclude it, and it does so in much the same way as Freud depicts how elements in the dream work elude the censor: by means of disguise and subterfuge. This being the case, the way to bring these concealed elements to light is to read Conrad's fiction much as Freud reads the dream – by searching for slips, double-meanings, unintended *doubles-entendres*, and other points at which the vigilance of the censor wavers.

I am far from rejecting Harpham's approach *in toto* – indeed I believe that it uncovers a number of significant textual details that have eluded the notice of previous critics. But I believe that Conrad is, actually, a far more knowing author than Harpham portrays him to be, one more in control of his meanings, and one more deliberate and knowledgeable in his portrayal of sexuality.

What I do *not* want to do in the pages that follow is merely to filter out the sexual and the erotic moments or elements from Conrad's fiction and to examine them in isolation. Some such filtering out is unavoidable if my case is to be made, but I want again to insist that right at the heart of Conrad's artistic achievement, at the core of his creative insight, is an understanding that the so-called public and private worlds interact and interpenetrate. Right at the heart and right from the start: in the trilogy of *Almayer's Folly*, *The Outcast of the Islands* and *The Rescue* the passionate and erotic desires of the characters are inseparable from – are indeed partly the product of – realities of class, race, and empire. In *Nostromo* the sterility of the Gould's marriage, and Charles Gould's symbolic unfaithfulness to his wife through his obsession with the silver mine, are important not primarily because they take us into the minutiae of a particular marriage, but more because they demonstrate, to invoke an anachronistic slogan, that the personal is political (and, concomitantly, that the political is one of the forces that moulds the personal). This insight into the intermingling of the personal and the political is depicted most powerfully and most overtly in the novel that follows *Nostromo – The Secret Agent*. Here again the particularities of a sterile and, it is hinted, a sado-masochistic marital relationship, are depicted as inseparable from the cruelties and sterilities of a commercialized and commodified culture.

It is with regard to this sense of the interpenetration of the private and the public that I am most at odds with Geoffrey Galt Harpham's view of the depiction of sexuality in Conrad's fiction. Harpham summarizes his own position as follows.

> I claim that a fugitive sexual energy, clustering in the fissures between primary and secondary meanings, provides Conrad's work with a personal urgency that it would not otherwise have, and gains, itself, in gravitas by being confused with public and political themes that seem remote from it. It is not the flickering and uncertain presence of sexuality as such that marks Conrad's work, but the partial exposure of a larger field of the repressed or transgressive in general that gives his work at its best its distinctive quality. (183)

The point at which I feel most uneasy in reading this passage is that at which the word 'confused' occurs. Reading the great political novels – *Heart of Darkness*, *Nostromo*, *The Secret Agent* and *Under Western Eyes* – I never have a sense that there is a confusion of the element of sexual energy with public and political themes. On the contrary: I detect a deliberate recognition of similarities and connections between the private (including the sexual) and the public. I use the word 'deliberate' rather than, for example, 'conscious', because I am not claiming that Conrad the man would or could have expressed the matter in these terms, but I do assert that at the level of his creative intelligence this recognition plays a decisive part in the process of fictional composition. Another way of putting it is to suggest that because Conrad typically perceives sexual relationships as, among other things, power relationships, the varied rôles played by sexual desire and erotic experience in his fictions cannot be isolated from other uses of power: political, economic and emotional. To ignore the sexual and the erotic in his fiction is not just to pass over an isolated, 'private', and self-contained component in his novels and short stories, but to disregard elements in them that are often organically linked to those elements that have, for many years, been deemed worthy of serious study.

In stressing the need to historicize our understanding of sexuality, Joseph Bristow points out that the OED dates the first use of the word 'sexuality' to 1836, and he adds that the word only achieves common currency in the late nineteenth and early twentieth centuries (1997, 3). During the period in which Conrad is writing, from the early 1890s to 1924, public understanding of, and attitudes towards, sexuality undergo major shifts. In the course of this period, and especially subsequent to the trials of Oscar Wilde, a concept of 'homosexuality' is refined and fixed in the public consciousness. (As Terry Collits points out [2005, 40], Wilde began his imprisonment just one month subsequent to the publication of Conrad's first novel.) During the same period the growth of the suffrage movement forced the attention of the public on to what we now call gender rôles. Public debate about the empire, and sharpening class struggle related to the growth of trade unionism and the formation of socialist parties, impacted on people's sense of the social prohibitions against inter-racial and inter-class sexuality. There is ample evidence in Conrad's work that at the level of his creative consciousness he understood that human sexuality was not a purely biological drive that assumed an invariable, universal form in all human cultures, but a biological drive that could only develop and express itself in and through historically and culturally specific forms.

My focus in this book is on Conrad's fiction and not on his life or non-fictional writings, but where appropriate I will make reference to extra-textual information, including biographical material. The monumental achievement of the Cambridge *Collected Letters* and the work of biographers such as Zdzisław Najder contains material that is indispensable to any investigation into the portrayal of sexuality and the erotic in Conrad's fiction. I will also make reference to material which Conrad is known to have read, and material that he *may* have read. Conrad's six weeks in Mauritius in 1888 seem to have had a major erotic significance for him, and I have spent some time looking at the content of newspapers to which he had access on the island at this time.

I do not move through Conrad's fiction chronologically. My first chapter traces the history of what, I believe, are too 'innocent' readings of Conrad's fiction, focussing initially on two test-cases, the short story 'Il Conde' (1908) and the short novel or novella *The Shadow-Line* (1917), before moving to other works which arguably involve homosexual or homoerotic elements. My second chapter moves back chronologically to Conrad's second published novel *An Outcast of the Islands* (1896) and to its depiction of the interpenetrations of sexuality, race, and gender, before tracing some similarities in the depiction of these same elements in *Heart of Darkness* (1899). My third chapter charts patterns of both sadism and masochism in a number of heterosexual relationships that are depicted in Conrad's fiction. My fourth and final chapter explores the important rôle played by a set of linked qualities in Conrad's fiction, including those of voyeurism, impotence, and masochism.

This does not claim to be a comprehensive study of the erotic and sexual elements in Conrad's fiction. I have chosen not to write at any length on 'The Secret Sharer', partly because the homoerotic element in this tale has been much discussed by previous critics and partly because for me the character Leggatt represents aspects of the narrator-captain's *own* sexuality and not another independent being to whom the captain can be sexually attracted. (The debt owed by this story to the tradition of the double or Doppelgänger is crucial to its ability to present Leggatt in such a way as to diminish his this-world reality for both the captain-narrator and the reader, and I have written about this elsewhere.[1])

I mention Conrad's treatment of female homosexuality in the character of Mrs Fyne, in *Chance*, only in passing. The treatment is worthy of note to the extent that it offers such strong evidence that Conrad was aware that lesbianism existed, which was not true of all his contemporaries. But I do not find the portrayal of Mrs Fyne and her liking for young women artistically rich. It is not, it seems to me, integrated into larger or deeper patterns of exploration in the novel.

1 Closeted Characters and Cloistered Critics in 'Il Conde', *Lord Jim*, *The Shadow-Line*, and *Victory*

Conrad's fiction and the innocent reader: 'Il Conde'

The critical history of Joseph Conrad's tale 'Il Conde' (1908) can conveniently serve to illuminate a general tendency among critics of the first three-quarters of the twentieth century to ignore or downplay sexual or erotic motifs – and especially those associated with various forms of tabooed or illicit sexuality – in Conrad's fiction. In his *The Deceptive Text: An Introduction to Covert Plots* (1984), Cedric Watts suggested that many of Conrad's fictions contain what he terms a 'covert plot', but the covert element in 'Il Conde' is not so much one that runs unrecognized alongside or beneath a 'main' plot, as one that, once recognized, quickly becomes the main, and only, plot. As with the critical history of Henry James's *The Turn of the Screw* (1898) there is an innocent reading of 'Il Conde' and there is a more knowing one. Moreover, as in the case of James's celebrated story, the innocent reading dominates the accounts of readers and critics in the years following the first publication of the tale, while the more knowing account is first granted public expression some years later – many years later in the case of 'Il Conde'. In the case of James's novella I side with those who have argued that James constructed his tale in such a way as to make it impossible to decide between these two readings,[2] but it seems to me that the dissemination of the knowing reading of 'Il Conde' has effectively destroyed the innocent one. And while the emergence of the knowing reading of 'Il Conde' has not led to the same sort of divide among critics as have Freudian and neo-Freudian readings of *The Turn of the Screw*, it has had two signal effects. The first of these is that it has transformed 'Il Conde' into a far more complex, artful, and sophisticated work than was believed to be the case when the innocent reading held sole sway. But the second and more substantial effect has been that of destabilizing meanings in other fictional works of Conrad; we might say that the faultlines that have opened up in 'Il Conde' have spread outside the territory of this single tale.

The innocent reading of the tale is usefully exemplified in the opening words of R. L. Mégroz's 1931 account.

> There is the lonely, proud man of fine feeling, an aristocrat asking from life little except an avoidance of the sordid. He is the victim of an outrage in Naples which we may infer is not unique or exceedingly rare. He is 'held up' by a secret-society gangster in a quiet side-street and compelled to hand over all his belongings. The gangster threatens ruthless murder, and is disgusted to find that the old man has hardly any money on him. (119)

Mégroz's account continues in like vein, accepting the Count's own report at face value and silently excising the rôle and even the presence of the intradiegetic narrator.

During the years of New Critical hegemony the innocent reading is developed in certain standard ways that stress the richness and complexity of the text without challenging its (or the Count's) innocence. Thus John Howard Wills's 1955 account of the story insists upon its 'almost perfect form and complex symbolism' (22) and adds two allegorical elements (the Fall or Expulsion from Eden and the Ivory Tower myth of the *fin de siècle*). However Wills's view of the Count is one that is very much in line with that of R. L. Mégroz.

> Now, the Count's tendency to avoid physical pain is symbolic of his tendency to avoid pain in general – and, ultimately, reality itself. Thus his 'rheumatic affection' (like Ransome's bad heart) symbolizes his own animality, his own mortality; and his 'dislike of the busts and statues of Roman emperors in the gallery of marbles' with their 'expressions of cruel discontent' ultimately symbolizes his own dislike of seeing animality in others. Like Axel in his castle, the old Count carefully barricades himself against the wilderness.
>
> But the wilderness will not be denied. It comes to meet him exactly as it comes to meet Lord Jim in Patusan, D'Hubert at his country retreat, Axel (and this name is certainly symbolic) Heyst upon his island. It follows him over the Alps into Naples. It follows him to the concert. Even then he desperately attempts to shake it off. At the concert he is pained by the expression of the young man who shares a table with him. He gets up and leaves. Being 'tired of the feeling of confinement,' he enters an alley of the gardens. Paradoxically, it is precisely there, while running away, within 'an atmosphere of solitude and coolness,' amid 'the sounds of music delightfully softened by the distance' that he meets the reality of himself. It is the Conrad recognition scene: Jim's meeting with Gentleman Brown, D'Hubert's with Feraud, Heyst's with his three infernal shades. (25)

In spite of these thought-provoking parallels – and in spite of the fact that Wills has earlier claimed that the old Count 'must look into the mirror of the Umberto (as the captain must look into the mirror of his "secret sharer")' – he is apparently totally unaware of the possibility that the young robber may indeed have been *selected* by his victim as a secret sexual sharer. Indeed, his formulation makes the young man the active agent so far as the sharing of the table is concerned, whereas the text of the tale makes it quite clear that it is the Count who *chooses* to sit at the table already occupied by the young man.

A decade following its publication Wills's account of the tale was to be subjected to considerable dismissive scorn by John V. Hagopian in his 1965 article 'The Pathos of "Il Conde"'. According to Hagopian, Wills's account is 'an essay which might be ignored except for the fact that it is the only extended study of this story and has recently been reprinted in a widely used anthology of Conrad criticism' (35). But Hagopian's account in its turn may be subjected to if not dismissal then at least ironic critique, for if Hagopian attacks Wills's account as a good example of 'the excesses of myth criticism', his own essay seems from our privileged position of hindsight to suffer from a paucity rather than an excess of interpretative ingenuity: rather than digging too deep and forcing meanings on to the tale, it skates along on the surface of the story's meaning blissfully unaware of the shadows below.

Hagopian, like Mégroz, takes the Count's rendering of his experiences at face value.

> The plot is simple. The aged Il Conde, who lives on the Gulf of Naples because it offers the only climate which does not aggravate his painful and dangerous rheumatic condition, is a fastidious, prudent and conventional man. He has never been involved in any adventure or violence, but one evening he experiences an abominable terror that makes him flee southern Italy, even though leaving is tantamount to committing suicide. In a dark path of the gardens at the Villa Nazionale, while the band is playing a concert in the distance, he is accosted by a dapper young man who at knife-point demands his valuables. (31)

Much of Hagopian's essay is written in the same no-nonsense style. He casts scorn on Frederick Karl's view that 'the sudden violence that overtakes him [the Count] is symbolic of the violence that was to overtake Europe in 1914. [...] Its surface is always human, and its dramatic climax is resolved in human terms, but the political meanings of the story are now common coinage of the contemporary intelligence', commenting that '[t]his is, of course, nonsense – the kind of nonsense that comes from retrospectively attributing to a work of literature a non-literary meaning derived from subsequent historical events' (35). Wills's view that the story details the Count's expulsion from Eden is ridiculed because it seems to locate Eden in three different places. There is a further objection to such a view, Hagopian insists: 'one might enquire why, if "Il Conde" is really a dramatization of the Fall and the Expulsion from Eden, there is no violation of a divine command, no Eve to tempt this aged Adam, no consequent sexual shame' (37). There are none so blind as those that will not see. From the perspective of a new millennium it seems incredible that having got so far as to search for a violation of a divine command, an Eve to tempt the ageing Adam, and a consequent sexual shame, Hagopian is unable to find them in 'Il Conde'.

A present-day reader of Hagopian's article has the odd sense of his continually sailing close to the rocks and reefs of the tale but merely grazing them and proceeding without any awareness of the scratches in his paintwork. For example, he draws attention to the manner in which the tale's 'very opening sentence calls our attention to the famous collection of bronzes from Herculaneum and Pompeii "whose delicate perfection has been preserved for us by the catastrophic fury of a volcano"', and poses the rhetorical question: 'Is this not Conrad's way of establishing at the beginning the principle that only a strength that can survive violence deserves our approval or esteem?' (32). The point is not invalid, but it skates over the fact that the tale opens with the narrator and the Count meeting while gazing at the statue of a beautiful and naked male youth whose posture is picked up later in the tale in the posture of the young robber. And it passes over, too, the associations with sexual excess – especially homosexual excess – enjoyed by Herculaneum and Pompeii, and slyly hinted at by Conrad (or perhaps by his narrator).

Even a writer on the lookout for sexual double-meanings such as Bernard C. Meyer in his 1967 study *Joseph Conrad: A Psychoanalytic Biography* fails to detect anything other than outraged gentility in Conrad's Count. For Meyer, ''Il Conde' is not a tale of a gross and venal older man who causes a boy's death, but of a vicious, snarling youth whose ruthless action leads to the ultimate destruction of an elderly gentleman' (196–7). Two years later, in 1969, Paul J. Dolan's article ''Il Conde': Conrad's Little Miss Muffett' also conveys the impression of a critic who is perpetually on the verge of reading Conrad's tale in a more knowing way, without ever quite managing so to do. Dolan sees the tale as 'an exact analogue of the nursery rhyme tragedy of "Little Miss Muffett". Their common theme is the fragility and impermanence of comfort and security in this world. Their plots reveal that life is filled with unpleasant little surprises and, with varying complexity of irony, they both reveal that the disturbance of one's life is most likely to happen at moments of serene contentment' (107). Given the fact that by 1969 the accounts of writers such as Sigmund Freud and Bruno Bettelheim had made it hard to sustain the view that fairy tales and nursery rhymes were pure accounts of the innocence of childhood, unsullied by any hint of sexuality, it is odd that Dolan's comparison does not cause him to question either the Count's account of himself, or the narrator's reliability. 'Almost immediately the narrator gives us, in one line, the essential fact about the count: "I have no doubt that his whole existence has been correct, well ordered, and conventional, undisturbed by startling events"' (108). (Conrad's text reads 'had' rather than 'has', and has no comma after 'ordered'.) The fact that the narrator has no doubt provides Dolan with sufficient reason for having no doubt himself. He has no fear that Conrad's narrator might be unreliable as a result of either imperceptiveness or duplicity. Dolan also tends to slide between basing his interpretation on the authority of the narrator, and basing it upon the authority of the tale's author.

> Conrad carefully skirts the questions of moral responsibility in regard to the count. He is a child-like hedonist and a most pleasant man. We regard him, in other words, with the same indulgence with which we regard children. Part of our shock of outrage at the 'abominable outrage' which befalls him is that we have been made to feel that his innocence preserved so long deserves to be preserved to the end of his life. (108)

It seems that although critics of the innocent persuasion seem unable to discuss this tale without introducing ideas of Eden, innocence, and corruption, none of them seems able to explore the implications of the fact that the expulsion from Eden and the loss of innocence followed not just temptation but also sin.

A few short years following Dolan's article, critics of Conrad's tale were themselves destined to lose their innocence for ever. Two articles in the same number of the journal *Conradiana* in 1975 proffer the apple of knowledge to Conrad's readers: the Count is no innocent, 'proud man of fine feeling' attempting to avoid the sordid. On the contrary, he is sexually interested in good-looking young Italian men, and he renders himself vulnerable to the 'outrage' he experiences by attempting to pick one up – the young man who robs him.

The longer and more developed of these two accounts – Douglas A. Hughes's 'Conrad's "Il Conde": "A deucedly queer story"' – argues that '[t]o the naive, credulous narrator and unwary reader, Il Conde represents the epitome of the proper gentleman, improbably correct in his social manners and bearing, but there is reason to believe that the Count is actually a lonely, vulnerable pederast who becomes involved in a sordid incident, the "pathetic tale" of the story's subtitle' (17–18). According to Hughes, critics have been able to offer disparate readings of 'Il Conde' for two reasons.

> First, most critics have either ignored or inconsistently explained what appear to be deliberately ambiguous details relating to the Count's character and his 'abominable adventure,' the central action of the story. Conrad himself refused to go beyond the mere intimation of these details. Secondly, and clearly related to these troublesome details, most critics and readers do not question the reliability of the narrator who conveys Il Conde's account of his experience. This paper contends that the Count's account of his 'adventure' may be an elaborate fabrication to preserve his reputation and that evidence that the old man may be lying is indicated by a series of suggestive details and the discrediting of the narrator's judgment. (17)

Hughes reads details concerning the places mentioned in the tale in an other than innocent manner.

> The place names, Naples, Capri, Baiae, Pompeii, and Herculaneum, which in the narrative are associated with the Count, to the ancient Romans were suggestive of decadence and immorality. It was here in Naples, the most Greek of Roman cities, that the citizens of Rome ventured to indulge their senses and lusts. For example, Capri, where the Count rents a villa, was once notorious for pederasty. Pompeii, which is mentioned in the first paragraph of the story as the Count and narrator gaze on the statue of a nude Hermes, was celebrated throughout the empire for its lewdness, and it was one of the few Roman cities in which the phallus was worshipped. (19)

Hughes even goes so far as to suggest that 'there is no *evidence* that the Count has been robbed; he still possesses his wallet, watches, and rings' (21).

In the same number of *Conradiana* Theo Steinmann's 'Il Conde's Uncensored Story' offers a comparable view of the Count and of the 'outrage' he experiences, basing his reading on some 'slips of the tongue and a few hardly veiled contradictions' in the tale that 'make the reader pause' (83). One such contradiction that he cites is that the Count, in telling the narrator of the 'outrage', chooses to share a table with 'a young man of just such a type', notices his moody expression, and thinks, 'He is sad; something is wrong with him; young men have their troubles. I take no notice of him, of course'. Steinmann comments: 'This last sentence is misleading, for he noticed him twice again in the crowd because "he had been struck by the marked, peevish discontent of that face" and "once their eyes met" or, as he later put it, "he had exchanged glances" with him' (84).

Let us for a moment move back from 'Il Conde' and focus on these two critical accounts of the work. It is significant that both accounts make reference to the reader – Hughes's to the 'unwary reader' and Steinmann's to remarks that make 'the reader' pause. But why should Hughes and Steinmann be, apparently, the first 'wary' readers of this tale, the first to be made to pause by some 'slips of the tongue and a few hardly veiled contradictions'? Why should it have taken 67 years before any commentator committed to print doubts as to the frankness and veracity of the Count? I shall return to this question below.

What is doubtless not the final but is certainly a decisive stage in the uncovering of the sexual covert plot of the tale is marked in 2005 by Keith Carabine's biographical-critical essay, "A very charming old gentleman': Conrad, Count Szembek, and "Il Conde"'. In this article Carabine publishes details from a letter written to Conrad's biographer Zdzisław Najder by Zygmunt Mycielski, the grandson of Count Zygmunt Szembek, who was the model for Conrad's Count. In the letter, dated 12 March 1981, Mycielski admits that his grandfather was homosexual and comments:

Quite clearly il conte accosted the boy in one of the dark alleys of the Chiaja gardens. Moreover, this entire set-up on Capri, which since the time of Tyberius was a 'paradise' of this kind, the early morning angling and the manner in which he tells the story, trying to reduce the whole affair to a 'simple criminal assault,' and finally Conrad's modulated irony – it all fits in! The great writer takes an interest in everything. He is fascinated by the illustrious nobleman whom he has met, by his upbringing and manners, by his fear of scandal, by his perfunctory and yet quite authentic culture – inborn – instilled through upbringing, by his social 'polish,' by the discreet elegance of his clothes, and ABOVE all this is a homosexual 'adventure'! (Carabine 2005, 58–9)

There is a delicious irony in the way in which Capri is yet again seen by a commentator as a paradise or Eden – but a paradise not for innocent, childlike souls, but for homosexual men who wish to cruise for young male sexual partners!

In his article Carabine reads 'Il Conde' in the light of the six letters that Conrad wrote to Count Szembek after his own departure from Capri, and he makes some perceptive and convincing arguments about the way in which the complexities of the persona and manner adopted by Conrad in these letters feed directly into those of the persona and manner of the tale's narrator. Carabine points out that Conrad would have disapproved strongly of Szembek's selling of his family estates – an action that his fellow-Poles would at that time have seen as unpatriotic – and he notes that the first draft of 'Il Conde' was finished only four days after the final letter was written.

Carabine finds a vein of suggestive double-meaning in both the letters and the tale, noting that 'there is even the suggestion that the changes of musical register slyly mimic the sexual act, moving from penetration ("crashed *fortissimo*"), through "slow movement" with "repeated bangs," ending with "a tremendous crash" of climax' (73).[3] He also notes that a letter written from Capri by Conrad to Ford Madox Ford makes clear the writer's sense of the associations enjoyed by the resort. ('The scandals of Capri – atrocious, u[n]speakable, amusing, scandals international, cosmopolitan and biblical flavoured with Yankee twang and the French phrases of the *gens du monde* mingle with the tinkling of guitars in the barbers' shops. [...] All this is a sort of blue nightmare traversed by stinks and perfumes [...]' [CL3, 241]. We may remember the Count's perfumed moustache at this point, while 'biblical' may well be a coded reference to homosexuality.)

In a letter to Ada Galsworthy (18 August 1908) Conrad responds to her praise of 'Il Conde' and admits: 'Truth is I am rather proud of that little trick' (CL4, 104). Picking up on Conrad's use of the word 'trick', Carabine suggests that the tale is written in such a manner as to 'deceive (say) the readers of a summer number of a magazine, but artfully designed to persuade the discriminating reader to detect another, untold, tale of a homosexual encounter that went badly wrong' (68–9). How many discriminating readers actually got the point in 1908 it is impossible to say; certainly there is at present no record of any committing their perceptions to print before 1975. And yet reading the tale, and Conrad's 'Author's Note' to *A Set of Six*, today, we cannot overlook the sly hints and suggestions that there is more to this 'pathetic tale' than meets the eye. In his 'Author's Note', for example, there is a marked sense that Conrad is playing with the reader when he writes that 'All I can say is that the personality of the narrator [i.e. the Count who narrates his experiences to Conrad, not the narrator of the tale] was extremely suggestive quite apart from the story he was telling me' (v). The OED gives 'apparently to suggest something indecent' as one euphemistic meaning of 'suggestive'. It is noteworthy that Henry James's Preface to volume XII of the New York edition of his works – which includes *The Turn of the Screw* – contains a comparable formulation: 'I need scarcely add after this that it is a piece of ingenuity pure and simple, of cold artistic calculation, an *amusette* to catch those not easily caught (the "fun" of the capture of the merely witless being ever but small), the jaded, the disillusioned, the fastidious' (James 1999, 125). This is first published in 1908, the same year in which Conrad's letter to Ada Galsworthy is written.

***

Although 'Il Conde' and James's *The Turn of the Screw* are very different works, there are striking parallels between the two so far as their critical histories are concerned. Once the 'knowing' reading is made public (James's governess does not see ghosts, they are the product of her sexual frustrations; Conrad's Count is not a saintly old man but a gay *roué* cruising for young men) the tale can never again be read in a totally innocent fashion. But while one of the most influential 'knowing' readings of James's tale – Harold C. Goddard's 'A Pre-Freudian Reading of *The Turn of the Screw*'[4] – was composed in the early 1920s (although not published until 1957), innocent readings of Conrad's tale went unchallenged, in public at any rate, until 1975. Moreover, whereas the innocent and the knowing readings of James's tale present themselves as mutually exclusive alternatives, the knowing reading of Conrad's tale seems to have succeeded in making it impossible to go on reading 'Il Conde' in an innocent manner.

It may well be that readers and critics prior to 1975 detected some of the hints in Conrad's story that made of the Count something other than the refined victim of an outrage, but it seems clear than many and probably most did not. Why should so many readers of the tale have been, to use Hughes's term, so 'unwary'?

The first answer to this question has to be that in the case of 'Il Conde' the knowing reading involves an unambiguous attribution of homosexual behaviour to the Count, whereas in the case of James's novella the tabooed forms of sexuality are (deliberately) not defined by James. The fact that the reader of Conrad's tale must consider the possibility of the Count's homosexuality in order to read the work's covert plot involves two different sorts of problem for students of the tale's critical reception. The first is that a present-day understanding of what homosexuality is (and that it may be more nuanced, multiple, and contradictory than we comfortably assume) cannot necessarily be attributed to either Conrad or his early readers. As Richard J. Ruppel points out, while for 'most people today, homosexuality is a fixed, profoundly defining feature of a person's identity', at the time when Conrad began publishing his work, 'this was not yet true' (1998, 20). The second problem is that however people conceived of or conceptualized homosexuality, for the first three-quarters of the twentieth century public discussion of the matter was either impossible or tolerated only in extremely indirect or specialized (for example, medical) forms.

Jósef Retinger (who is not the most reliable source of information about Conrad) reports that Conrad was a 'man of stern principles and straight lines in his private life' who 'despised weakness of character and the display of immorality'. Retinger adds that Conrad 'disliked consequently the works of Oscar Wilde, because he had a profound contempt for his way of living' (1941, 103). According to Richard J. Ruppel, the 'Cleveland Street Affair' (1889–90) and especially the trials of Oscar Wilde (1895), 'had an enormous influence on the development of the concept of homosexuality in British culture' (1998, 19). A range of critics have detected portrayals or echoes of the figure of Wilde in a number of 'dandified' characters in Conrad's fiction, including such unlikely contenders as James Wait in *The Nigger of the 'Narcissus'* and the immaculate accountant in *Heart of Darkness*, as well as more obvious figures such as Mr Jones in *Victory*.

As I shall discuss below, Conrad knew a number of male homosexuals personally, including Roger Casement and Norman Douglas, and there is evidence (firm in the case of Douglas) that he knew of their homosexual behaviour (which is not to say that he thought of them as 'homosexuals' in the sense in which the term is used today).

But this 'knowing' Conrad is not the Conrad who was familiar to readers for most of the twentieth century. Thus the second answer to the question that I posed above is one that I have already suggested: the knowing reading of 'Il Conde' took so long to be publicly formulated because the author was Joseph Conrad. Generations of readers have not suspected that there are figures in the carpet of Conrad's fiction, nor have they associated his works with illicit or 'perverted' sexuality. Had 'Il Conde' been published as one of Henry James's stories the knowing reading of the tale would surely been advanced rather earlier than 1975. The tale's opening scene, with the meeting between the narrator and the Count prompted by the latter's address to the former 'over the celebrated Resting Hermes which we had been looking at side by side' would have been enough to awaken the suspicions of readers: as I have noted, the statue in question is of a beautiful and naked male adolescent. But even knowing readers have perhaps paid too little attention to that phrase 'side by side'. I will return to this point below.

This answer is one that does not avoid the circularity mentioned in my introduction. Neither Conrad the man nor Conrad the author had the sort of reputation that invited readers to look for sexual sub-plots – especially of an illicit or tabooed nature – in his works. But because readers were able to remain satisfied with innocent 'surface' readings of Conrad's works, Conrad the man and Conrad the author retained the reputation that buttressed such readings. We can predict that once this circle is broken, then not only the works but also the man and the author will be considered in a new way – and in one sense that is just what the present work is attempting to achieve. But it is noticeable that even after – say – 1975, when articles propounding a knowing interpretation of 'Il Conde' were published, Conrad continued (perhaps even continues) to be read in a more innocent manner than is the case with the other major British modernist writers.

Of course, many readers not just of James but also of Forster and Lawrence failed for many decades to detect hints of homosexual desire or tabooed forms of sexual experience in their fiction. The prosecution of Lawrence's *Lady Chatterley's Lover* for obscenity in 1960 neglected to draw attention to the depiction of anal intercourse in the novel – presumably because it was not recognized for what it was. Even though Forster's homosexuality was common knowledge among his friends and acquaintances from early on in his life, it did not become a matter for public discussion or enter into open critical discussion of his work until after his death. And such matters as Lawrence's suppressed Prologue to *Women in Love* – which contains an explicit description of intense male homosexual desire – did not enter into public critical discussion of Lawrence's works again until comparatively late in the twentieth century. Even so, the fiction of all three writers has always seemed to represent a field of enquiry of which 'the sexual' is an important and unavoidable component. All three writers set the experience of passionate sexual love and desire at the centre of their major novels. The fiction of all three writers has been recognized as opaque and full of hidden depths, and James's fiction in particular makes secrecy and that which is in some way 'unspeakable' part of its declared subject matter. Even at the level of biographical criticism, James's and Forster's bachelor status and Lawrence's childless cohabitation with the married Frieda announce lives very different from that of Conrad, married for nearly thirty years to an outwardly conventional woman who bore him two sons.

Other answers would doubtless include Conrad's use of an narrator whose possible unreliability is not obvious on first reading, one who appears to take the Count's story and his explanations of his own conduct at face value, and who Conrad in his own 'Author's Note' explicitly invites the reader to identify with himself. Even without the publication of the 'Note', the tendency of the Common Reader to associate such personified, intradiegetic but anonymous narrators with the figure of the author if there is no obvious reason not to do so, would have made it less likely that readers would have seen the narrator as either unreliable or duplicitous. At the same time, a present-day reader cannot but be struck by the fact that a succession of Conrad's male intradiegetic narrators are presented either overtly or implicitly as without a female partner or wife. Clearly the most striking example of this is Charles Marlow who, although sharing many details of his professional life with his creator Joseph Conrad, is (unlike his creator) a bachelor. In the case of 'Il Conde', for example, Conrad's 'Author's Note' may invite the reader to identify the narrator with himself, but Conrad was accompanied by his wife and family when he met Count Szembek in Capri, while the narrator of the tale seems to have no family with him (he dines alone with the Count). Indeed, when the narrator has 'to leave Naples in a hurry to look after a friend who had fallen seriously ill in Taormina' (273), the strong implication is that he is either a widower like the Count or a bachelor. (The gender of the 'friend' is not specified, but at the time that Conrad is writing it would have been unusual to refer to a female acquaintance as 'a friend' in this manner. Moreover, had the friend had a partner or a close relative near by then the narrator's help would not have been needed.)

The detection of gay subplots or 'covert sexual plots' requires not just a wary reader but also an informed reader. For more than half of the twentieth century homosexuality is literally unmentionable in public discussion (including the public discourse of literary criticism), and when it involves the prostitution of the young by the old it is even more so. And that which is unmentionable often becomes, too, unthinkable. These are issue to which I shall return. At this point I would like to move to a closer scrutiny of 'Il Conde' and of what we can term its covert plot.

***

In the letter to Ada Galsworthy of 18 August 1908, Conrad reports that he wrote 'Il Conde' immediately after finishing the shorter, serial version of *The Secret Agent*. Although the tale and the novel seem different in almost every way one cares to think of, they may perhaps be linked through their shared if indirect relationship to the detective story. If the longer work announces this relationship through its use of the conventional elements of the genre (crime, detective, solution), the tale's relationship to the popular genre is more formal and technical than a matter of plot similarities. It is for example striking how hard critics find it to discuss the tale without using the word 'clue'. Moreover that experience of retrospective recognition and comprehension that is granted by the final pages of the detective story, when certain elements that have gone before now stand out as significant, is one that is granted to the reader of 'Il Conde' once he or she is prompted to reread the story from a more knowing and 'wary' perspective.

As with a detective story, all sorts of details that seemed unremarkable on a first (innocent) reading assume a new significance when the story is re-read from a more knowing perspective. I have already mentioned the narrator's meeting with the Count by the statue of Hermes. Not only is this statue of a beautiful youth, but the three figures of Eros, Hermes and Heracles are conventionally taken to form a homoerotic trinity presiding over homosexual relations. In a thoughtful discussion of 'Il Conde' Ted Billy points out that

> The Count's 'stony immobility' in the final scene calls to mind Conrad's emphasis on 'the celebrated Resting Hermes' at the outset of the story. This sculptural allusion is intriguing (literally *Hermes* means 'he of the stone heap') since Hermes traditionally is associated with mobility as the guide of souls to the underworld and as the patron god of travelers and thieves. (204–5)

Billy also draws attention to the way in which the 'young *Cavaliere* also unconsciously apes the pose of Resting Hermes' (205). Clearly, then, the implication is that as the Count has stopped by the statue and is looking at the statue, then we should not take at face value his claim that he is not interested in the young man who resembles this statue and who is occupying the table at which he chooses to sit.

Once we start to examine the story in the light of a suspicion that the Count is sexually interested in young men, then many other details may seem less innocent. Take for example these lines from the third paragraph of the story: 'For the servants he was *Il Conde*. There was some squabble over a man's parasol – yellow silk with white lining sort of thing – the waiters had discovered abandoned outside the dining-room door. Our gold-laced door-keeper recognized it and I heard him directing one of the lift boys to run after *Il Conde* with it' (269–70). Perhaps the parasol observed with less trusting eyes appears now a little effeminate? Is it altogether accidental that the doorkeeper directs one of the lift boys to run after the Count to return it? And is it even possible that the umbrella has been 'forgotten' deliberately, so as to enable him to get to know one of the lift boys?

There can be no definite answer to such questions; the details in question involve at the most hints and suggestions rather than unambiguous information. It is well-known that Henry James liked to prompt the reader's imagination in the direction of unstated but sexually suggestive meanings. In the Preface to the 1908 New York edition of *The Turn of the Screw*, for example, James is clear about his method: 'Make him [the reader] *think* the evil, make him think it for himself, and you are released from weak specifications' (128). It is important seriously to consider the possibility that Conrad was no less interested in getting his reader to 'think the evil' – or at least to imagine the unstated – so as to release himself from weak specification. Thus in a letter to Hugh Clifford written 9 October 1899, for example, Conrad comments on Clifford's prose as follows:

> The word *frightened* is fatal. It seems as if it had been withought* any thought at all. It takes away all sense of reality – for if you read the sentence *in its place on the page* You will see that the word *frightened* (or indeed any word of the sort) is inadequate to express the true state of that man's mind. No word is adequate. The imagination of the reader should be left free to arouse his feeling. (CL2, 201)

Given when this comment is written, in the middle of Conrad's composition of *Lord Jim*, it is worth bearing in mind that the word 'fear' is not used in the scene when Jim fails to join the cutter launched in rough seas to rescue the two sailors; it is only in retrospect that Jim thinks to himself: 'Not a particle of fear was left'. During the scene itself, the imagination of the reader is as Conrad puts it 'left free to arouse his feeling'.

Once the reader does indeed allow his or her imagination the freedom to 'arouse feeling', then many words and phrases in 'Il Conde' catch the attention.

> His white moustache, heavy but carefully trimmed and arranged, was not unpleasantly tinted a golden yellow in the middle. The faint scent of some very good perfume, and of good cigars (that last an odour quite remarkable to come upon in Italy) reached me across the table. It was in his eyes that his age showed most. They were a little weary with creased eyelids. (270)

> He had a piano, a few books: picked up transient acquaintances of a day, week, or month in the stream of travellers from all Europe. One can imagine him going out for his walks in the streets and lanes, becoming known to beggars, shopkeepers, children, country people; talking amiably over the walls to the contadini – and coming back to his rooms or his villa to sit before the piano [...] (271)

> 'The truth is that I have had a very – a very – how shall I say? – abominable adventure happen to me.'
> The energy of the epithet was sufficiently startling in that man of moderate feelings and toned-down vocabulary. The word unpleasant I should have thought would have fitted amply the worst experience likely to befall a man of his stamp. And an adventure, too. Incredible! But it is in human nature to believe the worst; and I confess I eyed him stealthily, wondering what he had been up to. In a moment, however, my unworthy suspicions vanished. There was a fundamental refinement of nature about the man which made me dismiss all idea of some more or less disreputable scrape. (274–5)

He got out of the cab and entered the Villa on foot from the Largo di Vittoria end.

He stared at me very hard. And I understood then how really impressionable he was. Every small fact and event of that evening stood out in his memory as if endowed with mystic significance. (276)

The technique here (whether it is Conrad's technique or his narrator's is a moot point) is reminiscent of that of Iago: raising a suspicion indirectly then denying it more overtly. The man wears perfume – but he smokes good masculine cigars; we are invited to imagine him picking up transient acquaintances – but then returning home alone to his piano; the narrator eyes him stealthily wondering what he has been up to – but then his unworthy suspicions vanish; the Count stares hard at the narrator as if to see how he responds to his decision to enter the Villa on foot – but then the narrator realizes that this is just a sign that every small fact and event of that evening is impressed in the Count's memory.

If we now turn to the passage in which the Count relates to the narrator the events leading in to the 'outrage', the reader whose suspicions have been raised starts – like Othello – to respond even to the slightest clues that the Count is not altogether without guilt in the matter.

There was, of course, a quantity of diverse types: showy old fellows with white moustaches, fat men, thin men, officers in uniform; but what predominated, he told me, was the South Italian type of young man, with a colourless, clear complexion, red lips, jet-black little moustache and liquid black eyes so wonderfully effective in leering or scowling.

Withdrawing from the throng, the Count shared a little table in front of the café with a young man of just such a type. Our friend had some lemonade. The young man was sitting moodily before an empty glass. He looked up once, and then looked down again. He also tilted his hat forward. Like this –

The Count made the gesture of a man pulling his hat down over his brow, and went on:

'I think to myself: he is sad; something is wrong with him; young men have their troubles. I take no notice of him, of course. I pay for my lemonade, and go away.'

Strolling about in the neighbourhood of the band, the Count thinks he saw twice that young man wandering alone in the crowd. Once their eyes met. It must have been the same young man, but there were so many there of that type that he could not be certain. Moreover, he was not very much concerned except in so far that he had been struck by the marked, peevish discontent of that face.

Presently, tired of the feeling of confinement one experiences in a crowd, the Count edged away from the band. An alley, very sombre by contrast, presented itself invitingly with its promise of solitude and coolness. He entered it, walking slowly on till the sound of the orchestra became distinctly deadened. Then he walked back and turned about once more. He did this several times before he noticed that there was somebody occupying one of the benches.

The spot being midway between two lamp-posts the light was faint.

The man lolled back in the corner of the seat, his legs stretched out, his arms folded and his head drooping on his breast. He never stirred, as though he had fallen asleep there, but when the Count passed by next time he had changed his attitude. He sat leaning forward. His elbows were propped on his knees, and his hands were rolling a cigarette. He never looked up from that occupation.

The Count continued his stroll away from the band. He returned slowly, he said. I can imagine him enjoying to the full, but with his usual tranquillity, the balminess of this southern night and the sounds of music softened delightfully by the distance.

Presently, he approached for the third time the man on the garden seat, still leaning forward with his elbows on his knees. (278–9)

It is not hard to find 'a few hardly veiled contradictions', to use Steinmann's phrase, in this passage. The Count says that he takes no notice of the young man at whose table he has chosen to sit, but he is able to describe his appearance and behaviour in some detail, and he has looked at him carefully enough to see him two more times. He even remembers meeting the young man's eyes. After this he moves off to a dark alley that presents itself 'invitingly' to him. He walks up and down it no fewer than three times, notices someone on one of the benches, and eventually 'approaches' this man for a third time. For the reader who is actively looking for an alternative reading the search is not long. The Count has chosen to sit at a table where a young man who attracts him is. He makes eye-contact with this man ('He looked up once, and then looked down again'). The man's tilting his hat may be understood as some sort of a signal. The Count then moves off, keeps in contact with the young man, signals to him again by means of eye-contact, then finds a suitably secluded spot for a sexual liaison. He waits to be approached, but when this does not happen he himself approaches the young man, and is successful in eliciting the standard pick-up line when the young man asks for a light. But from here on things go wrong as the young man is interested not in sex but in robbery, and correctly assumes that the Count will not want to risk exposure and report the robbery to the police. ('He might have said anything – bring some dishonouring charge against me – what do I know?' [281])

Conrad's count is, then, innocent neither in a sexual nor a moral sense. But what of Conrad's narrator in the story? Since the publication of Hughes's and Steinmann's articles in 1975 it has been generally accepted that the narrator of

'Il Conde' is what narratologists term an unreliable narrator. But before we leave 'Il Conde' it is worth asking whether this is the only thing about him that critics have failed to detect. Let us return to the opening of the tale.

> The first time we got into conversation was in the National Museum in Naples, in the rooms on the ground floor containing the famous collection of bronzes from Herculaneum and Pompeii: that marvellous legacy of antique art whose delicate perfection has been preserved for us by the catastrophic fury of a volcano.
>
> He addressed me first, over the celebrated Resting Hermes which we had been looking at side by side. He said the right things about that wholly admirable piece. Nothing profound. His taste was natural rather than cultivated. He had obviously seen many fine things in his life and appreciated them: but he had no jargon of a dilettante or the connoisseur. A hateful tribe. He spoke like a fairly intelligent man of the world, a perfectly unaffected gentleman. (269)

The two men meet while standing, side by side, looking at the statue of a beautiful, seated, adolescent boy, a representation that the narrator describes as a 'wholly admirable piece'. The Count initiates a conversation between the two men, and he chooses to talk to the narrator about the statue. When we learn that the count's 'taste was natural rather than cultivated', could this mean that his admiration is directed more at what is represented than at the aesthetic value of the representation?

The third paragraph of the story includes the episode with the mislaid parasol upon which I have already commented. The fourth reads as follows:

> Having conversed at the Museo – (and by the by he had expressed his dislike of the busts and statues of Roman emperors in the gallery of marbles: their faces were too vigorous, too pronounced for him) – having conversed already in the morning I did not think I was intruding when in the evening, finding the dining-room very full, I proposed to share his little table. Judging by the quiet urbanity of his consent he did not think so either. His smile was very attractive. (270)

If knowing critics of the tale make much of the fact that the Count himself chooses to sit at the same table as the seated young man who later robs him in the dark alley, what are we to make of the fact that after meeting through their shared admiration for the Resting Hermes in the morning, by the evening the narrator approaches the seated Count and asks to share his table? What too are we to make of the fact that the narrator reports that 'His smile was very attractive'?

Surely there are sufficient hints here to make us wonder how innocent the narrator himself is – especially given his own later suspicions of the Count ('it is in human nature to believe the worst; and I confess I eyed him stealthily, wondering what he had been up to'). Moreover the short sentence 'His smile was very attractive' prompts a very momentary pause on the part of the reader. Smiles can of course be attractive where there is no erotic or sexual charge, but the comment is ever so slightly arresting.

In short, if readers are well advised to treat the account of the narrating governess in James's *The Turn of the Screw* with circumspection, then perhaps they would be well-advised to manifest the same caution with regard to Conrad's narrator. Having said this, it is clearly the case that for the best part of a century, and a century including thirty years during which the innocence of the Count has been denied, readers have not done this. Why is this so?

Part of the answer to this question lies in what I have already suggested: if the reader of the tale entertains no suspicion of the Count and has no inkling of the existence of a sexual sub-plot then there is no reason to doubt the innocence of the narrator. But an additional reason can be found in a natural tendency to associate the narrator with Conrad himself. As I have noted, in his 'Author's Note' to *A Set of Six* Conrad encourages such an association, while the reader of 'The Turn of the Screw' is very much made aware that James's governess is both dead and a different sex from her creator. (More could however be said of James's frame narrator, and of his or her relationship with the narrator-character Douglas, which certainly carries the suggestion of some sort of emotional or erotic charge.) Given that the reader is encouraged to associate the narrator of 'Il Conde' with Conrad himself, the fact is that Joseph Conrad has enjoyed a reputation for being as thoroughly and conventionally heterosexual as can be imagined, while Henry James has certainly not. We may further note that James's use of a chain of narrators in his tale (Douglas, the governess, the shadowy frame narrator) makes it much more problematic to associate any of these with this figure of the author, while Conrad's narrator communicates with the reader without any such intermediate figures. We may feel that there are purely technical reasons why Conrad, although basing his narrator on himself, should choose to present him by implication as a man without wife or family. Such a choice makes it easier for the narrator and the Count to establish an intimate relationship in which embarrassing secrets are recounted. At the same time it would have been possible for Conrad to have had his narrator leave Capri to attend to a sick wife or child – and indeed during his time on Capri Conrad's son Borys was seriously ill. Instead the narrator has to attend to needs of his ungendered 'friend'.

My argument is that there is a case to be made that Conrad deliberately constructs this tale in such a way as to leave open the possibility that the narrator, too, knows more about tabooed or illicit forms of sexuality than most readers have appeared to have assumed. And this suggests that Conrad's designs on the reader may be rather more like those of James's designs on *his* reader than readers and critics have been prepared to accept.

Decoys and subterfuges: three echoes

Echo 1: 'Nice young men'

At this point I would like to use 'Il Conde' as a point of departure to make connections with a number of other works by Conrad. For if it is the case that for sixty-seven years critical discussion of 'Il Conde' remained oblivious of the deeper and darker meaning of the tale, then does this not raise the possibility that there are deeper and darker meanings awaiting critical discovery in some of Conrad's other fictions? I will attempt to lead in to this discussion by linking small but telling textual details in 'Il Conde' to a number of Conrad's other works.

Let us start with the scene late in 'Il Conde' in the Café Umberto, where the Count observes the man he assumes to be his robber and asks the 'old pedlar' Pasquale about him.

> Pasquale approached, the smile of deferential recognition combining oddly with the cynical searching expression of his eyes. Leaning his case on the table, he lifted the glass lid without a word. The Count took a box of cigarettes and urged by a fearful curiosity, asked as casually as he could –
>
> 'Tell me, Pasquale, who is that young signore sitting over there?'
>
> The other bent over his box confidentially.
>
> 'That, *Signor Conde*,' he said, beginning to rearrange his wares busily and without looking up, 'that is a young *Cavaliere* of a very good family from Bari. He studies in the University here, and is the chief, *capo*, of an association of young men – of very nice young men.'
>
> He paused, and then, with mingled discretion and pride of knowledge, murmured the explanatory word 'Camorra' and shut down the lid. 'A very powerful Camorra,' he breathed out. 'The professors themselves respect it greatly ... *una lira e cinquanti centesimi, Signor Conde*.' (286–7)

I wish to draw particular attention to the way in which we are told that Pasquale's 'smile of deferential recognition' combined 'oddly with the cynical searching expression of his eyes'. What are we to make of this? Should it remind us, perhaps, of the 'very attractive' smile with which the Count greets the narrator when the latter sits at his table? Clearly Pasquale recognizes the Count and treats him with the respect that his rank and his money require. But why the cynical searching expression of his eyes? Should we perhaps be warned that something other than the obvious is going on here – perhaps by the word 'oddly'? Does not his manner suggest that Pasquale is prepared to offer some less-than-respectable service to the Count, and is looking to see if it would be welcomed? When Pasquale hears the Count's question, he effectively warns the Count off: the young man is the head of a powerful Camorra. But before he does this, he expands his description of the 'association of young men' in a curious way: 'of very nice young men'.

This particular phrase has a strong and revealing echo in Conrad's later novella *The Shadow-Line*. Early in this work, the narrator – unemployed now after signing off his ship – is talking to Captain Giles after tiffin in the Officers' Sailors' Home about a fellow-guest who is clearly suffering from a very bad hangover. Captain Giles explains that the man is an officer of some Rajah's yacht which had come into port to be dry-docked.

> Must have been 'seeing life' last night, he added, wrinkling his nose in an intimate, confidential way which pleased me vastly. For Captain Giles had prestige. He was credited with wonderful adventures and with some mysterious tragedy in his life. And no man had a word to say against him. He continued:
>
> 'I remember him first coming ashore here some years ago. Seems only the other day. He was a nice boy. Oh! these nice boys!'
>
> I could not help laughing aloud. He looked startled, then joined in the laugh. 'No! No! I didn't mean that,' he cried. 'What I meant is that some of them do go soft mighty quick out here.' (11–12)

What, we may ask, is it that Captain Giles does not mean? The shared laughter clearly denotes a common understanding, and it is one that is triggered by the phrase 'nice boys'. Even on its own the passage is arresting and suggestive, but considered alongside Pasquale's explanatory comment – 'of very nice young men' – it seems difficult to avoid the conclusion that 'nice young men' and 'nice boys' are phrases that imply either that the young men are available for homosexual activity, or that they represent objects of male homosexual desire. Going back to the passage from 'Il Conde', then, we can surmise that what Pasquale is intimating to the Count is that yes, this young man – like those in his association – is indeed sexually attractive (perhaps even available), but that he is dangerous and thus not to be approached.

There are passages in other works by Conrad that strengthen the suspicion that Conrad was capable of suggesting a homosexual sub-plot or concealed meaning through such a use of coded comments. I pointed out above that 'Il Conde' was written after Conrad had completed the serial version of *The Secret Agent*; this novel also contains an example of a suggestive use of the word 'nice'. When the Assistant Commissioner goes to meet Sir Ethelred we are told that 'he was met at last by the volatile and revolutionary Toodles. That neat and nice young man concealed his astonishment at the early appearance of the Assistant

Commissioner' (162). The 'youthful-looking Private Secretary' Toodles is portrayed as foolish and absurdly fawning in his relationship to Sir Ethelred, but Conrad's use of the phrase 'nice young man' provides a legitimate reason to wonder whether Conrad is suggesting that the relationship between the older and the younger man is of a sexual nature. Whether the name Ethelred is chosen by Conrad to suggest unreadiness or to invite curtailment to 'Ethel' is hard to say, but 'Toodles' has a distinctly feminine ring to it (the name, we are told, was bestowed upon the young man by Sir Ethelred's daughters, and then adopted by their father).

There is evidence in Conrad's work that 'nice' *may* imply little more than naïve immaturity when linked to 'boy' or 'young man'. In *Nostromo* (1904) the word 'nice' is applied to a very minor character: 'At that moment young Scarfe of the railway staff emerged from the door of the part reserved for the Signori Inglesi. He had come down to headquarters from somewhere up the line on a light engine, and had had just time to get a bath and change his clothes. He was a nice boy, and Mrs. Gould welcomed him' (168). Scarfe displays obtuseness and immaturity in his brief appearance in the novel, but there is no suggestion that his 'niceness' has a sexual dimension.

'Freya of the Seven Isles' (1912) may also be said to confirm that the word was not necessarily possessed of sexual implications. In this tale Freya's father, Nelson, is unhappy that his daughter is seeing too much of Jasper Allen, because his trading habits do not recommend him to the Dutch authorities. In Nelson's opinion Jasper Allen is, among other things, 'a nice young man' (154), but the phrase appears to carry no sexual charge here.

Elsewhere in Conrad's fiction the force of the word is less easy to fix. In *Lord Jim* (1900) the bar-keeper Schomberg – who also appears in 'Falk' and *Victory* – refers to Jim as 'a very nice young man' (144) in conversation with Marlow. Schomberg's behaviour in *Victory* leaves no doubt as to his own heterosexual urges (if we are allowed to assume a transtextual consistency in the character), but it is just possible that he is delivering a slur here, and impugning Jim's sexuality. The issue of the sexual covert plot of *Lord Jim* is one to which I shall return later on.

One further passage merits consideration in this context, for even though it does not contain the word 'nice' it is strikingly similar to the discussion between Captain Giles and the captain-narrator that I cite above from *The Shadow-Line*. It comes from *Heart of Darkness*, during the discussion between Marlow and the Russian Harlequin, who is talking of his encounters with Kurtz.

'We talked of everything,' he said, quite transported at the recollection. 'I forgot there was such a thing as sleep. The night did not seem to last an hour. Everything! Everything! ... Of love too.' 'Ah, he talked to you of love!' I said, much amused. 'It isn't what you think,' he cried, almost passionately. 'It was in general. He made me see things – things.' (161–2)

If we ask what amuses Marlow, and what the Russian believes that Marlow 'thinks', then the fact that Marlow's reaction is triggered by the word 'love' suggests that the implied but rejected meaning is sexual in nature. And although the two men could have been talking about love between a man and a woman, Marlow's amusement (a reaction that is very similar to the narrator's 'laughing aloud' in response to Captain Giles's comment in *The Shadow-Line*) may suggest that it involves love of a less conventional sort.

What this chain or family of hints and suggestions establishes is that homosexual desire, especially the desire of an older man for an adolescent or young man, is something that ostensibly heterosexual men are aware of in the world of Conrad's fiction, and that they are able to treat with (perhaps embarrassed) amusement amongst themselves. This may seem a weak and unremarkable conclusion, but it should be set against a long-established critical assumption that Conrad the conventional family man was blissfully ignorant of tabooed or illicit forms of sexual desire or behaviour, and that to argue for the existence of such things in his works is to impose an anachronistic, present-day knowingness on an altogether more conventional and sexually innocent man and author.

Even so, many readers may still feel impelled to ask: 'So what? Such a process of intertextual tracking may indeed pick up some limited evidence that Conrad was not quite such a sexual innocent as has been assumed, but how aesthetically significant is such knowledge? It may allow us to read a minor work such as "Il Conde" in a fuller and more appropriate manner, but the fact that Marlow and the Russian Harlequin share a moment of knowledge about homosexual desire can hardly be argued to be more than extremely marginal to an interpretation of Conrad's best-known work.'

I think that the most important response to such a challenge would go something like this. Generations of readers and critics have, in spite of many disagreements, agreed that at the heart of Conrad's artistic vision is a powerful sense of human isolation and loneliness. If Conrad is – as again many have agreed is the case – a transitional figure, an author located on the cusp of nineteenth-century realism and twentieth-century modernism, this liminal position is manifested in his work by a simultaneous yearning for community and a grim recognition of existential isolation. Sexuality alone does not offer an escape from loneliness and alienation. But the human relationships that are brought about by, or imbricated in, sexual desires and consummations, have indeed been seen by many to offer a, perhaps the, way out of a despairing and destructive existential loneliness. In work after work we recognize that Conrad's characters are terrified of isolation, are appalled by the prospect of being left alone. We have too to face the fact that this terror is one that is repeatedly generalized and presented as a universal human experience by a succession of Conrad's narrators and authorial statements. In some cases the isolation is literalized, as it is in *Nostromo* when Decoud is left alone on the Isabels, cannot deal with such an abandonment, and after ten days, kills himself. Elsewhere, the isolation is more recognizably modernist, taking the form of a sense of existential aloneness that even the presence of other people cannot dissipate. Charles Gould and Adolf Verloc experience such a sense of abandonment even in the presence of their wives – and their wives, too, feel as tormentingly alone as does Decoud.

We have to ask, I think, why there is hardly any sense in Conrad's work that passionate, loving relationships of a sexual nature are able to offer a way out of the existential solitary confinement that his characters fear so much. No-one would claim that D.H. Lawrence is the novelist of marital happiness and contentment. Nonetheless, in Lawrence's work there is a consistent commitment to the belief that only through a powerful passionate relationship that is sexually and erotically charged and, eventually, consummated, can a human being escape from emotional sterility and isolation. In spite of enormous differences between three very different writers, much the same is true of the work of E.M. Forster and Virginia Woolf. But it can not be said of the work of Joseph Conrad. Tracing Conrad's treatment of sexuality, desire, and the erotic through a number of works is, then, far from marginal to his importance as a writer.

Echo 2: Bachelors, suicide and gold watches

Chapter 6 of Joseph Conrad's novel *Lord Jim* is one that is – even for such a digressive and episodic novel as this – notable for its digressive and episodic nature. It is the second chapter narrated by Marlow, following the four introductory chapters that are relayed to the reader by an impersonal, extradiegetic, and on occasions, in the traditional sense, 'omniscient' source. In the fifth chapter of the novel we have been introduced to Marlow, who has told the story of the arrival of the *Patna*'s officers in the 'Eastern port', and of the flight of all but Jim, who remains to face the Court of Inquiry. More details are filled in for Marlow and for the reader through Marlow's encounter with the hospitalized and delirious Chief Engineer of the ship.

Chapter 6 opens in such a manner as to lead the reader to expect that an account of Jim's trial is to follow. But it is as if Marlow, having mentioned that one of the three assessors is 'Big Brierly', is seduced into a digression involving this man. The paragraph detailing Marlow's account of Brierly's incomparably successful career – and of Brierly's arrogant sense of his own unique worth – is so heavily ironic that it comes as shock to the reader when it ends with the short sentence: 'He committed suicide very soon after'. From an impatient wish that Marlow should get back to giving an account of Jim and his fate the reader is suddenly jolted into a desire to know more about Brierly – about his uniquely successful career and his shockingly unexpected (both to those who knew him, and to us readers) end. This desire is soon satisfied: Marlow is able to provide the information about Brierly's last hours on earth that he was given by Brierly's 'grey-headed mate', Mr Jones. Jones tells Marlow of Brierly's actions immediately prior to his suicide: his extremely conscientious attention to the log and to the duties of the succeeding watch, and of his telling Jones to lock up his dog Rover in the chart-room. Jones's account continues:

> '"This was the last time I heard his voice, Captain Marlow. These are the last words he spoke in the hearing of any living human being, sir.' At this point the old chap's voice got quite unsteady. "He was afraid the poor brute would jump after him, don't you see?" he pursued with a quaver. "Yes, Captain Marlow. He set the log for me; he – would you believe it? – he put a drop of oil in it too. There was the oil-feeder where he left it near by. The boatswain's mate got the hose along aft to wash down at half-past five; by-and-by he knocks off and runs up on the bridge, – 'Will you please come aft, Mr. Jones,' he says. 'There's a funny thing. I don't like to touch it.' It was Captain Brierly's gold chronometer watch carefully hung under the rail by its chain.
>
> '"As soon as my eyes fell on it something struck me, and I knew, sir. My legs got soft under me. It was as if I had seen him go over; and I could tell how far behind he was left too. The taffrail-log marked eighteen miles and three-quarters, and four iron belaying-pins were missing round the mainmast. Put them in his pockets to help him down, I suppose; but, Lord! what's four iron pins to a powerful man like Captain Brierly. Maybe his confidence in himself was just shook a bit at the last. (44–5)

For the student of Conrad's fiction it is striking that the number of iron pins Brierly uses to ensure his own drowning matches exactly the number of silver ingots used by Martin Decoud to guarantee his own drowning in the later *Nostromo*. But there is an additional detail in this account that is worth paying some attention to.

Conrad was a great admirer of the fiction of Charles Dickens, and in *A Personal Record* he remarks of an acquaintance of his youth, Madame Delestang, that

> In her haughty weariness she used to make me think of Lady Dedlock in Dickens' 'Bleak House,' a work of the master for which I have such an admiration, or rather such an intense and unreasoning affection, dating from the days of my childhood, that its very weaknesses are more precious to me than the strength of other men's work. I have read it innumerable times, both in Polish and in English; I have read it only the other day, and, by a not very surprising inversion, the Lady Dedlock of the book reminded me strongly of the *belle Madame Delestang*. (124)

One of the most sinister characters in *Bleak House* is the lawyer Mr Tulkinghorn. Tulkinghorn discovers that Lady Dedlock has had a passionate relationship before marrying Lord Dedlock, and that Esther Summerson is the illegitimate fruit of that liaison. Tulkinghorn is portrayed as a man who obtains a perverted pleasure from torturing Lady Dedlock with his knowledge of her secret. He is a bachelor, who keeps his own secrets very close, and appears for a long while to have no intimate friends.

Chapter 22 of *Bleak House* opens with Tulkinghorn alone in his chambers at Lincoln's Inn Fields. He has dined alone and is now enjoying a glass from the 'priceless bin of port [...] which is one of his many secrets'.

> Mr Tulkinghorn, sitting in the twilight by the open window, enjoys his wine. As if it whispered to him of its fifty years of silence and seclusion, it shuts him up the closer. More impenetrable than ever, he sits, and drinks, and mellows as it were, in secrecy; pondering, at that twilight hour, on all the mysteries he knows, associated with darkening woods in the country, and vast blank shut-up houses in town: and perhaps sparing a thought or two for himself, and his family history, and his money, and his will – all a mystery to every one – and that one bachelor friend of his, a man of the same mould and a lawyer too, who lived the same kind of life until he was seventy-five years old, and then, suddenly conceiving (as it is supposed) an impression that it was too monotonous, gave his gold watch to his hair-dresser one summer evening, and walked leisurely home to the Temple, and hanged himself. (1971, 359)

The detail of the disposing of a gold watch, followed by an unexpected suicide, strikes an unexpected chord for anyone familiar with *Lord Jim* and its account of the suicide of Brierly. Both Brierly and Tulkinghorn's lawyer friend are bachelors, both function as figures of authority in legal inquiries, both are seemingly successful, and both kill themselves – although at very different stages in their lives and careers.

At the start of Marlow's discussion of Brierly, following the bald statement 'He committed suicide very soon after', Marlow expands on his knowledge of the assessor.

> 'No wonder Jim's case bored him, and while I thought with something akin to fear of the immensity of his contempt for the young man under examination, he was probably holding silent inquiry into his own case. The verdict must have been of unmitigated guilt, and he took the secret of the evidence with him in that leap into the sea. If I understand anything of men, the matter was no doubt of the gravest import, one of those trifles that awaken ideas – start into life some thought with which a man unused to such a companionship finds it impossible to live. I am in a position to know that

it wasn't money, and it wasn't drink, and it wasn't woman. He jumped overboard at sea barely a week after the end of the inquiry, and less than three days after leaving port on his outward passage; as though on that exact spot in the midst of waters he had suddenly perceived the gates of the other world flung open wide for his reception. (42–3)

While Marlow is able to ascribe much of his knowledge of Brierly and of his final moments of life to Brierly's first mate Jones, he is less than forthcoming about the source of some of the information provided here. 'I am in a position to know that it wasn't money, and it wasn't drink, and it wasn't woman'. Another detail catches the attention here; not 'it wasn't a woman', as would be idiomatic were the intention to explain that Brierly was not killing himself in consequence of an involvement with a specific woman, but 'it wasn't woman'.

There is a further, weaker echo of the passage in *Lord Jim* in the newspaper report of Winnie Verloc's suicide that Ossipon carries round with him at the end of *The Secret Agent*. A 'hand' on the cross-channel steamer discovers a wedding ring lying on the seat on which Winnie (described only as 'the lady in black') has previously been seen sitting. Inside the ring is inscribed a date: 24 June, 1879. The preciseness of this date – like the preciseness of the information that Brierly enters into the ship's log prior to his suicide – is of no help in revealing what has gone on inside the head of the owner of the ring. The ring, like the log-entry and the gold chronometer, provides those left behind with a very reliable point of temporal reference. But it grants no access to the inner life of Winnie Verloc.

The most obvious explanation for Brierly's suicide is that Jim's act of dereliction of duty causes him to doubt his own ability always to behave correctly. Unable to live with the possibility that he too might one day betray his trust, he prefers to kill himself. But the account of Brierly's life and death that is given the reader of *Lord Jim* is deliberately suggestive, and seems designed in an almost Jamesian fashion to encourage the reader to speculate on other possible explanations. What seems incontrovertible is that Brierly's suicide is triggered by his encounter with Jim and the case of the *Patna*. What, we may ask, is it about Jim that causes him to have such a profound emotional effect on a succession of adult men: Marlow, Brierly, Egström, Denver – and in a different way, Gentleman Brown?

Echo 3: The case of the effeminate captains

Brierly leaves two letters behind him, one addressed to the company that owns his ship the *Ossa* and one to Jones. In the former he does his best to recommend Jones to the company as his successor, and in the latter he writes to Jones 'like a father would to a favourite son'. But his efforts are in vain.

But no fear. The captain of the *Pelion* was shifted into the *Ossa* – came aboard in Shanghai – a little popinjay, sir, in a grey check suit, with his hair parted in the middle. 'Aw – I am – aw – your new captain, Mister – Mister – aw – Jones.' He was drowned in scent – fairly stunk with it, Captain Marlow. I dare say it was the look I gave him that made him stammer. He mumbled something about my natural disappointment – I had better know at once that his chief officer got the promotion to the *Pelion* – he had nothing to do with it, of course – supposed the office knew best – sorry. . . . Says I, 'Don't you mind old Jones, sir; dam' his soul, he's used to it.' I could see directly I had shocked his delicate ear, and while we sat at our first tiffin together he began to find fault in a nasty manner with this and that in the ship. I never heard such a voice out of a Punch and Judy show. I set my teeth hard, and glued my eyes to my plate, and held my peace as long as I could; but at last I had to say something. Up he jumps tiptoeing, ruffling all his pretty plumes, like a little fighting cock. 'You'll find you have a different person to deal with than the late Captain Brierly.' 'I've found it,' says I, very glum, but pretending to be mighty busy with my steak. 'You are an old ruffian, Mister – aw – Jones; and what's more, you are known for an old ruffian in the employ,' he squeaks at me. The damned bottle-washers stood about listening with their mouths stretched from ear to ear. 'I may be a hard case,' answers I, 'but I ain't so far gone as to put up with the sight of you sitting in Captain Brierly's chair.' With that I lay down my knife and fork. 'You would like to sit in it yourself – that's where the shoe pinches,' he sneers. I left the saloon, got my rags together, and was on the quay with all my dunnage about my feet before the stevedores had turned to again. (45–6)

Dickens was only one among many English novelists whose work was read and loved by Conrad. According to Joséf Retinger, 'Among English novelists nearest to him stood the eighteenth-century writers, and foremost among them Smollett and Richardson. He made me read their novels repeatedly and never tired commenting on them' (104–5). Retinger is not the most reliable of sources, and the idea of Conrad reading *Clarissa* or *Pamela* with pleasure requires a considerable effort of mind. But it is far easier to imagine his enjoying the fiction of Tobias Smollett, and especially those works that have a strong maritime flavour.

In Chapter 34 of Smollett's *The Adventures of Roderick Random* – probably the Scottish novelist's best-known and most widely read novel – the eponymous hero, who is working as a ship's surgeon, describes the arrival of a new captain on board ship, replacing the tyrannical Captain Oakhum.

Our tyrant having left the ship, and carried his favourite Mackshane along with him, to my inexpressible satisfaction, our new commander came on board, in a ten-oar'd barge, overshadowed with a vast umbrella, and appeared in everything quite the reverse of Oakhum, being a tall, thin, young man, dressed in this manner; a white hat garnished with a red feather, adorned his head, from whence his hair flowed down upon his shoulders, in ringlets tied behind with a ribbon. —His coat, consisting of pink-coloured silk, lined with white, by the elegance of the cut retired backward, as it were, to discover a white sattin waistcoat embroidered with gold, unbuttoned at the upper part, to display a broch set with garnets, that glittered in the breast of his shirt, which was of the finest cambrick, edged with right mechlin. The knees of his crimson velvet breeches scarce descended so low as to meet his silk stockings, which rose without spot or wrinkle on his meagre legs, from shoes of blue Meroquin, studded with diamond buckles, that flamed forth rivals to the sun! A steel-hilted sword, inlaid with gold, and decked with a knot of ribbon which fell down in a rich tossle, equipped his side; and an amber-headed cane hung dangling from his wrist: —But the most remarkable parts of his furniture were, a mask on his face, and white gloves on his hands, which did not seem to be put on with an intention to be pulled off occasionally, but were fixed with a ring set with a ruby on the little finger of one hand, and by one set with a topaz on that of the other. —In this garb, Captain Whiffle, for that was his name, took possession of the ship, surrounded with a crowd of attendants, all of whom, in their different degrees, seemed to be of their patron's disposition; and the air was so impregnated with perfumes, that one may venture to affirm the climate of Arabia Fœlix was not half so sweet-scented. (Smollett 1999, 194–5)

Smollett's account of Captain Whiffle continues for the rest of this chapter and spills into the following one. It emphasizes his effete and effeminate nature, and the imputation of homosexuality is unmistakable when Whiffle insists that no-one but his personal surgeon Simper or his own servants be permitted to come into his cabin without first sending in to obtain leave. The narrative continues: 'These singular regulations did not prepossess the ship's company in his favour: but on the contrary, gave scandal an opportunity to be very busy with his character, and accuse him of maintaining a correspondence with his surgeon, not fit to be named' (199).

Just as Conrad stresses the sharp contrast between the scented ex-captain of the *Pelion* and the rough and course-mouthed Jones, so too Smollett engineers a similar encounter of opposites between the perfumed new commander and the scruffy, Welsh, Surgeon's First Mate Morgan. The effect (or one of them) is the same in both fictional works: the quarrel sets the 'rough' Mate in opposition to the effeminate Captain, stresses the former's masculinity and heterosexual 'normality', and thus allows him to be depicted in close, emotional relationships with another man without risking that these be interpreted as in some way or another homoerotic in nature by the reader. We can see the same effect in Virginia Woolf's novel *Mrs Dalloway* (1925) in which the negative portrayal of the character Miss Kilman as a stereotypical lesbian, along with Clarissa Dalloway's dislike of her, serves to deflect the force of the homoerotic relationship between Clarissa Dalloway and Sally Seton. This use of an overtly homosexual character to mask the homoerotic nature of a relationship between two ostensibly heterosexual characters is one that Conrad uses elsewhere in his fiction – most notably, as I shall argue, in *The Shadow-Line*.

The homosocial and the homosexual

In recent years a number of critics have argued that a more knowing stance on the part of the reader will reveal a significant strain of homoerotic impulses and relationships in Conrad's fiction. In *Heart of Darkness* Marlow, recounting his interrupted and danger-strewn journey towards Kurtz, remarks of it that 'the approach to this Kurtz grubbing for ivory in the wretched bush was beset by as many dangers as though he had been an enchanted princess sleeping in a fabulous castle' (146–7). This is not the only reference to an enchanted princess in Conrad's fiction. In the later *The Shadow-Line* the captain-narrator comments on his as-yet unseen command: 'She was there waiting for me, spell-bound, unable to move, to live, to get out into the world (till I came), like an enchanted princess'. I will return to a consideration of the passage in which this sentence appears below.

Richard J. Ruppel – the critic who has perhaps explored the issue of the homoerotic in Conrad's fiction most extensively – includes Marlow's comment among a number of telling quotations from Conrad's best known novella to underpin his case that in this and other works of Conrad there are many hitherto unrecognized examples of the homoerotic. In his article '"Girl! What? Did I mention a girl?" The economy of desire in *Heart of Darkness*', Ruppel claims that

> Conrad's novels and stories contain many representations of homosexual desire. In *Lord Jim* (1900), the eponymous hero – though sexually passive – is desired not only by the heroine, Jewel, but also by the mill owner he works for and by Marlow himself. In *Under Western Eyes* (1911), the language-teacher narrator can be seen as a rather bitter, closeted homosexual, sexually attracted to Razumov. In Natalia Haldin, the narrator has found a 'virile' young woman whom he can admire, even sexually, and the somber, disappointed tone of the novel might be attributed to his knowledge that a union between them is impossible. (2003, 152)

This short paragraph contains a number of assertions that, I believe, range from the well-founded to the dubious. If we start with *Lord Jim* we can concede that Jim is indeed desired by Jewel, to whom he is married in all but name, and who makes strenuous efforts to protect him from assassins and to dissuade him from returning to a certain death at the hands of Doramin. At the same time it is worth noting that Marlow's descriptions of the relationship between Jim and Jewel contains no hint of the erotic: they appear like good friends, a well-established couple, but on the evidence of Marlow's account, hardly a site of smouldering passion.

So far as the mill owner is concerned, we enter here the realm of speculation. This is Mr Denver – the friend to whom Marlow writes a letter after Jim's trial, a man Marlow describes as 'my friend (he was a cynical, more than middle-aged bachelor, with a reputation for eccentricity, and owned a rice-mill)' (135). Denver is named only once in the novel; Marlow normally refers to him only as 'my friend'. Six months after sending Jim to him, Marlow receives a letter from 'my friend', who enlarges on Jim's 'perfections'.

> These were apparently of a quiet and effective sort. 'Not having been able so far to find more in my heart than a resigned toleration for any individual of my kind, I have lived till now alone in a house that even in this steaming climate could be considered as too big for one man. I have had him to live with me for some time past. It seems I haven't made a mistake.' It seemed to me on reading this letter that my friend had found in his heart more than tolerance for Jim, – that there were the beginnings of active liking. Of course he stated his grounds in a characteristic way. For one thing, Jim kept his freshness in the climate. Had he been a girl – my friend wrote – one could have said he was blooming – blooming modestly – like a violet, not like some of these blatant tropical flowers. He had been in the house for six weeks, and had not as yet attempted to slap him on the back, or address him as 'old boy,' or try to make him feel a superannuated fossil. He had nothing of the exasperating young man's chatter. He was good-tempered, had not much to say for himself, was not clever by any means, thank goodness – wrote my friend. It appeared, however, that Jim was clever enough to be quietly appreciative of his wit, while, on the other hand, he amused him by his naïveness. 'The dew is yet on him, and since I had the bright idea of giving him a room in the house and having him at meals I feel less withered myself. The other day he took it into his head to cross the room with no other purpose but to open a door for me; and I felt more in touch with mankind than I had been for years. Ridiculous, isn't it? Of course I guess there is something – some awful little scrape – which you know all about – but if I am sure that it is terribly heinous, I fancy one could manage to forgive it. For my part, I declare I am unable to imagine him guilty of anything much worse than robbing an orchard. *Is it* much worse? Perhaps you ought to have told me; but it is such a long time since we both turned saints that you may have forgotten we too had sinned in our time? It may be that some day I shall have to ask you, and then I shall expect to be told. I don't care to question him

myself till I have some idea what it is. Moreover, it's too soon as yet. Let him open the door a few times more for me. . . .' (135–6)

The next letter that Marlow receives from his bachelor friend reports that Jim has left, 'leaving on the breakfast-table a formal little note of apology, which is either silly or heartless. Probably both – and it's all one to me' (136).

I quote at length here, because the quoted matter constitutes the sum total of the textual evidence available to support the claim that the mill owner experiences sexual desire for Jim. How convincing, how conclusive is this evidence? Read from the perspective of Ruppel's assertion it must be conceded that the passage contains a succession of hints that, taken together, do suggest that something more than innocent, asexual male companionship is being proposed to the reader. Key elements in this passage include Mr Denver's bachelor status (something that he shares with Marlow, just as both the widowed Il Conde and the narrator of his tale are without a female partner), the unspecified nature of his reputed eccentricity, his conceit that had Jim been a girl 'one could have said he was blooming – blooming modestly – like a violet' (a flower not so far distant from a pansy), his inviting Jim to live with him in his own house, and the vague connotations of the biblical fall that accompany the supposition that Jim cannot have been 'guilty of anything much worse than robbing an orchard'. There is, too, the appeal to shared knowledge in the comment to Marlow that 'it is such a long time since we both turned saints that you may have forgotten we too had sinned in our time?' – an appeal that is proleptic of Gentleman Brown's appeal to a common background in his fatal discussion with Jim much later in the novel. And there is, too, that word 'scrape' – the same word that springs to the mind of the narrator of 'Il Conde' when, following his having entertained unworthy suspicions of the Count, he finds that they vanish because 'There was a fundamental refinement of nature about the man which made me dismiss all idea of some more or less disreputable scrape'.

On its own, not one of these elements would constitute anything like conclusive evidence to substantiate Ruppel's claim. Conrad certainly uses the word 'scrape' about heterosexual escapades. (In 'To-morrow' Harry comments to Bessie: 'Anything for a woman of the right sort. The scrapes they got me into, and the scrapes they got me out of!' [271].) If the orchard robbing has biblical connotations then these should involve heterosexual temptation – and so on. But it is undeniably the case that, taken as a whole, the succession of hints does have a cumulative force, one of which it seems hard to believe that Conrad was totally unaware.

But what of the claim that Marlow too experiences homosexual desire for Jim? Or that the teacher of languages experiences a similar desire for Razumov? In the same article from which I have already quoted, Richard J. Ruppel also argues that

The relationship between the harlequin and Kurtz presents the most obvious example of same-sex attraction in *Heart of Darkness*. The harlequin is devoted to Kurtz – as his conversations with Marlow amply reveal. 'They had come together unavoidably,' Marlow explains, 'like two ships becalmed near each other, and lay rubbing sides at last.' (2003, 159)

and he draws attention to the femininity of the Russian harlequin: 'the sunshine made him look extremely gay and wonderfully neat'; 'A beardless boyish face, very fair, no features to speak of' (160).[5] It seems that the Conradian fiction that Ruppel leaves us with may resemble Henry James's fiction far more than has hitherto appeared to be the case.

***

Let me return to the technique of using an overtly homosexual – what we might anachronistically[6] term a 'camp' – character to deflect suspicion that there might be an erotic component in the relationship between two overtly heterosexual male characters. Conrad seems to have felt the need for such a technique more in his later than his earlier work. If we compare the early *The Nigger of the 'Narcissus'* (1897) with the late *The Shadow-Line* (1917) we see a sharp contrast between the presentation of powerful emotional relationships between men in the two works. *The Nigger of the 'Narcissus'* and *The Shadow-Line* are the most exclusively male-populated of Conrad's longer works. Women appear in them only in terms of the memories of male characters (James Wait's 'Canton Street girl', the 'awful, mature, white female with rapacious nostrils and a cheaply ill-omened stare in her enormous eyes' [48] in the later work with whom the late captain becomes involved in Haiphong), at the margins of the text (Charlie's mother), or in metaphorical form (primarily the two ships, and especially the captain's command in *The Shadow-Line*). In *The Nigger of the 'Narcissus'* even the cat is male, and his description as a 'black tom' is doubtless deliberately chosen to link him with James Wait. When Charlie throws the rope-end at him the cat goes off 'with the tail carried up stiff and upright, like a small flag pole' (11), a detail that is doubtless intended as a racist marker of sexual potency – tom cats are known for their sexual appetite.

It can of course be countered that it is not surprising that there are no women characters in two works that are set on board ship. But in both *Youth* and *Chance* Conrad contrives to convey a woman on board a ship, and in the all-male shipboard community of 'Karain' the stories and memories of both Karain and Hollis cast women in a central rôle. When the sailors of *The Nigger of the 'Narcissus'* talk, they talk of what constitutes a gentleman, or about a male do-gooder and a Plimsoll man. 'Dirty' Knowles delivers an 'opinion' to the crew and makes them all laugh, but the joke is not shared with the reader – although 'the sailmaker, charged with an anecdote about a Commodore, looked sulky'

(25–6).[7] The actual voyage of the narrator-captain's new command in *The Shadow-Line* starts more than a third of the way into the text, and yet not a single female character – cook, maid, or whatever – has appeared by the time the ship leaves harbour.

Of the two works, however, *The Nigger of the 'Narcissus'* is the more unself-conscious when it comes to the portrayal of an all-male community within which men form relationships and adopt rôles that mirror those found in a community composed of both men and women. What I mean by this is that whereas a permanent awareness of the homoerotic seems as it were to linger in the suburbs of *The Shadow-Line*, *The Nigger of the 'Narcissus'* is in contrast characterized by a sort of innocence when it comes to the question of intimate male-male relationships. After the storm 'Men chummed as to beds', the two young Scandinavians are always referred to as a pair if not a couple, and we are told that they 'sat on a chest side by side, alike and placid, resembling a pair of love-birds on a perch, and with round eyes stared innocently'. Belfast addresses James Wait as 'Jimmy darlint!', steals an Edenic apple pie for him, and refuses to join his shipmates in celebration at the end of the voyage, telling the narrator:

> 'When I think of Jimmy ... Poor Jim! When I think of him I have no heart for drink. You were his chum, too ... but I pulled him out ... didn't I? Short wool he had ... Yes. And I stole the blooming pie ... He wouldn't go ... He would go for nobody.' He burst into tears. 'I never touched him – never – never!' he sobbed. 'He went for me like ... like ... a lamb.' (126)

In contrast to such a display of innocent openness *The Shadow-Line* strikes the reader as a work that is deliberately structured in such a manner as to deflect attention away from the possibility of any suspicion that the captain-narrator's relationship with the steward Ransome is in any way imbued with a sexual element. It does this, it seems to me, by intentionally alerting the reader to the possibility of homosexuality but then locating it elsewhere than on the ship.

I have already discussed the scene in which the narrator and Captain Giles talk about the 'supine' and 'insensible' stranger who, after having been 'seeing life' the night before, is now badly hung over. But this is not the only place in the first, land-based half of the novella in which the possibility of homosexuality is evoked and then located away from the narrator and those to whom he is close. The most obvious example of this procedure involves the Chief Steward of the Officers' Sailors' Home. When the narrator tells the Chief Steward that he wishes to stay at the Home, the latter's response is couched in a form that might nowadays be termed camp.

> 'Perhaps you would like to pay in advance?' he suggested eagerly.
> 'Certainly not!' I burst out directly I could speak. 'Never heard of such a thing! This is the most infernal cheek. . . .'

He had seized his head in both hands – a gesture of despair which checked my indignation.

'Oh, dear! Oh, dear! Don't fly out like this. I am asking everybody.' (8–9)

Even in this first encounter it is striking how the Chief Steward's petulant and plaintive discourse serves as it were to masculinize the narrator, who speaks in the language of assertive, upper-class, male assurance. (Later on in the text when the Chief Steward is trying to persuade Hamilton to seek the captaincy that the narrator is eventually to be offered, he makes 'plaintive expostulations' to the supercilious Hamilton.) The reader's sense of the narrator is thus formed at this early stage of the novella in terms of his disdain for a weak and 'effeminate' opponent, and this process is consolidated each time that the narrator encounters the Chief Steward.

I am afraid my behaviour to the Steward became very rough indeed. But it wasn't in him to face out anything or anybody. Drug habit or solitary tippling, perhaps. And when I forgot myself so far as to swear at him he broke down and began to shriek.

I don't mean to say that he made a great outcry. It was a cynical shrieking confession, only faint – piteously faint. It wasn't very coherent either, but sufficiently so to strike me dumb at first. I turned my eyes from him in righteous indignation [...]. (22)

Here the narrator is figured as dominant, even brutal husband, bullying a tearful and submissive wife. While such a figuration stresses the narrator's masculinity it does so in a risky way, as it forms this masculinity in an opposition created within a male-male relationship.

The Chief Steward is not the only feminized male in *The Shadow-Line* whose effeteness serves to stress the narrator's masculine qualities. When the narrator reaches Harbour Office his first contact is not with the Harbour Master Captain Ellis, but with the head Shipping-Master, who hops down from his elevation and hurries along the mats to meet the narrator.

He had a Scottish name, but his complexion was of a rich olive hue, his short beard was jet black, and his eyes, also black, had a languishing expression. He asked confidentially:

'You want to see Him?' (24)

As I have remarked elsewhere, the word 'but' in this short description seems to imply a racial slur: in spite of his Scottish name the head Shipping-Master's complexion, beard, eyes and expression suggest that he has Asian, or perhaps

Jewish, blood. This is not the only way in which this individual is presented as being other than that which he presents himself to be.

> I said: 'Oh! He has asked for me twice. Then perhaps I had better go in.'
> 'You must! You must!'
> The Shipping-Master led the way with a mincing gait around the whole system of desks to a tall and important-looking door, which he opened with a deferential action of the arm. (25)
> He stepped right in (but without letting go of the handle) and, after gazing reverently down the room for a while, beckoned me in by a silent jerk of the head. Then he slipped out at once and shut the door after me most delicately.

The man's way of talking (once again the probably anachronistic term 'camp' seems appropriate), the way he shuts the door 'most delicately', and his reverential attitude to the capitalized 'He' Captain Ellis – an attitude reminiscent of that displayed by 'Toodles' to Sir Ethelred in *The Secret Agent* – clearly imply effeminacy. But the most unambiguous signalling of homosexuality comes in the word 'mincing', denoting a walk involving quick small steps. Three other characters in Conrad's fiction have cognates of the word 'mincing' applied to them. In *Romance* (1903) which Conrad co-authored with Ford Madox Hueffer (later Ford), a prosecution witness called to testify against John Kemp is described by Kemp as a 'mincing swell', and the reader is told that 'A tiny, fair man, with pale hair oiled and rather long for those days, and with green and red signet rings on fingers that he was forever running through that hair, came mincingly into the witness-box' (523–4). In my third chapter I will discuss the case of the chief clerk in 'A Smile of Fortune' who numbers among his effeminate characteristics the fact that he walks 'mincingly', and who may share a real-life model with the Shipping-Master.

Then there is Privy Councillor Wurmt in *The Secret Agent* who, when first seen by Verloc, walks up to the table 'with a rather mincing step', and at the end of his interview with Verloc goes out 'with mincing steps' (18, 20). The term is stereotypically associated with a gait attributed to effeminate males. That great expert in cultural stereotypes, Agatha Christie, presents us with a representative example of the stereotype in her 1939 novel *Murder is Easy* in which the paleness and the long hair match those of the witness against John Kemp (Councillor Wurmt, too, has a 'pasty complexion'): 'Mr Ellsworthy was a very exquisite young man dressed in a colour scheme of russet brown. He had a long pale face with a womanish mouth, long black artistic hair and a mincing walk' (49). The characteristic is of a sort to encourage mockery, as Christie's character Mrs Pierce confirms.

'It was just his fun, sir, that was all. Tommy was always good at imitations. Make us hold our sides with laughing the way he'd mince about pretending to be Mr. Ellsworthy at the curio shop [...]. (71)

While the Shipping-Master is in feminized awe of the gruff and patriarchal Captain Ellis, the narrator stands up to Ellis, treats him as an equal, and displays his own non-subservient independence in discussion with him.

Thus by the time that the narrator has assumed a command and has joined his ship, his masculinity has been set in relief by a succession of meetings with feminized males: the hungover guest, the Chief Steward, and the Shipping-Master. Moreover he has informed the reader that 'This is not a marriage story', and has witnessed a sort of proxy marriage and a symbolic sexual consummation with his feminine ship (see the discussion below on p. 133). On joining his new ship, looking at his reflection in the mirror of his cabin, he pictures himself as the latest in an all-male dynasty of captains, the product of a succession of fathers-without-mothers, engendered without female intervention or help. And he learns that the late captain's mental and moral collapse was accompanied by – if not the result of – his involvement with the 'awful mature, white female' in Haiphong.

At this point – it is well over a third of the way into the text – the new captain meets Ransome. And Conrad now attempts the difficult feat of depicting an intimate, tender, relationship between the all-seeing Ransome and the insecure captain that is one of extreme emotional affect and dependence but that at the same time appears – at least on the surface – sexually chaste. *The Shadow-Line* thus presents the reader with a male-male relationship that is both intriguing and tantalizing. From the moment of his introduction into the narrative more than a third of the way into the text of the novella, both the personality of Ransome and the complex intimacy of his relationship with the captain-narrator dominate the reader's sense of the captain's experience as he confronts one problem after another. The scenes in which Ransome appears constitute only a relatively small part of the text of the novella, and yet this quantitative insignificance is in sharp contrast to the powerful qualitative effect of these passages. No other member of the ship's company occupies such a central rôle in the novella, or is seen to enjoy such a rich and intimate relationship with the captain-narrator.

The precise nature of this intimacy is not easy to specify. This is partly because Ransome's rôle in the novella is – like the rôle of Leggatt in 'The Secret Sharer' – important both on a realistic and on a symbolic plane. On the realistic plane, Ransome takes over the duties of the steward who dies shortly after the new captain takes command of his ship, combining them with his existing duties as cook. But symbolically he also takes over where the Chief Steward of the first part of the novella leaves off, presenting the reader with an opposition between a bad steward and a good steward that has strong Biblical associations. The name Ransome is also evocative of the ransom paid by Christ by dying to redeem mankind from the sins of the world.

On the realistic plane, the strong sense of intimacy between the captain and Ransome is the result of a number of textual elements. Perhaps most important, there is in the depiction of the exchanges between Ransome and the captain a marked emphasis on non-verbal communication. In the scenes in which the captain and Ransome are both present in the novella Ransome's voice is referred to no fewer than eleven times, while his eyes are mentioned eight times. Ransome's smile is referred to eleven times, the collocation 'wistful smile' is found six times while there are four mentions of his 'faint smile'. Ransome's face is mentioned six times, and the words 'gaze' or 'gazing' occur three times.

But it is the range of adjectives applied to voice and eye that have such a powerful effect on the reader. Ransome's voice is 'pleasant' (twice), 'quiet', 'soft', 'cultivated', 'low' (twice), 'equable', 'unperturbed', and 'natural'. His eyes are twice referred to as 'grey', and five times as 'intelligent'. The adjective 'quiet' is applied a total of six times to him (to his eyes, voice, face, and gaze) while the adverb 'quietly' is associated a total of six times both with him, and with the captain when in his presence. Other important adjectives and adverbs associated with Ransome are 'intelligent' (five times), 'natural' (three times), 'pleasant' and 'pleasantly' (eight times), 'serene' (three times, along with one occurrence of 'serenity'). Three times the word 'natural' is associated with him, and twice the words 'attractive' and 'low'. The collocations 'unfailing Ransome' and 'uneasy heart' both occur twice. There are also single occurrences of the words 'soft', 'tenderly', 'sympathy', 'faithful', and 'immune'.

Even though the narrator and Ransome talk a fair amount to each other, the reader cannot but be struck by the text's insistence upon their non-verbal interaction. 'He answered me in his pleasant, quiet voice and with a faint, slightly wistful smile' (60); 'He turned his head, and something in his eyes checked my modest elation' (64); 'Ransome's eyes gazed steadily into mine. We exchanged smiles' (65); 'He turned away from the sideboard with his usual pleasant, quiet gaze' (72); 'And then I would know nothing till, some time between seven and eight, I would feel a touch on my shoulder and look up at Ransome's face, with its faint, wistful smile and friendly, grey eyes, as though he were tenderly amused at my slumbers' (81); 'Ransome gave me one of his attractive, intelligent, quick glances and went away with the tray' (85); 'From time to time I murmured to him: 'Go steady' – 'Take it easy, Ransome' – and received a quick glance in reply' (100). Given this succession of intense moments of non-verbal intimacy it is thus striking that at the end of the work Ransome avoids eye-contact with the captain. 'His eyes were looking away from me – nowhere'; 'His eyes, not looking at me, had a strained expression' (109).

What does all this add up to? The relationship certainly involves emotional intensity and a seemingly shared sense of intimacy, and I think that clearly it has to be located somewhere along what Eve Kosofsky Sedgwick has referred to as the male homosocial continuum. But many of the descriptions of the interaction between the narrator and Ransome evoke more of a maternal than a sexual relationship (I am thinking of words such as quiet, soft[ened], serenity, tenderly, sympathy, unfailing, unperturbed, and natural). If I have earlier suggested that Ransome in a sense replaces the dishonest and scheming Chief Steward of the early part of the novella, it can also be argued that he takes over too the rôle performed on land by Captain Giles. For if the captain has earlier exclaimed to the older man 'I wonder what this part of the world would do if you were to leave off looking after it, Captain Giles?' (32), he later remarks of Ransome (twice described as the 'unfailing Ransome'): 'That man noticed everything, attended to everything, shed comfort around him as he moved' (99). It seems, then, that when Captain Giles leaves off looking after the captain's 'world', Ransome takes over his duties as he takes over the duties of the dead steward.

I have located most of these suggestive elements on a realistic plane in the novella, and yet their cumulative force is not of a realistic nature. There is something other-worldly in Ransome's presentation and rôle in the novella, something almost uncanny or unearthly. This is so notwithstanding the emphasis upon his physical reality – and especially the bodily reality of his damaged heart; encountering Ransome late in the work, the narrator comments that 'He possessed an unimpaired physical solidity which was manifest to me at the contact', and mentions later his 'powerful chest'. In spite of his weak heart Ransome is muscular and well-formed, but even while insisting upon Ransome's physical attractiveness (the narrator goes so far as to apply the word 'comeliness' to Ransome at the end of the novella) the narrator seems to insist upon the inseparability of physical and moral attributes. Consider the following passages.

> Even at a distance his well-proportioned figure, something thoroughly sailor-like in his poise, made him noticeable. On nearer view the intelligent, quiet eyes, a well-bred face, the disciplined independence of his manner made up an attractive personality. (55–6)

> Ransome gave me one of his attractive, intelligent, quick glances and went away with the tray. (85)

> Here a faint smile altered for an instant the clear, firm design of Ransome's lips. With his serious clear, grey eyes, his serene temperament – he was a priceless man altogether. Soul as firm as the muscles of his body. (93)

It is almost as if there is a process of deflection taking place here – that as soon as attention is drawn to Ransome's physical or bodily attractiveness, the text veers over to a comment on his moral or intellectual qualities; his intelligence, his breeding, his disciplined independence (a nice yoking together of qualities, that if not opposites certainly tug in different directions!). In the first two quotations the word 'attractive' appears to herald a comment on Ransome's physical appearance, but the text twists away to focus upon his non-bodily qualities (his personality, his intelligence). In the third quoted passage the text steers even more dangerously close to physical admiration of an erotic sort in the reference to 'the clear, firm design of Ransome's lips', but shifts to a concern with his 'serene temperament' and to an almost religious assessment of his worth: he is 'a priceless man', possessed of a (capitalized) 'Soul as firm as the muscles of his body'. As I will note later on, a comparable process of deflection can be observed in admiring comments made by the teacher of languages about Nathalie Haldin in *Under Western Eyes* (see below p. 148).

In one respect Ransome can be compared to Leggatt in Conrad's earlier tale 'The Secret Sharer'. Although these two works are very different in many ways, they share a common pattern involving an isolated and lonely captain who, in the course of his testing first command, forges a sustaining and powerfully emotional relationship with another man. Once the captain has passed at least the first part of this test this other man disappears – the murderer Leggatt striking out to the life of 'a fugitive and a vagabond' and Ransome (who is also in a sense under sentence of death) demanding the right to an existence that allows him to maintain a hold on 'this precarious hard life'. Perhaps more important is the fact that in both works there is a continual sliding between the realistic and the symbolic, the literal and the metaphoric. Conrad's unambiguous evocation of the tradition of the double or *Doppelgänger* in 'The Secret Sharer' means that however grittily material the realistic detail provided in the novel may be, the reader is continually aware that Leggatt's importance does not reside purely on the realistic plane in the tale. In *The Shadow-Line* something similar takes place, as the extreme intimacy of the relationship between the captain and Ransome again implies that the character's importance – and, especially, his importance for the captain – is not to be sought through scrutiny of what could be termed his 'real-world function'. In both works, moreover, there is a sense in which the escape from loneliness and isolation provided by an intimate and private relationship with another man is only partly satisfying (for the two captains, that is, *and* for the reader). It is only partly satisfying because in both cases the relationship is with a character who seems almost to be internal to the two captains – almost an aspect of their own subjectivity.

Victory: The homosexual as Satan

According to Richard J. Ruppel, the 'only absolutely unequivocal homosexual in Conrad's fiction is the evil Mr Jones, the antagonist in *Victory*' (1998, 22). Jones is characterized from his first arrival upon the scene in *Victory* as a hater of women. Upon meeting the hotel-keeper, Schomberg, Jones introduces Ricardo as 'My secretary', adding: 'He must have the room next to mine' (78) – an arrangement that duplicates the one insisted upon by Smollett's Captain Whiffle, who has 'a cabin made for him [his "personal surgeon", Simper] contiguous to the state-room, where Whiffle slept' (Smollett 1999, 198–9). Soon afterwards, we are told that Jones 'fired out another question', asking Schomberg:

> 'You have no women in your hotel, eh?'
> 'Women!' Schomberg exclaimed indignantly, but also as if a little frightened. 'What on earth do you mean by women? What women? There's Mrs. Schomberg, of course,' he added, suddenly appeased, with lofty indifference.
> 'If she knows how to keep her place, then it will do. I can't stand women near me. They give me the horrors,' declared the other. 'They are a perfect curse!'(81)

While the word 'curse' here prepares the reader for Jones's satanic intrusion on Heyst and Lena on their Edenic island, Jones's attitude towards women is not just one of hatred, but of disgust, and Conrad takes care to remind the reader of this at regular points. Indeed, this reaction of disgust performs an important rôle in the development of the novel's plot, as it is when Jones learns that there is a woman staying with Heyst, and that Ricardo has concealed this fact and is with her, that he reacts with powerful disgust and sets out to kill Ricardo – although his stated reason for this mission is that he recognizes that both his and Heyst's lives are in danger from Ricardo.

Ricardo explains to Schomberg that he first met Jones on a treasure-hunting yacht manned by a group of gentleman.

> 'At first there were only nine of them adventurous sparks, then, just a day or two before the sailing date, *he* turned up. Heard of it somehow, somewhere – I would say from some woman, if I didn't know him as I do. He would give any woman a ten-mile berth. He can't stand them. Or maybe in a flash bar. Or maybe in one of them grand clubs in Pall Mall. (99)

Jones's liking for male-only clubs and company does not exclude younger companions; Ricardo tells Schomberg of his master's boredom, and of the time that Jones lay all day long in a dark room in a one-horse Mexican pueblo.

> 'Drunk?' This word escaped Schomberg by inadvertence, at which he became frightened. But the devoted secretary seemed to find it natural.
> 'No, that never comes on together with this kind of fit. He just lay there full length on a mat, while a ragged, bare-legged boy that he had picked up in the street sat in the *patio*, between two oleanders near the open door of his room, strumming on a guitar and singing *tristes* to him from morning to

night. You know *tristes* – twang, twang, twang, aouh, hoo! Chroo, yah!'
(116)

Conrad includes what is (for him) a broad and unsubtle hint just to make sure
that the reader gets the message. When Schomberg asks Ricardo about this
aversion of his master's, Ricardo implies that the presence of Lena may make it
difficult to get Jones to face Heyst.

> He funks women. In that Mexican pueblo where we lay grounded on our
> beef-bones, so to speak, I used to go to dances of an evening. The girls there
> would ask me if the English *caballero* in the *posada* was a monk in disguise,
> or if he had taken a vow to the *santísima madre* not to speak to a woman, or
> whether – You can imagine what fairly free-spoken girls will ask when they
> come to the point of not caring what they say; and it used to vex me. Yes, the
> governor funks facing women.' (123)

The dash following 'or whether' clearly signals a suggestion too shocking for
Ricardo (or for Conrad) to specify, and the implication is as clear as it can be.

Hatred of women is not as it happens a characteristic of male homosexuality,
although clearly a lack of sexual interest in women is. Did Conrad believe that
male homosexuals disliked, or were repulsed by, women? As it happens he knew
a number of homosexuals, and knew that some of these got on well with women
– his own wife Jessie included. Of Norman Douglas, for example, Jessie writes
that 'His success with my sex was certain and assured' (1935, 97) although she
knew at the time of writing that Douglas had fled England in 1917 to avoid
prosecution for indecent assault on a schoolboy, as she and her husband took
Douglas's son Robin in to their household after the father's abandonment of
England.

Conrad also knew Sir Roger Casement, and had indeed shared a tent with
him when they met in the Congo. In the second of her memoirs of her husband
Jessie Conrad recalls that Casement, who she describes as a 'fanatical Irish
protestant', was the Conrads' guest soon after they returned from Capri.

> He was a very handsome man with a thick dark beard and piercing, restless
> eyes. His personality impressed me greatly. It was about the time when he
> was interested in bringing to light certain atrocities which were taking place
> in the Belgian Congo. Who could foresee his own terrible fate during the war
> as he stood in our drawing-room passionately denouncing the cruelties he
> had seen. (1935, 103–4)

Her husband's public assessment of Casement was one that changed over time.
As Barra Ó Séaghdha points out, there is a contrast between comment on
Casement in his Congo diary, in which Conrad refers to Casement as 'most

intelligent and very sympathetic', and that in a 1916 letter to John Quinn, written after Casement's arrest, in which Conrad writes that already in Africa he had judged that Casement 'was a man, properly speaking, of no mind at all. I don't mean stupid. I mean that he was all emotion. By emotional force (Congo report, Putumayo – etc) he made his way, and sheer emotionalism has undone him. A creature of sheer temperament – a truly tragic personality: all but the greatness of which he had not a trace' (Séaghdha 2005, 86, citing CL5, 598). After Casement was arrested for treason the British authorities leaked details alleged to have come from his diary that confirmed Casement as homosexual and paedophile. The authenticity of these leaked details is still a matter of debate, although the consensus seems to be that they are genuine. To what extent Conrad was aware of the leaked material, or suspected such leanings, is impossible to fix with certainty, but there is some evidence that he was so aware. Jane Ford (1995) points out that in a letter written to H.W. Nevinson in 1928, after Conrad's death, Conrad's friend Robert Cunninghame Graham commented of Casement that 'He was presumably a brave man, and did splendid work both in the Congo and on the Putumayo. The abnormality of his private life, which I hear from Conrad, from Englishmen who had known him in Paranagua and Rio de Janeiro, did not weigh with me at the least. ... it is not a disease that is catching. ... He dies like a brave man, and for that I respect him, as I respect the consistent courage that he showed throughout his life' (Ford 1995, 130, citing Watts 1969, 151–2). A much less reliable commentator, Jósef Retinger, reports that Conrad 'despised' Casement, and adds 'I remember when after his trial and his condemnation during the War somebody, I believe it was Fisher Unwin, the publisher, circulated an appeal for pardon and asked Conrad's signature, he refused it with vehemence, telling me at the time that he once shared a hut on the Congo with Casement, and that he ended by utterly disliking the man' (1941, 40).

Ford makes a case for Casement as a possible model for Kurtz, listing his voice, his writing poetry, and his writing for the newspapers (127) as possible links. She also argues more speculatively that 'Conrad's contact with Casement probably forced him to confront his own inherent bisexuality', and that 'this factor contributed to the atmosphere' of *Heart of Darkness* (124).

Bernard C. Meyer (237) claims that Mr Jones denounces women as basically dirty. The relevant passage in *Victory* occurs when Jones, who has just learned of Lena's existence and has deduced that Ricardo is interested in her, observes Ricardo seated on the floor in Heyst's bungalow, at some distance from the seated Lena – just before he compares himself and Ricardo to Acis and Polyphemus (see the discussion of this passage on p. 122).

'This is serious,' he went on, distilling his ghostly venom into Heyst's very ear. 'I had to shut my eyes many times to his little flings; but this is serious. He has found his soul-mate. Mud souls, obscene and cunning! Mud bodies, too – the mud of the gutter! I tell you, we are no match for the vile populace. I, even I, have been nearly caught. He asked me to detain you till he gave me the signal. It won't be you that I'll have to shoot, but him. I wouldn't trust him near me for five minutes after this!'

He shook Heyst's arm a little.

'If you had not happened to mention the creature, we should both have been dead before morning. He would have stabbed you as you came down the steps after leaving me, and then he would have walked up to me and planted the same knife between my ribs. He has no prejudices. The viler the origin, the greater the freedom of these simple souls!' (295)

What seems apparent when we look at this passage carefully and bear in mind its dramatic context, however, is that Jones's obsessive repetition of the word 'mud' is aimed not at women in general or at Lena in particular, but at Ricardo, or possibly at Ricardo and Lena. Mr Jones and Axel Heyst have just seen Heyst's mistress Lena, dressed in black and sitting in the light of eight candle-flames. Mr Jones's servant and fellow criminal Ricardo is sitting on the floor at some distance from Lena, 'one side of his upturned face showing the absorbed, all-forgetful rapture of his contemplation' (294). And here Jones's obsessive hatred of women starts to make sense. He hates them not because of what they are in themselves, but because they are his rivals for Ricardo, who has had his 'little flings' with them 'many times'. Meyer also refers to Conrad's 'The Planter of Malata' (1914), claiming of the story's main male character, Renouard, that he 'too is unable to separate his image of the beautiful Felicia from ideas of filth in the course of his wooing: "and if I saw you steeped to the lips in vice, in crime, in mud, I would go after you [...]"' (304). Here, too, the association of mud and dirt is more the result of a disgusted aversion to the idea of the sexual desire of a man for a woman, than with woman as woman, although here there are complex ideas of both self-abasement (Renouard's willingness to soil himself with the 'mud' of femininity) and sadism (the woman inspires sexual interest when she is clearly 'soiled' and degraded). The association between mud and male heterosexual passion can also be found in Conrad's *An Outcast of the Islands*, as I will discuss in the next chapter.

Writing to B. Macdonald Hastings some time between September 1916 and February 1917 in connection with the dramatization of *Victory*, Conrad responds to what must have been a query about Jones's hatred of women. His reply is evasive.

As to his dislike of women I am damned if I know what to say. They have spoiled so many of his little games before perhaps? Don't forget however that there is a strain of peculiar craziness about the gentleman. The novel only faintly suggests it. On stage it may pay if Irving will try honestly.

Something temperamental rather than mental. He's in fact an unusual sort of crank. Voyez-Vous ça? (CL6, 4)

It is almost as if the slightly exasperated Conrad is expostulating: 'Do I have to spell it out to you?' here, with the letter's final recourse to French perhaps shrouding his embarrassment ('Do you see?'). Exactly what sort of 'little games' have been spoiled by women is not specified, but the evidence of the novel supports the view that they may be little games with younger men.

Ironically, in view of his professed hatred of women, Jones's own feminine appearance is insisted upon in the text. When Jones is first introduced to the reader (on the steam launch taking him to Schomberg's hotel) we witness him leaning 'the back of his head against the stanchion of the awning'. The narrative continues: 'In this pose, his long, feminine eyelashes were very noticeable, and his regular features, sharp line of the jaw, and well-cut chin were brought into prominence, giving him a used-up, weary, depraved distinction' (81). Here Jones is both Satanic gentleman and debauched homosexual, and his aristocratic airs and aspirations evoke conventional associations of both the 'Prince' of Darkness and the upper-class 'deviant'.

Martin Bock claims that 'the extent to which Conrad was conscious of homosexuality, either in his life or fiction, is ultimately an unknown' (2002, 75). Bock's conclusion, that accordingly the 'concept of the continuum of male homosocial desire is useful, for it is less a finite measure than a broad spectrum from homosocial to homoerotic' (2002, 75–6) is not one with which I wish to disagree. However I feel that there is perhaps more evidence in Conrad's writings concerning the extent to which he was 'conscious of homosexuality' than is admitted by Bock. Some of this evidence is what we can call 'positive', as in the case of Il Conde and Mr Jones. But some is 'negative', in the sense that it stems from Conrad's clear attempts to avoid the imputation of homosexuality with regard to a character or an emotion. This negative evidence becomes more common in Conrad's middle and later periods – with *Lord Jim* as the watershed work.

***

In Chapter 37 of *Lord Jim* Marlow meets the now-abandoned Jewel, who greets him with a telling comment: 'She recognised me at once, and as soon as I had stopped looking down at her: "He has left me," she said, quietly; "you always leave us – for your own ends"' (253–4). In its immediate context the natural conclusion drawn by the reader is that 'you' refers to European men while 'us' denotes 'native' women. But in the fictional worlds of Joseph Conrad the remark could apply to more or less all emotionally charged relationships that are infused with some sexual, erotic or passionate element. Jim abandons the *Patna*, his father, Denver, Jewel, and even Marlow. Nina leaves Almayer, Willems attempts to leave Aïssa, Kurtz leaves both his Intended and his African mistress, Charles Gould abandons his wife emotionally if not physically, Winnie Verloc attempts to leave her husband and when he prevents her from doing so she kills him, and so on and so on. And highly charged relationships between two men last little longer. James Wait leaves Belfast, Kurtz leaves the harlequin, Leggatt leaves the captain, and Ransome leaves his captain, too. I mentioned earlier in this chapter Conrad's great admiration for the fiction of Charles Dickens. Dickens's novels are not exactly crowded with happy marriages, but there are some. If for example we return to *Bleak House*, we could cite the relationship between George Bagnet and his wife as a good example of an affectionate, mutually supportive and long-lasting married relationship. It is true that such relationships tend to exist on the margins of the Dickens world, in the ranks of the minor characters. But there are few such examples in the world of Conrad's fiction. Like Il Conde, the men in Conrad's fiction tend to return home alone.

2 The Exotic and the Erotic in *An Outcast of the Islands* and *Heart of Darkness*

The Conradian erotic is very far from being exclusively or even primarily homoerotic, although because the homoerotic could only be expressed in fiction in concealed or displaced form during Conrad's lifetime its depiction offers a convenient starting point for the exploration of concealed or disguised erotic elements in the fiction. But right from the start of his writing career Conrad's fiction includes an important concern with heterosexual erotic excitement and enslavement by passion. His first two published novels, *Almayer's Folly* (1895) and *An Outcast of the Islands* (1896) have plots that are powered by, among other things, men and women in the grip of sexual passion. In both novels the depiction of this passion relies upon, but also goes beyond, stereotyped associations of the erotic with the exotic. Both novels presented their contemporary readers with patterns of sexual enslavement that were familiar from popular narratives of the exotic, but both novels inject original and non-stereotypical elements into their depiction of heterosexual passion. In *An Outcast of the Islands* in particular, I will argue, we can see early evidence of Conrad's fascinated interest in the association of unequal power relationships between a man and a woman with sexual excitement. In what follows I want to concentrate on Conrad's second published novel as it offers, I think, a richer delineation of the obscure roots of Conradian sado-masochistic heterosexuality than does its predecessor.

Chronologically speaking, in the world of Conrad's fiction, sex starts in the forest. This is partly as a result of the fact that Conrad's early fiction is set in parts of the world – notably the Malay archipelago and Africa – where wild natural scenery offers a convenient place for sex, and especially extra-marital sex, to take place. But it seems clear that there are literary and cultural as well as geographical reasons for this association. If the literary treatment of natural scenery frequently slides into a concern with sexuality and the erotic, the literary treatment of sexuality and the erotic is often displaced into the depiction of natural scenery. There are powerful traditions associated with the biblical myth of the fall that link natural scenery through original sin to 'the original Adam' and sexuality. Moreover, while the myth of Eden makes available a symbolic exotic garden associated both with innocence and with sin, the massive increase in human mobility associated with colonialism and imperialism gave those who travelled access to real exotic landscapes that could serve the same representative purpose. If the flora of tropical lands struck the visiting European as more lush and fecund than the plants and trees back home, it was tempting to extrapolate a view of tropical sexuality as similarly exaggerated. A good example of the way in which the symbolic force of the contrast between local and exotic vegetation could be exploited is to be found in Chapter 25 of Virginia Woolf's *Night and Day* (1919), the action of which takes place in Kew Gardens. Katharine Hilbery is surprised to discover that while for her the flowers are 'variously shaped and coloured petals, poised, at different seasons of the year, upon very similar green stalks' (349), for Ralph Denham they are 'in the first instance, bulbs or seeds, and later, living things endowed with sex, and pores, and susceptibilities which adapted themselves by all manner of ingenious devices to live and beget life' and that are fashioned by processes 'which might reveal the secrets of human existence' (350). When the two move on from British plants to the exotic blooms of the Orchid House, however, Katharine needs no instruction from Ralph. Observing the orchids – 'fantastic plants, which seemed to peer and gape at her from striped hoods and fleshy throats', she stretches her ungloved hand to touch one of the fantastic plants 'in defiance of the rules' (351) in a manner that signals a desire to embrace a bodily sexuality that cannot be addressed directly. While Ralph speaks like a botanist, categorizing the plants in terms of the distinct stages of their development, Katharine seems almost mesmerized by the fleshy and phallic displays of the orchids, and is prompted to defy a prohibition and make physical contact with them. As is so often the case in Woolf's fiction, men compartmentalize while women combine.

I have already noted that Woolf was an admirer of the fiction of Joseph Conrad, and the distinction between a masculine world of distinct categories and prohibitions, and a female world of desire that involves the breaking of 'look but don't touch' rules that is presented in *Night and Day*, is one that Woolf could well have had suggested to her by a reading of Conrad's fiction. Tropical florae in Conrad's fictions, especially those set in the Malay Archipelago and Africa, also carry a complex and multi-layered symbolic burden. In Conrad's novels and stories, references to tropical foliage typically condense a number of associations that together form a meaning-cluster standing in binary opposition to an opposed family of associations denoting European control. Consider, for example, the following brief passages taken from four of Conrad's fictions.

The narrow creek was like a ditch: tortuous, fabulously deep; filled with gloom under the thin strip of pure and shining blue of the heaven. Immense trees soared up, invisible behind the festooned draperies of creepers. Here and there, near the glistening blackness of the water, a twisted root of some tall tree showed amongst the tracery of small ferns, black and dull, writhing and motionless, like an arrested snake. The short words of the paddlers reverberated loudly between the thick and sombre walls of vegetation.

Darkness oozed out from between the trees, through the tangled maze of the creepers, from behind the great fantastic and unstirring leaves; the darkness, mysterious and invincible; the darkness scented and poisonous of impenetrable forests. ('The Lagoon', 188–9)

We called at some more places with farcical names, where the merry dance of death and trade goes on in a still and earthy atmosphere as of an overheated catacomb; all along the formless coast bordered by dangerous surf, as if Nature herself had tried to ward off intruders; in and out of rivers, streams of death in life, whose banks were rotting into mud, whose waters, thickened into slime, invaded the contorted mangroves, that seemed to writhe at us in the extremity of an impotent despair. (*Heart of Darkness*, 115)

She was turning her back on the Cage, the fore-part of the deck and the edge of the nearest forest. That great erection of enormous solid trunks, dark, rugged columns festooned with writhing creepers and steeped in gloom, was so close to the bank that by looking over the side of the ship she could see inverted in the glassy belt of water its massive and black reflection on the reflected sky that gave the impression of a clear blue abyss seen through a transparent film. And when she raised her eyes the same abysmal immobility seemed to reign over the whole sun-bathed enlargement of that lagoon which was one of the secret places of the earth. (*The Rescue*, 285)

But Captain Whalley, who had now no ship and no home, remembered in passing that on that very site when he first came out from England there had stood a fishing village, a few mat huts erected on piles between a muddy tidal creek and a miry pathway that went writhing into a tangled wilderness without any docks or waterworks. ('The End of the Tether', 181)

Conrad had first-hand knowledge of the natural scenery that he describes in these passages, but these are more descriptions of the effect of such scenes of tropical fecundity on a European observer than they are attempts to present accurate botanical information to his readers; indeed in three of the four passages these European observers are made explicit. All four passages contain forms of the verb 'to writhe', a verb that elsewhere in Conrad's fiction is associated with the movement of a snake, a connection that in one of the quoted passages is made overt in the comparison to an arrested snake, and in two others is half-suggested in the reference to creepers. Three of the four passages also contain words denoting forms of interlacing or confused mingling of some sort: 'twisted root', 'tangled maze', 'contorted mangroves', 'tangled wilderness'. From the very start of his writing career, then, Conrad contrasts the fecund self-interlacings of tropical nature with the imposed and ordered compartmentalizations of European control. A repeated element in Conrad's depiction of tropical nature is the impression of serpentine weaving-together that the European observer confronts, one that is used to suggest an uncontrolled urge to merge and reproduce on the part of the non-European that is in sharp contrast to a European order consisting of, and maintained by, boundaries and self-enclosed, sharply defined identities.

At the same time, a form of psychological displacement allows Europeans to project their own promiscuity on to the peoples they exploit: if green things grow, reproduce and die more quickly in tropical climates than they do in the cold north, then it is easy to assume and to assert that the same is true of the people who live there. If natural growth is more clearly seasonal in Europe, with periods of winter hibernation or barrenness, in hot places it never stops. And the people who live in these hot places – by European standards inadequately clad and thus tempting the eye with their naked or semi-naked flesh – are for the European easy to imagine in a state of continual rut.

Rut, and also rot: processes of decay and corruption are also more rapid and harder to prevent when the temperature is high. Three of the quoted passages associate the fecund and writhing vegetation of the tropics with fetid and toxic substances: 'oozed', 'scented and poisonous', 'rotting into mud', 'thickened into slime', 'a muddy tidal creek and a miry pathway'. And from this fascinating but horrifying mucoid and fertile base grow 'immense trees', a 'great erection of enormous solid trunks, dark, rugged columns' – or, in their absence, mud huts 'erected on piles'. If these descriptions are indeed displacing human sexuality and gender characteristics into vegetable nature, then they suggest that at least one element in Conrad's view of sex is a horrified disgust at forms of rottenness that are partly hidden – words such as 'black(ness)', 'dark(ness)', 'sombre' and 'secret' all link corruption with concealment and death. This family of associations is present in Conrad's fiction from the very start. Referring to the scene in Conrad's first published novel *Almayer's Folly* in which Nina and Dain kiss for the first time, Thomas Moser notes that although the scene 'begins glamorously enough with an account of the lovers paddling into a miniature bay "under a low green archway of thickly matted creepers" where immense red blossoms send "down on their heads a shower of great dew-sparkling petals ... in a continuous and perfumed stream"', the tone suddenly shifts 'from enjoyment of this beauty to horror at its sources – death and decay' (1957, 53).

In *An Outcast of the Islands*, the link between man as erect tree and woman as parasitic creeper threatening to pull him down into swampy corruption is made overt. When the outcast Willems finally persuades the desirable Aïssa to embrace him, she clasps her hands behind his neck and 'swung off the full length of her arms' – presumably by lifting her feet from the ground.

Her head fell back, the eyelids dropped slightly, and her thick hair hung straight down: a mass of ebony touched by the red gleams of the fire. He stood unyielding under the strain, as solid and motionless as one of the big trees of the surrounding forests; and his eyes looked at the modelling of her chin, at the outline of her neck, at the swelling lines of her bosom, with the famished and concentrated expression of a starving man looking at food.[8] (109)

In botanical terms, however, it is the creeper that feeds off the tree and not the other way round: in the long run creepers destroy the trees upon which they feed. This truth has already been insisted upon in *Almayer's Folly*. In the opening lines of Chapter 11 of this novel we meet the isolated Dain, stretched in front of the glowing embers of a fire.

> On three sides of the clearing – appearing very far away in the deceptive light – the big trees of the forest, lashed together with manifold bonds by a mass of tangled creepers, looked down at the growing young life at their feet with the sombre resignation of giants that had lost faith in their strength. And in the midst of them the merciless creepers clung to the big trunks in cable like coils, leaped from tree to tree, hung in thorny festoons from the lower boughs and sending slender tendrils on high to seek out the smallest branches, carried death to their victims in an exulting riot of silent destruction. (124)

When Nina appears to the waiting Dain, she throws 'both her arms round his neck with a sudden gesture', and then, as the fire starts to burn again and a 'bright hot flame shot upwards' in a piece of crude erotic symbolism, Nina completes her conquest of Dain.

> [S]he drew back her head and fastened her eyes on his in one of those long looks that are a woman's most terrible weapon; a look that is more stirring than the closest touch, and more dangerous than the thrust of a dagger because it also whips the soul out of the body but leaves the body alive and helpless, to be swayed here and there by the capricious tempests of passion and desire. – A look that enwraps the whole body, that penetrates into the innermost recesses of a being bringing terrible defeat in the delirious uplifting of accomplished conquest. It has the same meaning for the man of the forests and the sea as for the man threading the paths of the more dangerous wilderness of houses and streets. Men that had felt in their breasts the awful exultation such a look awakens become mere things of to-day – which is paradise; forget yesterday – which was suffering; care not for to morrow – which may be perdition. They wish to live under that look for ever. It is the look of woman's surrender. –
>
> He understood and as if suddenly released from his invisible bonds fell at her feet with a shout of joy and embracing her knees hid his head in the folds of her dress, murmuring disjointed words of gratitude and love. (128–9)

Who, we may wonder, is surrendering to whom here? Taken together, these two passages suggest that for a man the supreme sexual experience is that of masochistic surrender. Nina has learned her skill as a seductress well: 'The thing was done. Her mother was right. The man was her slave. As she glanced down at his kneeling form she felt a great pitying tenderness for that man she was used to call – even in her thoughts – the master of life' (129). Earlier on in *Almayer's Folly* there is a scene that mirrors this one, but with the rôles reversed. Nina here takes Dain's face between her hands and looks into his eyes 'with a fond yet questioning gaze'. Finding confirmation of Dain's words of love in his face, 'An immense wave of gratitude and love welled forth out of her heart towards him' (55). While each feels at different times 'gratitude and love' while gazing into the eyes of the other, there is no example of both feeling these emotions at the same time. Passion, love, erotic excitement are rarely experienced in a mutual, equal exchange by a man and a woman in Conrad's fiction.

Towards the end of *An Outcast of the Islands* Aïssa's clinging is clearly sucking the life out of Willems: 'She clung to him. There was nobody else. Nothing else. She would try to cling to him always – all the life!' (190). When Aïssa does eventually kill Willems the event can hardly be said to come unheralded.

Discussing this and other passages in *An Outcast of the Islands*, Rebecca Stott comments that the 'clinging, caressing, cloying quality of the jungle and of the native women is likened to the great jungle vines which cling to the giant trees, felling them by erotic strangulation' (138). Stott devotes a chapter of her book *The Fabrication of the Late-Victorian Femme Fatale: The Kiss of Death* to Conrad's second novel, and she detects a consistent pattern in Conrad's fiction up to and including *Heart of Darkness*, a pattern that involves sharply defined Europeans and deadly non-Europeans – especially non-European women – whose indistinct contours merge into their jungle surroundings (131). However not all Europeans are sharply defined in Conrad's fiction. In *Lord Jim* Marlow says of Jim that 'I am fated never to see him clearly' (175) – a comment that follows immediately on from 'an indistinct shout' from Jim that Marlow is unsure that he has understood correctly. Rather than undermining Stott's argument, however, this exception proves her point: Jim is no longer clearly defined to Marlow because the younger man's betrayal of his responsibilities has effectively removed him from the ranks of the 'whites'. It is a mark of this loss of status that in Jim's relationship with Jewel, gender relationships are reversed. When Stott compares a passage from *Lord Jim* in which Jewel clings to Jim with one in which Aïssa hangs around Willems's neck, she ignores the crucial difference that in *Lord Jim* Jewel is the active, strong partner who protects and saves a complacent and sleeping Jim when an attempt is made on his life.

Stott recognizes the link between loss of European status and loss of definition in *An Outcast of the Islands*. She makes the illuminating comment that 'Willems' "fall" is described as a loss of self and of *outline*: he feels "lost amongst shapeless things that were dangerous and ghastly"' (145). If the novel's first sentence tells us of Willems's stepping off 'the straight and narrow path of his peculiar honesty', this refusal to respect a dividing-line leads eventually to his smudging the defining outline of his self. Throughout *An Outcast of the Islands* the opposition between European and 'native' is imaged in terms of an opposition between a reality separated into distinct and labelled categories, and a reality within which there are no fixed categories but rather an unceasing and writhing turmoil of interpenetrating exchange.

Moreover, although the primary focus of passages such as the one quoted above is to indicate a cultural divide, such passages can also – as Stott notes – be used to assert purportedly universal truths about the sexual natures of man and woman. (Recall that in the passage I quote above that details Nina's enslavement of Dain by means of her look of surrender, the narrative insists that this look 'has the same meaning for the man of the forests and the sea as for the man threading the paths of the more dangerous wilderness of houses and streets'.)

It is a critical commonplace that in *Heart of Darkness* Conrad uses the loss of restraint experienced by Europeans in Africa to expose that which is allegedly present in Europeans but repressed in Europe as a result of the discipline of external restraints. In his *Joseph Conrad and Psychological Medicine* (2002), Martin Bock argues that in

> *Heart of Darkness*, the woman/wilderness 'getting hold of something' in the man who is then 'lost' to civilization represents the feminine act of cannibalism and the failure of masculine restraint to maintain itself. Kurtz has been incorporated by the wilderness, which 'had taken him, loved him, embraced him, got into his veins, consumed his flesh' […]. (94)

Bock's comment is representative in terms of its assumption that Conrad uses depictions of the unrestrained sexuality of the tropics to display aspects of male and female sexuality that are culture-independent. As Bock implies, such depictions thus perform a double rôle, illustrating both the untrammelled sexuality of uncivilized 'natives' and also the 'real' nature of men and women that is concealed in the civilized world. It is thus relevant to ask what the force of the four passages quoted at the beginning of this chapter is. Do they picture for the reader the unrestrained and horrific sexuality of the tropics, or do they rather use a tropical setting to depict in displaced form more universal truths about human sexuality? More specifically: do they sanction the view that for Conrad the desirable woman – *any* desirable woman, whether 'native' or European – is both parasite and destroyer, beautiful but corrupt, a scented but dirty and vampiric presence that will if not repulsed destroy the erect but vulnerable male?

In *An Outcast of the Islands*, following his first meeting with Aïssa, the besotted Willems cannot remember how and when he parted from her, but he catches himself 'drinking the muddy water out of the hollow of his hand, while his canoe was drifting in mid-stream past the last houses of Sambir' (57). As befits a sailor, Conrad almost invariably associates the verb 'to drift' with moral decline, and Willems's moral collapse after meeting the desirable Aïssa is also figuratively expressed by his ingesting mud. In my previous discussion of the scene in the later *Victory* in which the furious Mr Jones catches sight of Ricardo in rapturous contemplation of Lena I noted that Jones's outburst ('Mud souls, obscene and cunning! Mud bodies, too – the mud of the gutter!') associates male heterosexual desire with mud and dirt – and thus by implication with a self-debasement that both excites and disgusts (see p. 58).

If the sexual desire experienced by Conrad's male characters is frequently compared to hunger (the tale 'Falk' [1903] offers a classic and extended example), the consummation of such desire often seems to conclude with the woman somehow ingesting the male. In *The Secret Agent* (1907) the knife that Verloc uses to slice a joint of beef that he is eating is used by his wife Winnie to stab him to death. The desirable woman in Conrad's fiction, displaced into mud and creepers, tempts, undermines, corrupts, and finally kills and consumes the vulnerable man. Man does not even experience the sexual abandon that seems to be promised: in the passage from *Heart of Darkness* the contorted mangroves 'seemed to writhe at us in the extremity of an impotent despair'. Whether it is indeed the mangroves that are impotent, or the European male observers who feel their impotence in the confrontation with this lavish display of shameless tropical coupling, is a moot point.

This is by no means the only place in his fiction where Conrad links the verb 'to writhe' with impotence, and the collocation is unsurprising when we remember that in the first quotation from Conrad's fiction that I cite in this chapter the forests are described as 'impenetrable'. In *Lord Jim* the Rajah Tank Allang 'writhed weirdly on his mat, gesticulating with his hands and feet, tossing the tangled strings of his mop – an impotent incarnation of rage' (181), while in the non-fictional *The Mirror of the Sea* (1906) the despicable Cesar, once knocked down on the deck by Dominic's 'brawny arm', 'would writhe on the deck, gnashing his teeth in impotent rage' (166). It seems likely that one association that is being called on here is that of the impotence of Satan in the Garden of Eden (another transgressor of boundaries), enviously observing an innocent sexuality to which he has no access. In 'The Return' (1898) the bourgeois home of Alvan Hervey exhibits a bronze dragon which, 'nailed by the tail to a bracket writhed away from the wall in calm convolutions' (124). In the same story Hervey, considering ways of ending his marriage, rejects the divorce court, which appears to him 'rather as an unclean and sinister cavern where men and women are haled by adverse fate to writhe ridiculously in the presence of uncompromising truth' (132). In *An Outcast of the Islands* Willems, 'stood for a while, his hands grasping the lintels on each side of the door, and writhed about, glaring wildly, as if he had been crucified there' (196). In *The Arrow of Gold* (1919) M. George is left alone with 'an articulated dummy without head or hands but with beautifully shaped limbs composed in a shrinking attitude' (21). His response to the dummy suggests an impotent fear of the female: 'From time to time I looked at the dummy. I even got up once from the couch on which I had been writhing like a worm and walked towards it as if to touch it, but refrained, not from sudden shame but from sheer despair' (248).

Later on in the same novel, while walking with Señor Ortega, M. George meets 'in the light of the street lamp his [Ortega's] own stealthy glance directed up at me with an agonized expression, an expression that made me fancy I could see the man's very soul writhing in his body like an impaled worm' (276). In 'An Anarchist' (1908) the advertisement for the beef extract 'represents in vivid and shining colours a large and enraged black bull stamping upon a yellow snake writhing in emerald-green grass' (135). Finally, another of Conrad's classically disempowered and impotent male voyeurs – Renouard in 'The Planter of Malata' (1914) – notes 'the sombre, as if secret, night-splendour' of the frigid Felicia Moorsom's eyes, 'under the writhing flames of her hair' (75). One fundamental truth about the writhing sexuality depicted in Conrad's fiction is that *it is usually being observed, not indulged in, by the voyeuristic but impotent European male.* Observing oriental sexuality he admires and desires, but is unmanned by the spectacle.

In his 'Author's Note' to *An Outcast of the Islands* Conrad says of the novel that 'though it brought me the qualification of "exotic writer" I don't think the charge was at all justified. For the life of me I don't see that there is the slightest exotic spirit in the conception or style of that novel. It is certainly the most *tropical* of my eastern tales' (282). The Author's Note was first published in 1919, twenty-three years after the initial publication of the novel, and it has to be read with this gap of time in mind. Nevertheless the comment prompts one to ask from what exactly it is that Conrad is attempting to distance himself or his novel when he rejects the label 'exotic'. Generally speaking Conrad uses the word 'exotic' to indicate the bemusement of a European observer when confronted by the alien but unthreatening life – natural and social – of non-European locations. For example, after his departure from Sta. Marta, the chairman of the railway in *Nostromo* feels 'that he had utterly lost touch with the feeling of European life on the background of his exotic surroundings' (36–7), and in *Victory* Lena walks up to Heyst, 'exotic yet familiar, with her white woman's face and shoulders above the Malay sarong, as if it were an airy disguise' (192).

In Conrad's fiction, then, the exotic typically involves a European's feeling of what we can call controlled strangeness when confronted by everyday aspects of the life of the oriental Other. The exotic is the oriental Other tamed and rendered harmless for the European. It is significant that in *An Outcast of the*

Islands, when Aïssa veils herself in defiance of Willems's wishes, he does *not* find her appearance 'exotic' but is rendered 'exasperated, amazed and helpless' (99) by this evidence that he is unable to assimilate her into his own culture.

Writing his 'Author's Note' so many years after the publication of *An Outcast of the Islands* Conrad may be protesting too much. There is no doubt that some of the clichés and stereotypes of exotic fiction are indeed to be found playing a structurally significant rôle in this novel. The white man who 'goes native', a process which typically involves enslavement by an oriental temptress, clearly represents one such stereotype. Of Jim's relationship to Jewel in *Lord Jim* Marlow comments: 'I suppose you think it is a story that you can imagine for yourselves. We have heard so many such stories, and the majority of us don't believe them to be stories of love at all' (199). One such story might well be *An Outcast of the Islands*, a tale not of love but of the enslavement of a white outcast besotted with a non-European women. Revealingly, Marlow refers to the familiarity his listeners have not with *actual* relationships between a white man and a 'native' woman but to *stories* about such relationships – a strong indication that we are dealing with an ideologically loaded stereotype. Among the many reasons why *Lord Jim* is a better novel than *An Outcast of the Islands* is precisely that it more effectively isolates, interrogates, and challenges many of the stereotypical elements that are substantially reinforced by and in the earlier work. The account of Jim and Jewel, Marlow insists, is *not* another of the stories Conrad's readers could imagine for themselves, whereas to a significant extent the account of Willems and Aïssa is.

As the passage quoted from 'The End of the Tether' at the start of this chapter indicates, aboriginal 'mire' precedes the docks and waterways of European control; to step off the path of honesty into wayside quagmires is to step out of the modern European community and into a retentive and soiling primeval mud. Prior to his Adamic fall, Willems attempts to walk in the middle of the European path, as far away from the non-linear and inchoate native nature as possible. When he first encounters Aïssa it is, appropriately, not on the white man's street but on a 'narrow way between the bushes' (53). Stunned by his encounter with her he looks first at her, and then at the vegetation that surrounds her.

> Who was she? Where did she come from? Wonderingly he took his eyes off her face to look round at the serried trees of the forest that stood big and still and straight, as if watching him and her breathlessly. He had been baffled, repelled, almost frightened by the intensity of that tropical life which wants the sunshine but works in gloom; which seems to be all grace of colour and form, all brilliance, all smiles, but is only the blossoming of the dead; whose mystery holds the promise of joy and beauty, yet contains nothing but poison and decay. He had been frightened by the vague perception of danger before, but now, as he looked at that life again, his eyes seemed able to pierce the

fantastic veil of creepers and leaves, to look past the solid trunks, to see through the forbidding gloom – and the mystery was disclosed – enchanting, subduing, beautiful. He looked at the woman. Through the checkered light between them she appeared to him with the impalpable distinctness of a dream. She seemed to him at once enticing and brilliant – sombre and repelling: the very spirit of that land of mysterious forests, standing before him, with the vague beauty of wavering outline; like an apparition behind a transparent veil – a veil woven of sunbeams and shadows. (54–5)

She 'appeared to him', 'seemed to him' – it is clear that Conrad does not present Aïssa to us as she is to herself or her own people, but as she is perceived by Willems. And Willems perceives her after having moved his eyes from her to 'the serried trees of the forest' and back again. This is both an odd and also a familiar displacement. As Rebecca Stott notes, the need (on Conrad's part – or on Willems's?) to see the desirable native woman in terms of an attractive but deadly vegetation here prefigures the same sort of perspectival movement in *Heart of Darkness* with regard to the 'savage and superb' African woman. By as it were shifting the camera from Aïssa to the forest, Conrad associates Willems's view of her with an 'intense' tropical life that is both attractive and corrupt, beautiful and poisonous, promising joy but guaranteeing death. (As both Andrea White [1993] and Linda Dryden [2000] have pointed out, Aïssa's name recalls that of the ultimate oriental temptress, Ayesha from Rider Haggard's 1889 novel *She*.)

In another passage that serves almost as a parody *avant la lettre* of the self-censorship of the post Hays Office Hollywood film, the eventual sexual consummation of Willems's and Aïssa's mutual desire is again displaced into the shrubbery. After Willems comes to the enclosure where Aïssa has been secreted by Babalatchi, he lifts her up and then, 'with immense strides, he dashed up the planks and disappeared with his burden in the doorway of the big house'. Shortly after this we read:

The boughs of the tree nodded and trembled in the unsteady currents of the light wind. A leaf fluttered down slowly from some high branch and rested on the ground, immobile, as if resting for ever, in the glow of the fire; but soon it stirred, then soared suddenly, and flew, spinning and turning before the breath of the perfumed breeze, driven helplessly into the dark night that had closed over the land. (84)

The fire of desire is burning itself out, leaving Willems helpless in that darkness that always seems to accompany the perfume of femininity in Conrad's work.

The phrase 'blossoming of the dead' associates both the 'native' and the 'feminine' with the rich vegetative life of the tropics that is fecund because it is fed and constituted by decaying organic matter. By association, then, Aïssa's beauty is also a blossoming of the dead, and one that holds too the promise of death for Willems. Indeed, following his first embrace of Aïssa, Willems whispers, 'I wish I could die like this – now!' (109). This wish may appear to confirm Willems's madness at this point, but it actually echoes an earlier statement that appears to be granted authorial support in the novel.

> There are in our lives short periods which hold no place in memory but only as the recollection of a feeling. There is no remembrance of gesture, of action, of any outward manifestation of life; those are lost in the unearthly brilliance or in the unearthly gloom of such moments. We are absorbed in the contemplation of that something, within our bodies, which rejoices or suffers while the body goes on breathing, instinctively runs away or, not less instinctively, fights – perhaps dies. But death in such a moment is the privilege of the fortunate, it is a high and rare favour, a supreme grace. (57)

If the juxtaposition of 'big and still and straight' trees and the 'fantastic veil of creepers' evokes once again an extreme phallic masculinity and a frighteningly 'clinging' femininity, it nonetheless gestures towards a feeling of envy for Willems's loss of self in his contemplation of Aïssa's desirability. Even as Conrad unpicks the contradictory impulses generated by the desirable exotic woman: 'at once enticing and brilliant – sombre and repelling', Willems's state of enrapture is surely portrayed to the reader as a desirable one. It is also worth noting that this is one of these moments at which the generalizing thrust of the narrative encourages the reader to see Willems's experience not as a particularly oriental one, but as one familiar to the European (male) reader. The phrase 'our lives' invites an assent from the European male reader that is based upon shared cultural assumptions.

While in *An Outcast of the Islands* Willems understands Aïssa by looking round at the serried trees of the forest, in *Heart of Darkness* it is the personified land itself that witnesses its own reflection in the African woman.

> She was savage and superb, wild-eyed and magnificent; there was something ominous and stately in her deliberate progress. And in the hush that had fallen suddenly upon the whole sorrowful land, the immense wilderness, the colossal body of the fecund and mysterious life seemed to look at her, pensive, as though it had been looking at the image of its own tenebrous and passionate soul. (168)

In both this passage and the previously quoted one there is mystery: 'the mystery was disclosed', 'the colossal body of the fecund and mysterious life'. Images of darkness – 'gloom' (twice) and 'tenebrous' reinforce this idea of the desirable 'native' woman as both mysterious and deadly and as an extension of the forests with which she is associated. The binary division is clear: on the one side there is the sequence 'twisted-dark-corruption-nature-native-female', and on the other side the opposing sequence 'tall-light-strong-culture-European-male'.

However the difference between *An Outcast of the Islands* and *Heart of Darkness* is that while these opposed binaries remain constant throughout the earlier work, in *Heart of Darkness* they are disrupted and challenged. When Marlow encounters Kurtz's Intended at the close of the novella she is presented in terms that shatter these neat oppositions. In the room in which Marlow waits for the Intended there is a 'tall marble fireplace' that has 'a cold and monumental whiteness' but there is also a grand piano 'with dark gleams on the flat surfaces like a sombre and polished sarcophagus' (182–3). The Intended is all in black but she has a pale head; she has fair hair, a pale visage, and a pure brow, but also dark eyes. Her forehead is smooth and white and it remains 'illumined by the unextinguishable light of belief and love' (184), but she is not strong; she represents culture and Europe but she is not male, and as Marlow speaks to her the scene of light becomes a scene of darkness. Thus although at one level *Heart of Darkness* duplicates a central pattern presented in *An Outcast of the Islands* – a European man leaves a woman associated with his own culture and becomes passionately and self-destructively involved with a 'native' woman (or perhaps, rather, involved with a passionate native woman) – this pattern co-exists with other, complicating patterns in the later work.

Moreover although many readers and critics (including myself) have assumed that the 'savage and superb' African woman is Kurtz's sexual partner, this is never made explicit in the way it is with regard to the relationship between Willems and Aïssa in *An Outcast of the Islands*. While the heads on the poles that Marlow sees when approaching Kurtz's compound are unambiguous markers of brutality and open up for the possibility of other 'horrors' such as cannibalism, the reader is left free to infer the nature of the relationship between the African woman and the white man – although words such as 'passionate' and 'fecund' help to link her in the reader's mind with sexuality.

In *Heart of Darkness*, then, sexuality is never so overt as it is in *An Outcast of the Islands*, while passion is less explicitly linked with sex. This lack of explicitness is partly the result of Conrad's much greater writerly sophistication in the later work, a work in which he leaves the reader more work to do. Late in his life, in separate letters written within a couple of months of each other, Conrad was to place a high premium on the inexplicit. In a letter to an unknown recipient dated 23 February 1922, Conrad insists: 'You can't call upon an artist to be *explicit*. It is not his province' (CE7, 424). And in a letter to Richard Curle of 24 April, 1924, Conrad repeats the point: 'Explicitness, my dear fellow, is fatal to the glamour of all artistic work, robbing it of all suggestiveness, destroying all illusion' (CE7, 457).

The new Oxford World's Classics edition of *An Outcast of the Islands* uses a detail from Henri Rousseau's *Woman Walking in a Tropical Forest* (1905) as its jacket illustration – an inspired choice, showing a tiny, white-clad woman dwarfed and partly obscured by lush, threatening, intertwined and enormous plants and trees. The chasteness of the woman which is suggested by her white clothes is questioned and subverted by the fecundity of the vegetation that threatens to engulf her. In the tropical forest woman's hidden sexuality, corruption, and threat are made visible by being displaced into her surroundings. A passage from Conrad's novel which describes Willems's observation of Aïssa could – apart from the difference of the woman's posture and position – be a comment on Rousseau's painting.

> And he looked at her, standing above him, her head lost in the shadow of broad and graceful leaves that touched her cheek; while the slender spikes of pale green orchids streamed down from amongst the boughs and mingled with the black hair that framed her face, as if all those plants claimed her for their own – the animated and brilliant flower of all that exuberant life which, born in gloom, struggles for ever towards the sunshine. (60)

As with the African woman in *Heart of Darkness*, tropical life is characterized by a merging of the female with the 'exuberant life' of the vegetation, while European settlement, in contrast, involves the establishing of a firm demarcation between 'the natural' and 'the human'. When Willems forsakes even a metaphorical 'path' in the opening lines of *An Outcast of the Islands* he thus makes a decisive and, it transpires, an irreversible move from European order to 'native' disorder, from a disciplined compartmentalization to an uncontrolled intermingling. For him the words applied by Marlow to Jim in *Lord Jim* apply equally well: 'Woe to the stragglers!' (162).

Towards the end of the novel, when Almayer pretends to be trying to find and rescue Willems, he conspires to strand the boat carrying himself and his deceived helpers in another of Conrad's scenes of tropical corruption.

> It was a sombre creek of black water speckled with gold, with the gold of scattered sunlight falling through the boughs that met overhead in a soaring, restless arch full of gentle whispers passing, tremulous, aloft amongst the thick leaves. The creepers climbed up the trunks of serried trees that leaned over, looking insecure and undermined by floods which had eaten away the earth from under their roots. And the pungent, acrid smell of rotting leaves, of flowers, of blossoms and plants dying in that poisonous and cruel gloom, where they pined for sunshine in vain, seemed to lay heavy, to press upon the shiny and stagnant water in its tortuous windings amongst the everlasting and invincible shadows. (249)

Again images of deathly corruption serve as the foundation for more displays of intertwining sensuality – climbing creepers and 'tortuous windings'. Here the masculine and 'insecure' trees are not only being encircled by the parasitic female creepers, they are being undermined and unmanned by the floods. Such passages indicate how a long tradition that expresses a misogynistic view of woman as outwardly attractive but inwardly corrupt can be grafted on to an orientalist warning of the dangers of miscegenation.

In the closing pages of the novel, the 'chance visitor from Europe' who is talking to Almayer 'many years afterwards' is shocked to learn that the 'doubled-up crone' who serves their meal is Aïssa. Almayer explains: 'They age quickly here' (279). The frantic and unrestrained coupling of tropical existence consumes life rapidly. If for Wallace Stevens in 'Sunday Morning' death is the mother of beauty, for Conrad it is beauty that is the mother – and daughter – of death. In this novel it is as if Conrad is unable to mention blossoms or perfume (both evoking the female) without thinking of mortality. Early on in the novel Willems is wrapped up in 'in the soft and odorous folds of air heavy with the faint scent of blossoms and with the acrid smell of decaying life' (59). The parallel is clear: just as there are no flowers without decaying life at their roots, so too there is no attractive woman who does not carry with her and in her the promise of corruption and death.

***

In his highly influential study *Orientalism* (first published in 1978), Edward Said suggests that 'Once we begin to think of Orientalism as a kind of Western projection onto and will to govern the Orient, we will encounter few surprises' (95). There is a sense in which the patterns that I have discussed in this chapter can be seen as an attempt to project certain stereotypical patterns on to the people of the Malay archipelago in order to legitimize European domination and control of them. But Conrad's fiction does actually present a few surprises to the reader who expects to find in it little more than a legitimation of European domination of non-Europeans. First there is the complicating factor that, as I have attempted to demonstrate, colonialist ideology is mixed in with sexual politics in complex ways. Then there is the problem that it is often the most corrupt Europeans who assert their racial and cultural superiority most insistently in Conrad's Malayan and African fictions. In *An Outcast of the Islands* it is indeed the character who is subjected to most authorial scorn, irony, and direct criticism – Willems – who insists most vocally and most absurdly on his right to privileges that are his because he is white. The further he falls, the more he advances such claims, and in an increasingly ludicrous manner.

> He thought of escape – of something to be done. What? A raft! He imagined himself working at it, feverishly, desperately; cutting down trees, fastening the logs together and then drifting down with the current, down to the sea into the straits. There were ships there – ships, help, white men. Men like himself. Good men who would rescue him, take him away, take him far away

where there was trade, and houses, and other men that could understand him
exactly, appreciate his capabilities; where there was proper food, and money;
where there were beds, knives, forks, carriages, brass bands, cool drinks,
churches with well-dressed people praying in them. He would pray also. The
superior land of refined delights where he could sit on a chair, eat his tiffin
off a white tablecloth, nod to fellows – good fellows; he would be popular;
always was – where he could be virtuous, correct, do business, draw a salary,
smoke cigars, buy things in shops – have boots ... be happy, free, become
rich. (252–3)

On one level this can be read as a warning of what happens to white men who
leave the beaten path of western morality and indulge their desires with 'native'
women. But more subversively it displays and mocks precisely those pretensions
that, often in unstated form, are used to underpin the legitimacy of European
control. The absurd collocations that constitute Willems's sense of European
civilization are reminiscent of the vain and foolish Carlier's equation of
civilization with 'Quays, and warehouses, and barracks, and – and – billiard-
rooms' (9) in Conrad's 'An Outpost of Progress' (1897). It is surely not
accidental that Willems is an accomplished player of billiards. Indeed when the
narrator of *An Outcast of the Islands* describes Almayer and Willems as '[t]hose
two specimens of the superior race' (49) the reader is strongly reminded of the
narrative irony at the expense of Carlier and Kayerts in the short story, in which
the two characters are described as 'the two pioneers of trade and progress' (8).

It is perhaps more helpful to think of a novel such as *The Outcast of the
Islands* as a sort of ideological palimpsest, one in which the surface of the
narrative can indeed be read along the lines suggested by Said, but one possessed
too of subversive depths in which more complex and contradictory meanings
contend. If the decline and fall of Willems displays what happens to the white
man who 'goes native', the narrative unexpectedly recognizes his loss of self as
a desirable experience. If the novel at one level privileges a European, masculine
world of well-defined identities and clearly demarcated borders, at another level
it bespeaks a mesmerized desire for the writhing, death-linked intimacies and
interminglings of an exotic, erotic and feminized space. Faced with the exotic
Conrad is shocked and repelled, while at the same time, like Woolf's Katharine,
fascinated by the force it exerts, he and his male characters are tempted to reach
out in defiance of the rules.

3 The Erotics of Cruelty in 'A Smile of Fortune', 'The Planter of Malata', *The Secret Agent*, *Victory*, and 'Freya of the Seven Isles'

One of the most chilling moments in *Nostromo* – a novel that contains much to disturb the reader – occurs when the narrative is tracing Dr Monygham's nightmare recollections of the time he was tortured by Father Beron.

> He would dream of Father Beron sitting at the end of a long black table, behind which, in a row, appeared the heads, shoulders, and epaulettes of the military members, nibbling the feather of a quill pen, and listening with weary and impatient scorn to the protestations of some prisoner calling heaven to witness of his innocence, till he burst out, 'What's the use of wasting time over that miserable nonsense! Let me take him outside for a while.' And Father Beron would go outside after the clanking prisoner, led away between two soldiers. Such interludes happened on many days, many times, with many prisoners. When the prisoner returned he was ready to make a full confession, Father Beron would declare, leaning forward with that dull, surfeited look which can be seen in the eyes of gluttonous persons after a heavy meal. (372)

Father Beron's surfeited look confirms that a need or desire of his has been satisfied, and the hard-to-avoid implication of the passage is that the torturing priest obtains a satisfaction from the inflicting of pain that is sexual in nature. We do not need to cross-relate this passage to the explicit comparison of the sexual drive to the compulsion to eat in 'Falk' to realize that Conrad is very clear that while torture may ostensibly be inflicted in order to extract information (or a 'confession') from its victim, its primary cause may involve the satisfaction of a perverted sexual need on the part of the torturer.

Sadistic cruelty forms a sort of permanent backdrop to the action of *Nostromo*, but it is in some of Conrad's shorter fictions that the interpenetration of the desire to inflict or experience hurt, and sexual excitement, is most assiduously investigated. My starting point in this chapter is what is arguably the most successful study of the heterosexual erotic in Conrad's oeuvre, the novella 'A Smile of Fortune', which was written in 1910 and first published in 1911. I contend that the intermingling of the erotic with the sadistic and the masochistic in Conrad's fiction is most clearly depicted in this work. I then move on to trace the contours of one part of this complex – that connected with sadism and sexually stimulating cruelty – in two of Conrad's full-length novels: *The Secret Agent* and *Victory* (1915). If my trajectory defies chronology so far as composition and publication are concerned, it can be said to respect a chronology of a different sort. As the investigations of a number of researchers and biographers have established, 'A Smile of Fortune' relies very heavily on experiences that Conrad underwent during his seven-week stay in Mauritius in 1888, while *The Secret Agent*'s London setting associates it with Conrad's visits to that city on many occasions from 1878 up to the time of writing the novel. Although the erotic relationship in 'A Smile of Fortune' no longer involves a 'native' woman, the fascinating Alice is a child born of the hopeless (and masochistic) passion experienced by her European father for a 'gypsy' circus entertainer, and it unfolds not just in a generally exotic setting (the 'Pearl of the Ocean') but more locally in a lush and Edenic walled garden. Thus although the passion depicted in this story involves two Europeans, it is also saturated with that association between the erotic and the exotic that I have traced in *An Outcast of the Islands*. Moreover, although the implied setting of 'A Smile of Fortune' is the unnamed Mauritius, as I will show it is packed with allusions and references to events in Europe, and particularly in London. Furthermore, while *Victory* must be classified as a later work given its publication date, it too owes much to Conrad's youthful acquaintance with the Malay Archipelago, and it too depicts a passion that instead of prompting an expulsion from Eden, rather inspires the desire to seek refuge there.

In the *Introduction to a Contribution to a Critique of Political Economy* Karl Marx famously comments that the anatomy of man is a key to the anatomy of the ape – meaning, presumably, that we understand a less developed organism by looking at it in its more developed, and more sophisticated analogues. My contention is that the movement from 'A Smile of Fortune' to *The Secret Agent* – although in one sense a movement backwards in time – is a movement from the depiction of a simple complex of sado-masochistic desire in an individual character's psychosexual makeup, to the perception of an analogous pattern in the structure of a whole society. So far as *Victory* is concerned, the island setting of the novel makes such direct social commentary impossible, but Mr Jones's comment to Heyst that he is 'the world itself, come to pay you a visit ' reminds us that the characters in the novel bring to Heyst's island the fruits of life elsewhere.

Included in my discussion of 'A Smile of Fortune' are some comparative comments on another, and later, short fiction of Conrad's: 'The Planter of Malata'. I include this discussion in order to support my contention that when the element of power expressed through sado-masochistic stimulation is removed from Conrad's depiction of heterosexual desire, the result is a wholesale dissipation of erotic force. And it is this erotic intermingling of sexual need with the desire to inflict or endure physical or psychological pain – with those forms of erotically charged cruelty that we term sado-masochistic – that provides Conrad with patterns of association that can be applied to the cruel exercise of forms of power that are not individual but social, cultural, and political.

'A Smile of Fortune' and 'The Planter of Malata'

Critical assessments of 'A Smile of Fortune' and 'The Planter of Malata' have been mixed.[9] In my own opinion the former is one of Conrad's finest short fictions, while the latter is a failure, mainly of interest to the literary pathologist. 'A Smile of Fortune' was the first work Conrad produced after his three-month convalescence subsequent to the breakdown he experienced after completing the manuscript of *Under Western Eyes*, the work that Thomas C. Moser and others see as his final major 'achievement' as a writer of prose fictions. This, along with the fact that the novella is concerned with its young captain-narrator's abortive sexual obsession with a young woman, might lead us to expect the story to serve as copybook example of Conrad's decline, if only in incipient or partial form. To the extent that the work can be taken to be Conrad at his near-best it serves rather as a copybook example of the awkward limb that sticks out of the Procrustean bed of Moser's double thesis that when Conrad turned to matters of love and sexuality his writing suffered, and that subsequent to *Under Western Eyes* his creative powers went into decline.

In brief, my argument is that while 'A Smile of Fortune' is a modernist work in which sexuality and the erotic are conceptualized and analysed in ways appropriate to modernity and informed by the insights of contemporary understanding, sexuality in 'The Planter of Malata' is understood and depicted in terms of an anachronistically melodramatic outlook. While the earlier story sees desire and the erotic inextricably connected to class, power, and violence, in 'The Planter of Malata', in contrast, sexuality and desire are mediated through courtly-love and fairy-tale conventions that involve self-sacrifice, chastity, and knightly devotion. Because these are not of the time *in* which or *about* which Conrad is writing, they prevent his making contact with the erotic as he or his contemporaries lived it. *Chance*, the latter part of which was written at about the same time as these stories, involves *both* a chivalric and courtly-love element (seen strongly in its chapter titles) *and* a modernist element, in its engagement with feminism, lesbianism, and hints of sadistic arousal. Separating out these elements into two very different stories allows us to perceive the modernist element's strength and the chivalric one's weakness.

The settings of both of the shorter works owe much to a brief period of Conrad's life. If not an *annus mirabilis*, 1888 provided him with experiences that he used in a succession of works written at different points in his career. It is striking that many of his fictions that contain an erotic element have some connection with this period. Appointed Master of the *Otago* in January, Conrad sailed from Bangkok on 9 February 1888 to Singapore and then on to Sydney, arriving in the Australian capital on 7 May. After a return voyage to Melbourne, he sailed to Port-Louis, Mauritius on 7 August, staying for seven weeks after his arrival on 30 September. 'The Planter of Malata' opens in a 'great colonial city', which Conrad's manuscript identifies as Sydney, while the 'Pearl of the Ocean' of 'A Smile of Fortune' is clearly modelled on Mauritius.[10]

Both stories trace the history of solitary but active and independent young men who become obsessed with a woman while dealing with complications in which the woman's father is involved. In both stories the father seems anxious that the relationship be legitimately consummated. In both cases, the young man initiates passionate physical contact, only for the relationship to end in separation, and in the case of 'The Planter of Malata', in death. Both works, in short, deal with the sort of male heterosexual fixation and obsession that can easily become the stuff of melodrama but that can also be used to display the manner in which sexual desire is constructed with building-bricks taken from social relationships more generally.

A Smile of Fortune

If both stories owe much to Conrad's experiences in 1888, 'A Smile of Fortune' is linked to that year by more compelling textual evidence. This story details the captain-narrator's growing obsession with the young Alice Jacobus. (According to the captain's informant, the eldest brother of one of the old French families, 'She must be over eighteen now' [38]). Alice is the illegitimate daughter of the merchant and ship's chandler Alfred Jacobus, who although married, ran off with a female circus-rider who became Alice's mother. Because of her scandalous origins Jacobus keeps his daughter in social and physical seclusion, confined to the house and its suggestively luxuriant walled garden. Looked after by 'an elderly female relative' (38), who serves as her *gouvernante*, she gleans what she knows of the world from 'newspapers provided for the captains' room of the "store"' and brought home 'in a very stained and ragged condition' (60). (Both 'A Smile of Fortune' and 'The Planter of Malata' share a contemptuous attitude to journalism and the press, though they are far from the only works in Conrad's canon to have this in common.)

In 1888, newspapers did not lack for sensational copy: 'At that time the batches of papers brought by the last mail reported a series of crimes in the East End of London, there was a sensational case of abduction in France and a fine display of armed robbery in Australia' (61). The 'series of crimes in the East End of London' must be meant to invoke the reader's knowledge of the 'Jack the Ripper' murders of autumn 1888. Conrad's memory did not play him false on this: study of the newspapers published in Mauritius while he was there confirms that they did indeed contain stories of 'crimes in the East End of London'. The mainly French-language *Journal de Maurice* for 16 October, for example, includes a news item entitled 'Les crimes de Whitechapel' and subtitled 'femmes éventrées'. It reports that

On télégraphie de Londres, 9. septembre:

Le meurtre de Whitechapel, suivent à bref intervalle d'autres crimes analogues restés impunis, produit dans Londres une immense émotion. Le corps de la victime, dont les jupes étaient relevées jusqu'à la poitrine, étaient littéralement ouvert de bas en haut. Une parti des entrailles était enroulée autour du cou, comme une collier. Le cœur et le foie de la malheureuse étaient placés derrière sa tête.

[…]

On suppose que cette femme s'appelle Annie Siffey [...]

[…]

Dans la journée d'hier, les propriétaires de la maison dans la cour de laquelle le corps a été trouvé faisaient payer dix centiments aux personnes qui voulaient voir le lieu du crime. La recette à été considérable. Une foule énorme était massée dans les roues adjacentes.

[…]

L'homme a tablier de cuir était israélite, c'est aux juifs que la foule s'en prend. De groupes nombreux poussent des cris de menace à leur adresse.

[By telegraph, London, 9th September.

The Whitechapel murder, taking place shortly after other comparable and still-unsolved crimes, has produced a powerful emotional response in London. The body of the victim, whose skirts had been raised to her bosom, had been literally opened up its entire length. A part of the victim's intestines had been wound around her neck, like a necklace. The unfortunate woman's heart and liver were placed behind her head.

[…]

It is believed that the victim's name is Annie Siffey.

[…]

All yesterday the owners of the house in the courtyard of which the body was found were charging ten centimes per person for the privilege of witnessing the scene of the crime. The income from this offer was considerable. An enormous crowd gathered in the streets adjacent to the building.

[…]

The man wearing a leather apron was Jewish, and it is to the Jews that the crowd has taken itself. Large groups of individuals have uttered threatening shouts where Jews reside.]

In its issue for 20 November the same newspaper reprints a news item from the *République Française* of 20 October, under a banner headline 'DEUX FEMMES ASSASSINEES A LONDRES' which reports that

> Toute l'Angleterre est mise en émui par cette découvert simultanée de deux cadavres de femmes, horriblement mutilées, qui a été faites à Londres, dans la nuit de samedi à dimanche. On est sans doute en présence de nouveaux forfaits du misérable qui a commis déjà trois crimes semblables (les crimes de Whitechapel), et l'opinion publique est surexcitée au plus haut point par ces actes de sauvagerie incroyable.

> [Two women murdered in London

> The whole of England has been set in turmoil by the simultaneous discovery in London of two female corpses, horribly mutilated, during the night of Saturday to Sunday. We are no doubt witnessing new crimes committed by the miserable wretch who is already responsible for three similar outrages (the Whitechapel murders). Public opinion has reached a high pitch of excitement in response to these acts of unbelievable savagery.]

The report names the victim as Annie Fitzgerald and reports that she was discovered by two participants in a conference on '*Judaïsme et le Socialisme*' [Judaism and socialism] at a Jewish club. It also reports that two hours later another victim was discovered, and provides grisly details of her evisceration. There are also details about a suspect, a 'gentleman', 'grand, vetu de noir', [tall, dressed in black] along with the information that the murderer apparently sent a letter to the *Central News* which was dated 25 September.

The English-language newspaper *The Commercial Gazette* carries briefer reports of these same crimes, but its issue of 27 October has a column headed 'Undiscovered Crimes' of precisely the sort that might have terrified Alice Jacobus or her *gouvernante*.

> It was the boast of Mr. Howard Vincent, at the time he was head of the Criminal Investigation Department, that London is the safest city in the world; and so it would seem to be – for the assassin. The undiscovered murders of recent years make a long list. Passing over the murder of Mrs Squires and her daughter in their shop a[t] Hoxton in broad daylight; the killing of Jane Maria Clousen in Kidbrooke-lane, near Eltham; the murder of the housekeeper to Bevingtons, of Cannon-street, we come to, perhaps, the best remembered and most sensational of the mysterious crimes of the past. On the morning of Christmas Day, 1872, Harriet Buswell was discovered with her throat cut. She was a ballet-girl, employed at the Alhambra, and had been accompanied to her home, 12, Great Coram-street, by a 'gentleman,'

supposed to have been a German, who on the way purchased some apples, one of which was left in the room, and bore the impression of his teeth. This half-eaten apple was the sole clue to the murderer, who was never found. A German clergyman named Hessel was arrested at Ramsgate on suspicion three weeks after the murder, but a protracted magisterial investigation resulted in his complete acquittal.

Mrs. Samuel was brutally done to death at her house in Burton-crescent, and a few doors further up Annie Yeats was murdered under precisely similar circumstances to those attending the death of Harriet Buswell.

Miss Hacker was found dead in a coal-cellar in the house of one Sebastian Bashendorff, in Euston-square, and Hannah Dobbs was tried, but acquitted. An almost identical case happened in Harley-street. In this case the victim was unknown.

Another unknown woman was discovered lying in Burdett-road, Bow, murdered.

Mrs. Reville, a butcher's wife, of Slough, was found sitting in a chair with her throat cut, but no one was apprehended.

There was the murder of an unfortunate in her home near Pye-street, Westminster. A rough fellow was known to have gone home with her, and he left an old and dirty neckerchief behind, but he was never found.

Mrs. Samuel was killed with impunity in the Kentish Town Dairy.

The murderer of Miss Clark, who was found at the foot of the stairs in her house, George street, Marylebone, has gone unpunished.

The account then notes that 'Besides these there are the cases in which the victims have been men', and proceeds to give a comparable list of male victims. The distinction between female and male victims is itself noteworthy, as is the fact that it is the female ones who are reported first.

Alice would however have had scant basis for a belief that life was safer where she lived, as on the same page of *The Commercial Gazette* there is a brief report headed 'Assizes', which reads:

The calendar for the fourth criminal session of this year has been posted up at the Supreme Court. It contains eighteen cases, *i.e.* larceny with breaking 4, forgery 2, embezzlement 1, possession of mould for coining 1, attempt on chastity 1, wounds and blows causing death 1, crimes against nature 8, manslaughter and attempt at manslaughter 3, murder and attempt at murder 2.

Exactly which 'crimes against nature' are meant is not specified, but the issue of the same newspaper for 15 November reports cases of bestiality (6 months hard labour) and rape (7 years penal servitude).

On the French abduction and the Australian armed robbery these newspapers have nothing obvious to offer (Ned Kelly's armed robberies occurred earlier: he was hanged in 1880). Conrad may be remembering something from his reading in either Sydney or Melbourne prior to sailing to Mauritius. But even a brief perusal of the local newspapers that would have been available to Alice's non-fictional counterpart (and there may too have been foreign newspapers as well) is sufficient to confirm that if her reading of these publications formed her view of the world-at-large then it would not have been surprising if 'she had formed for herself a notion of the civilised world as a scene of murders, abductions, burglaries, stabbing affrays, and every sort of desperate violence' (60). Thus when the 'elderly female relative' remarks: 'I don't know what your precious papa is plotting with that fellow. But he's just the sort of man who's capable of carrying you off far away somewhere and then cutting your throat some day for your money' (61), Alice takes the warning seriously, and the captain's position is not helped by the fact that she perceives no irony in his response:

'Yes, that's what we do with girls in Europe,' I began in a grimly matter-of-fact tone. I think Miss Jacobus was disconcerted by my sudden appearance. I turned upon her with cold ferocity:
  'As to objectionable old women, they are first strangled quietly, then cut up into small pieces and thrown away, a bit here and a bit there. They vanish –' (62)

Conrad's earliest surviving reference to 'A Smile of Fortune' comes in a letter to John Galsworthy of 17 May 1910, in which he announces: 'I am going to begin to morrow a short story. [...] It's to be comical in a nautical setting and its subject is (or *are*) potatoes. Title: A Smile of Fortune' (CL4, 329). The reader is invited to find passages such as that just quoted 'comical', but only later does the reader discover that Alice firmly believes that the captain and her father are planning her abduction (or worse), and that she is, literally, terrified. Ted Billy has described 'A Smile of Fortune' as a 'seriocomic romance' (1997, 88), and throughout the story references to violent and tragic events are juxtaposed with humorous and comic elements: at the opening a bereaved captain mourning his son gives way to a bereaved captain ludicrously mourning the loss of his ship's figurehead. (Is it too far-fetched to relate the captain's ironic description of objectionable old women being cut up into small pieces to Alfred Jacobus's description of Captain H— of the *Stella* and his wife who, after the experience of having the chief officer of the ship lost overboard and then experiencing the death of their child 'a few hours before reaching port', are both 'terribly cut up' [11]?)
  The relationship between the tragic and the comic elements in the tale is by no means a simple one. Although these elements are inevitably in a sort of tension, they can also be understood as different perspectives on the same

events: a hopeless love affair has its comic elements for onlookers, but not for the one hopelessly in love. Whatever the case, this is a story that includes very dark elements that Conrad's humour repeatedly obscures, lightens or displaces. The one I wish to draw attention to is that of the captain's alternate (or even simultaneous) masochistic and sadistic arousal by Alice's expression of both contempt and fear for him.

If Conrad's memory of his time in Mauritius in 1888 and his romantic involvements with one and perhaps two young women constitutes a basis of personal experience from which he constructed 'A Smile of Fortune', it is noteworthy that writing the story twenty-two years later he also recalled that at that time the papers were full of reports of the 'Ripper' murders – and perhaps, too, of a French abduction, and an Australian armed robbery.

On the basis of evidence from letters written by Conrad, the composition of the first handwritten draft of 'A Smile of Fortune' took place between 18 May 1910 (the date suggested in the letter to Galsworthy) and the end of August of the same year (Conrad acknowledges receipt of £40 from his agent Pinker for the completed manuscript in a letter written 3 September). In the middle of this period of composition the British newspapers started to print reports of what became known as the Crippen murder case. From 15 July the London *Daily Mail* carried regular reports of what it first dubbed 'The Mystery of Hilldrop-Crescent', making use here of the address at which Dr Crippen murdered and interred his wife before fleeing England with his mistress Ethel Le Neve, who was disguised as a boy. Conrad is likely to have been reading the *Daily Mail* at this time, as the day following the *Mail*'s first report, on 16 July, the newspaper published one of a number of columns that Conrad wrote for it. Conrad's review of a book on spiritualism entitled 'The Life Beyond' was followed on 23 July by a further review, this time entitled 'A Happy Wanderer'.

The Crippen case was a journalist's dream: the fugitive pair were reported to be on the ship the *Montrose*, which Crippen boarded with his mistress Ethel le Neve at Antwerp, bound for Quebec. Scotland Yard detectives were sent to intercept the ship, travelling to Canada on a faster vessel. Thus while Crippen and Le Neve were sailing to Canada in the belief that their whereabouts were unknown, the whole of England was reading about them and their crimes in the daily press. After Crippen and Le Neve's arrest in Canada, Conrad was asked by the *Daily Mail*'s literary editor to review the books that Crippen had with him on the *Montrose* (Ray 1990, 63).[11]

During both the time *about which* and *at which* Conrad was writing 'A Smile of Fortune', the newspapers were full of reports of a violent murderer who killed one or more women.[12] Violence to women does not merely lurk at the text's borders: in the newspapers Alice reads, it spills into the text and sensitizes readers to a continued suggestion that male heterosexual desire in the story is linked sadistically and masochistically to pain, fear and humiliation. When Alice first sets eyes on the captain, he reports that 'Under her amazement there was a

hint of fear, and then came a flash as of anger' (43). It becomes apparent that
these two responses – fear and anger – both have erotic force for the captain. As
his obsessive need to visit Alice deepens from day to day, the captain attempts
to distinguish between her reality as a person independent of himself, and his
puzzled, if not tormented, awareness of his desire for her:

> I was looking at the girl. It was what I was coming for daily; troubled,
> ashamed, eager; finding in my nearness to her a unique sensation which I
> indulged with dread, self-contempt, and deep pleasure, as if it were a secret
> vice bound to end in my undoing, like the habit of some drug or other which
> ruins and degrades its slave. (62)

What is it about his desire that he associates with 'dread, self-contempt, and deep
pleasure'? How is his attraction comparable to a drug habit?[13] Soon after this
passage, Alice asks him why he keeps on 'coming here'. The captain's response
to himself is at least honest: 'I could not have told her. I could not even tell
myself with sincerity why I was coming there' (63). What is that 'strange, half-
evil, half-tender sensation which had given its acrid flavour to so many days,
which had made her appear tragic and promising, pitiful and provoking' (78) and
that disappears during his final meeting with Alice?

In the captain's attempts to come to terms with, and to isolate and
understand, his desire, is a recurrent yoking together of opposites: self-contempt
and deep pleasure; half-evil, half-tender, 'tragic and promising, pitiful and
provoking' (78). At the heart of this contradiction-filled desire lies his shameful
perception of the contradictory nature of his attraction to Alice, an attraction
sadistically fuelled by her fear and by his perception of her vulnerability and his
potential power over her, and masochistically by her contempt for and
indifference to him. Even Alice's physical appearance manages to combine the
autocratic and the subservient. 'She was like a spellbound creature with the
forehead of a goddess crowned by the dishevelled magnificent hair of a gipsy
tramp' (59). The passage continues with the captain's comment that 'Even her
indifference was seductive. I felt myself growing attached to her by the bond of
an irrealizable desire, for I kept my head – quite ' (59). It is, surely, not so much
a case of 'even' but more of 'especially'; the captain after all goes on to admit
that it is the fact that his desire is 'irrealizable' that constitutes the bond that links
him to her. And as we shall see, once it becomes clear that his desire is actually
not irrealizable, then the bond is severed.[14]

On the narrative's surface, the captain is presented as a kind man, heartily
shocked and disgusted by Ernest Jacobus's violent bullying of his
unacknowledged mulatto son. But under the surface – both of the captain's
depicted self-awareness and of the narrative's tracing of his relations with Alice
– the captain recognizes a guilty pleasure in his sense of power over Alice, in his
realization that he inspires fear in her, that he has the power to hurt her, and is,

indeed, doing just that. If the two Jacobus brothers betoken, respectively, sadism and masochism, the respectable and the outcast, the captain's confusion of Ernest and Alfred indicates that similar contrary impulses are to be found in his own make-up.

If this sounds unlike Conrad, it is worth remembering that 'A Smile of Fortune' is not his only work to associate male heterosexual excitement with perverse or perverted pleasure. In *Chance*, half-finished at the time 'A Smile of Fortune' was written, the first meeting between Captain Anthony and Flora – during which Anthony saves Flora from committing suicide – is replete with strong indications that the captain is erotically aroused by Flora's suffering and his sense of power over her:

> What seemed most awful to her was the elated light in his eyes, the rapacious smile that would come and go on his lips as if he were gloating over her misery. But her misery was his opportunity and he rejoiced while the tenderest pity seemed to flood his own being. [...]
>
> 'Flora had tried more than once to free herself, but he tightened his grasp on her arm each time and even shook it a little without ceasing to speak. The nearness of his face intimidated her. He seemed striving to look through her. It was obvious the world had been using her ill. And even as he spoke with indignation the very marks and stamp of this ill-usage of which he was so certain seemed to add to the inexplicable attraction he felt for her person. It was not pity alone, I take it. It was something more spontaneous, perverse and exciting. (223–4)

'Spontaneous, perverse and exciting': the emotions explored at this point in *Chance* are very close to those charted and investigated in 'A Smile of Fortune', while Anthony's grasp on her arm and aggressive nearness and aggressive eye-contact are all in consort with a desire to exert control over Flora. It seems clear that this passage hints at a tension between the indignation at Flora's ill-usage that Anthony expresses verbally, and a deeper enjoyment, and even continuation, of this ill-usage.

In his 'psychoanalytic biography' of Conrad, Bernard C. Meyer argues that there are strong echoes of Leopold Sacher-Masoch's *Venus in Furs* in Conrad's novel *The Arrow of Gold*, and he proposes that Conrad may well have read Sacher-Masoch's novel in his youth. The parallels between the two texts seem too striking to have occurred without Conrad having had some knowledge of Sacher-Masoch's text, and I will return to this topic in my final chapter. It is, accordingly, tantalizing to note that the Mauritian French-language newspaper *Le Progrès Colonial* had started to serialize Sacher-Masoch's novel *La Pecheuse d'Âmes* on the 1 September. So that when Conrad arrived at Port Louis on 30 September the newspaper's 'feuilleton' was being published in every issue, but publication was interrupted on the 5 October when it was discovered that a section was missing, then only resumed again on the 29 October. Extracts were still being published when Conrad left the island on the 20 November. Thus although Conrad could not have read the entire novel from the newspaper, the name of Sacher-Masoch may well have reminded him of this author's more scandalous work, a work also concerned with a man's drug-like, masochistic obsession.

In one of the deepest ironies of 'A Smile of Fortune', the captain's sexual obsession with Alice is revealed as part inverted mirror-image, part duplicate, of Alfred Jacobus's ignominious pursuit of her mother, the circus horseback-rider by whom he becomes obsessed. As Jerome Zuckerman puts it: 'the narrator's plight comes to parallel that of Jacobus, an indication of the partnership that develops between them and their mutual weakness and guilt. Just as Jacobus' passion had enslaved him to the circus-rider, so now the captain becomes helpless in his passion for Alice' (1964, 100).

It may well be that the account in this story of the time when 'a wandering circus came to the island and my Jacobus became suddenly infatuated with one of the lady-riders' (36) can also be traced back to Conrad's own experiences in Mauritius in the autumn of 1888. The bilingual *Le Progrès Colonial* of this period carries a series of reports about a visiting circus. On 6 October the paper announces the visit of the

CIRCUS TROUPE
KNOWN UNDER THE NAME OF
WALLETT'S CIRCUS

and consisting of Mr and Mrs W.H. Wallett and nine children. The issue of 8 October confirms the presence of the circus 'depuis hier', from 'Natal' (in Conrad's tale Alfred Jacobus follows the circus-rider 'to the Cape'). The first performance of Wallett's Circus in Mauritius took place 15 October, and of the following performances one was advertised to take place 8 November. Conrad might well have been present at either or both of these.

The newspaper's report of the first performance in its issue for 19 October gives a fair idea of the range of its attractions. It includes the following details.

L'intallation [sic] intérieure du Cirque es des plus couvenables et est très coque tement [sic] faite.

L'orchestre, tenue par les musicien [sic] Italiens et quelques artistes et amateurs de la colonie, égaie le public par ses mélodieux flonflons.

Les applaudissements n'ont pas fait defaut aux sujets que M Wallett à préséntes au public. Baby Bondin, F??d Diaz, Littles Georgie, Clara Brilliauso et autres ont émerveillé les spectateurs par l'audace et la précision de leur travail, le jeune Baby Blondui [??] est charmant; les clowns avec leurs lazzis sont très amusants.

[…]
[…] n'oublions pas de dire que les animaux sauvages ne manquent pas […]

[The inside of the Circus is both comfortable and very stylishly turned out.

The orchestra, consisting of both Italian musicians and some artists and amateurs drawn from the colony, cheered the public with its melodious pieces.

The public was provided with plenty of acts to applaud by Mr. Wallett. Baby Bondin, F??d Diaz, Little Georgie, Clara Brilliauso and others astonished onlookers by the audacity and precision of their performances. Baby Blondui [??] is a charmer; the jeering clowns are most amusing. […]

[…] did we mention that there is no shortage of savage animals […]?]

It is tempting to wonder whether at this or at another performance Conrad witnessed a seductive lady circus-rider – or even whether it was during such a performance that he saw something that served as inspiration to the comparison he uses to express Inspector Heat's sudden rush of insecurity in *The Secret Agent*: 'He felt at the moment like a tight rope artist might feel if suddenly, in the middle of the performance, the manager of the Music Hall were to rush out of the proper managerial seclusion and begin to shake the rope' (92). (There is also a reference to a 'tight-rope walker' in 'The End of the Tether', and in *Under Western Eyes*, the 'squeaky stress put on the name "Razumov – Mr. Razumov"' by Necator, 'pierced the ear ridiculously, like the falsetto of a circus clown beginning an elaborate joke' [196].)

If Alfred seems to derive a perverted masochistic pleasure from being humiliated by the object of his desire, the narrator-captain's secret vice has both sadistic and masochistic aspects. The captain presents Alfred Jacobus's degrading obsession with the circus-rider as clearly 'Other', as unlike himself, but the fascination the story exerts on his imagination warns that his attempt to distance himself from Jacobus's humiliation is only partly convincing:

He followed that woman to the Cape, and apparently travelled at the tail of that beastly circus to other parts of the world, in a most degrading position. The woman soon ceased to care for him, and treated him worse than a dog. Most extraordinary stories of moral degradation were reaching the island at that time. He had not the strength of mind to shake himself free. . . .

The grotesque image of a fat, pushing ship-chandler, enslaved by an unholy love-spell, fascinated me […]. (36)

The captain's condescending contempt turns out to be premature: later he has recourse to words similar to those used here to represent Alfred Jacobus's passion, in order to describe his own sexual obsession for Alfred's daughter Alice: 'It was like being the slave of some depraved habit' (59); 'like the habit of some drug or other which ruins and degrades its slave' (62). If the circus-rider treated Alfred 'worse than a dog'– the captain is told of 'the depth of passion under that placid surface, which even cuts with a riding-whip[15] (so the legend had it) could never ruffle into the semblance of a storm' (56) – the captain realizes with 'sudden dismay' that 'I would be no longer able to come into this verandah, sit on this chair, and taste perversely the flavour of contempt in her indolent poses, drink in the provocation of her scornful looks, and listen to the curt, insolent remarks uttered in that harsh and seductive voice' (65).

Whereas Alfred Jacobus sticks by his circus-rider and even, apparently, plots to ensnare the captain into marrying the daughter he had with her, the captain deserts Alice at the point at which his desire dies and she appears before him as an independent individual. Why? The implied answer is that whereas the circus-rider continues to treat Jacobus with contempt, feeding and satisfying his masochistic impulses, Alice rids herself, first, of her fear of the captain and, some time later, of her contempt for, or indifference to, him. At this point, when he has to deal with her as an equal interested in and attracted to him, his desire evaporates. For the captain, it would appear, equality is not erotic.

About two-thirds through the story, when the captain tells Alice that he will set sail the next day, 'She murmured a distinctly scared "So soon," and getting up quickly, went to the little table and poured herself a glass of water'. As Alice walks past him with 'rapid steps and with an indolent swaying of her whole young figure above the hips' the captain feels 'with tenfold force the charm of the peculiar, promising sensation I had formed the habit to seek near her' (64–5). He has to exercise sudden self-control to prevent himself from 'jumping up to stride about, shout, gesticulate, make her a scene' and realizes that 'It was just the relief of violence that I wanted', although outwardly he attempts to keep his lips in a 'half-indulgent, half-mocking smile which was my shield against the shafts of her contempt and the insulting sallies flung at me by the old woman' (65). The key words here are 'scared' and 'violence' (his sadistic desire) and 'contempt' (his masochistic desire). This is not the first time he entertains a fantasy of treating Alice violently; in an early scene his frustration with her leads him to feel 'as if I could have done her some violence – shaken her, beaten her maybe' (54). If this enslavement by Alice's fear, on the one hand, and indolence and contempt, on the other, this drinking-in of her provocatively scornful looks and seductively curt and insolent remarks, merit the verdict of 'perverse', with its shadowy hint of 'perverted', the captain's full 'perversity' becomes most apparent at that point of the tale that has typically surprised the first-time reader of the novella: his sudden loss of desire.

Thomas C. Moser focuses attention on to the captain's changing interest. First, he characterizes this interest as voyeuristic: 'Since Alice seldom speaks to the captain and since she usually has a chaperone in attendance, his desire for her seems, as he says, "unrealizable." In fact, he wants it that way. He comes only to *look* at her in her thin wrapper that reveals a "young supple body"' (1957, 97). (The word used by the captain to describe his desire is, actually, the neologism 'irrealizable'.) Moser justifies his diagnosis by referring to the passage already quoted ('I was looking ... slave' [62]), then goes on to argue that 'Simply looking at Alice sufficiently satisfies the young captain, until she shows her indifference. This is such a blow to his vanity that he desires her, in order to prove his manhood' (98). If we return to Conrad's text, however, neither claim can be justified. The captain does *not* simply want to look at Alice; he wants to satisfy his sadistic and masochistic tendencies by enjoying her fear and contempt, and his desire starts well before she becomes indifferent to him. Moser is right, however, that the story is able to delve deeply and analytically into the captain's sexuality by tracing the stages through which his desire progresses. In particular, the captain's sudden loss of desire, a heretofore so powerfully obsessive force, is especially significant: this loss is the final stage in a sequence of rapid alterations in the nature of the relationship between the captain and Alice.

The first of these alterations comes after the captain has solemnly promised Alice that he will do nothing to her, nor will he allow her father to force him to harm her. On this declaration, her behaviour is transformed.

> To watch the change in the girl was like watching a miracle – the gradual but swift relaxation of her tense glance, of her stiffened muscles, of every fibre of her body. That black, fixed stare into which I had read a tragic meaning more than once, in which I had found a sombre seduction, was perfectly empty now, void of all consciousness whatever, and not even aware any longer of my presence. [...]
>
> But, man being a perverse animal, instead of rejoicing at my complete success, I beheld it with astounded and indignant eyes. (68)

The captain's perverse indignation is the result of his loss of power to inspire dread in Alice, now 'not even aware any longer of my presence'. No longer able to derive sadistic pleasure from observing her fear, he does not yet lose his desire as he can still derive masochistic pleasure from her contempt. But when both fear *and* contempt disappear to be replaced by her romantic interest in him, he, perversely, loses interest in her. The 'sombre seduction' of Alice's 'black, fixed stare' is replaced by emptiness, by a void – and the change evokes astonishment and indignation in the captain.

Three things are necessary for the captain's desire to evaporate: first, Alice must cease to be afraid of him; second she must cease being contemptuous of, or indifferent to, him; and, finally, she must take the initiative in encouraging romantic contact. If her fear satisfies his sadistic impulses and her contempt and indifference are productive of a masochistic pleasure, her genuine romantic interest in him requires a corresponding commitment on his part and accordingly kills his desire and encourages him to flee. For the captain, it would appear, the romantic without the exercise of power is not erotic.

When it is merely a matter of Alice's being indifferent to him, the captain witnesses her 'revelling contemptuously in a sense of relief, easing her limbs in freedom after all these days of crouching, motionless poses when she had been so furious and so afraid', acting 'with supreme indifference, incredible, offensive, exasperating, like ingratitude doubled with treachery', and offering 'to pass by me as if I were a wooden post or a piece of furniture'. At this point he attempts to replace her indifference with a new version of the superior-subservient relationship: he places both arms round her waist, 'and the first kiss I planted on her closed lips was vicious enough to have been a bite' (69).

Suddenly Alice is transformed for the captain: 'I felt her there, close against me, young, full of vigour, of life, a strong desirable creature, but as if she did not care in the least, in the absolute assurance of her safety, what I did or left undone' (69). After she escapes from him, he is confounded, hesitating between violence and love: 'I could not make up my mind whether to shake my fist in that direction or blow a kiss' (70). As I will argue below, there are elements in the scene in *The Secret Agent* which culminates in Winnie's murder of her husband Adolf Verloc that are very similar to aspects of the captain's contradictory feelings about Alice.

Alice's 'vigour' and 'life' do not stimulate the captain's desire. Indeed, her subsequent display of interest in him finally kills his erotic excitement. For if this moment of her indecision ends the tale's fifth section, the following section opens with the captain's awareness that Alice's father has observed his sexual wrestling. The next time he meets Alice, she appears not when he calls for her but some time afterwards:

> The girl, when I turned my head at a slight noise, appeared to me very tall and slender, advancing with a swaying limp, a floating and uneven motion which ended in the sinking of her shadowy form into the deep low chair. And I don't know why or whence I received the impression that she had come too late. She ought to have appeared at my call. She ought to have ... It was as if a supreme opportunity had been missed. (76–7)

This is a small but crucial detail: 'She ought to have appeared at my call'. She has displayed her independence of him. In the lines that follow the captain discovers that his desire has vanished:

'If you buttoned the strap you would not be losing your shoe, Miss Don't Care,'[16] I said, trying to be playful without conviction. I felt more like wailing over the lost illusion of vague desire, over the sudden conviction that I would never find again near her the strange, half-evil, half-tender sensation which had given its acrid flavour to so many days, which had made her appear tragic and promising, pitiful and provoking. That was all over. (77–8)

Once his ability to make her afraid or to bathe in her contempt has evaporated and the captain has to face Alice as a sexual equal, his desire evaporates: 'That was all over'. Thomas C. Moser argues that 'Conrad's moral sense, demanding that his characters act upon their own volition, conflicts with his misogyny. Woman in action, woman as the competitor of man, is insufferable. Thus, Conrad's sympathy for the homeless waif vanishes as soon as she makes a gesture of self-assertion' (160). I am not convinced that it is, at least in the case of the captain's loss of desire for Alice, a question of misogyny, but more that when Alice faces the captain as an equal rather than as contemptuous or afraid of him, she no longer provokes sexual excitement in him.

The Crippen case involved not simply a wife's murder but the murdering husband's obsession with a younger woman who fled with him dressed as a boy.[17] If, as I have suggested above, Conrad's writing of 'A Smile of Fortune' was influenced by his reading of press reports of the Crippen case, he may also have read a number of articles about cross-dressing women that were published during this same period in the *Daily Mail*. In the *Mail* for 15 August 1910, for example, there is a brief report from New York headed 'Woman's Life as a Man: 5 Years' Masquerade', with a follow-up report published 17 August. Three days later the issue for 18 August has another report entitled 'Reply to the Girl-Man. Another Masquerade Experience. Masculine Virtues'. Just at the time Conrad was finishing his first draft of the story, on 27 August, the *Mail* published a half-page account headed 'Women Who Pose as Men', by 'Lieutenant-Colonel E. Rogers'. The article includes four pictures, including two that show the woman who was the subject of the first article dressed both as woman and as man. In her article 'Turn-of-the-century male impersonation: rewriting the romance plot' (1996) Martha Vicinus argues that the entire nineteenth century 'is rife with cross-dressed heroines and heroes in theater, opera, and fiction, as well as numerous historical characters' (187), and she provides a number of representative examples from the period 1890–1914. If we extend this period by three years to 1917 it includes more or less every work of artistic value written by Conrad. Although Vicinus does not mention the circus, it is worth noting that most of the well-known examples of females dressing as men that she discusses are associated with the stage.

Alice Jacobus, like other Conradian heroines, notably Nathalie Haldin in *Under Western Eyes*, is characterized by a certain 'masculinity'. She has a 'fine, somewhat masculine hand' (63), and her 'attitude, like certain tones of her voice, had in it something masculine' (65). The *Daily Mail* of 27 July, 1910 includes an account of the 'Crippen Chase' based on an interview with the landlady of the hotel in Brussels where Crippen and Le Neve stayed prior to sailing for Canada. The first sub-head in the column reads: 'Betrayed by Hands', and reports that the landlady was suspicious that the young man kept his hands in his pockets all the time, and that when the two dined 'we saw that her hands were beautiful and white, with well-kept nails – a woman's hand quite obviously'.

The narrator-captain of 'A Smile of Fortune', when presented with flowers by Alfred Jacobus, 'assured him jocularly [...] that he made me feel as if I were a pretty girl, and that he mustn't be surprised if I blushed' (22–3). The episode prepares for the challenge to his sense of his masculinity that awaits him in the fertile and seductive garden from which these flowers have been picked, and, taken together, these different episodes prepare the reader for a narrative in which any conventional belief that gender roles and identities are allotted unproblematically on the basis of sex is likely to be challenged and undermined.[18] Early in the story the captain is told of the dispute between the two Jacobus brothers by 'the chief clerk' who talks 'primly', walks 'mincingly', and 'resembled an old maid ... shocked by some impropriety' (14).[19] As with the effeminate Chief Steward in *The Shadow-Line*, the early introduction of this character prepares for a world in which sexual identity does not guarantee conventional gender characteristics. Monika Elbert has pointed out that 'A Smile of Fortune' is 'a harbor story, a liminal setting which collapses boundaries between feminine and masculine' (2001, 139), and there is certainly a sense in which the harbour functions as a sort of border country in which conventional attributes and behaviour – including those associated with sex and gender – can be modified. The title *'Twixt Land and Sea*, the collection in which the story was published, may well puzzle: if the sea meets the land, then there is nothing between them. But perhaps 'land' and 'sea' are not absolute, all-embracing terms; perhaps there are areas such as the harbour that are both land and sea; and perhaps there is also an area *'Twixt Man and Woman* in which more of us live more of the time than is generally admitted.

This questioning of gender boundaries parallels the way in which other binaries are seen to be less precise and more fluid than conventionally expected. The *Hilda*'s captain mourns his wooden figurehead much as – and as much as – the *Stella*'s captain mourns the death of a flesh-and-blood child, while the flesh-and-blood captain-narrator, amazed when the aged *gouvernante* suggests that Alice put on a corset and petticoat, asks himself: 'Was I of no more account than a wooden dummy?' (48). (I have already referred to the subsequent passage in which the captain expresses his anger at Alice's 'movement to pass by me as if I were a wooden post or a piece of furniture'.) In the fourth paragraph the captain reports that, faced by the seductive beauty of the 'Pearl of the Ocean', 'horrid thoughts of business interfered with my enjoyment of an accomplished passage' (3–4), and as commentators have noted, it proves impossible for the captain, and for the reader, to separate out Alfred Jacobus's business interests from his desire to marry off his daughter. Is his daughter a tool to entrap the captain into unwanted 'trading', or is the forced purchase of potatoes merely the second-best conclusion to a plot aimed at the captain's single status rather than his pocket? Is the garden in which Alice is confined a prison or an Edenic retreat from the world? (It is potatoes rather than the traditional, if unbiblical, apple that the cunning Jacobus persuades the captain to take from the paradise, but Conrad would have known that 'potato' in French is *pomme de terre*: the potato seems an appropriate earthly variant of the Edenic fruit.) Is Alice herself victim or tormenter? Was her father the circus-rider's victim or a willing participant in his savoured degradation?

That neat distinction between Alfred Jacobus's apparently masochistic obsession with the circus-rider, and the captain's incipient drawing of sadistic pleasure from Alice's fear, a distinction that might underwrite the captain's claim to a manliness based on power, must be set against scenes in which the captain appears fascinated and aroused by the young woman's contempt:

> 'Surely, Miss Alice, you will not let them drive me out into the street?'
> Her magnificent black eyes, narrowed, long in shape, swept over me with an indefinable expression, then in a harsh, contemptuous voice she let fall in French a sort of explanation:
> '*C'est papa.*' (45–6)

It seems appropriate that Alice's contempt is linked here to her mention of her father. At the start of the fifth section the captain reports of his relationship with Alfred Jacobus that 'A sort of shady, intimate understanding seemed to have been established between us' (51), an understanding that may involve their shared knowledge of the captain's obsession with Alice, or their shared understanding of the masochistic pleasure to be derived from being badly treated by the object of such an obsession. If at the novella's opening the captain wishes to preserve boundaries – flowers should not be grown on board as salt water may rot them – by the end he recognizes the inevitable untidiness of the world and of our relations to it.

This blurring of binaries leads both the captain and the reader to recognize that the world is not always a place in which things human are susceptible to neat categorization. What makes 'A Smile of Fortune' such a rich work is that there is nothing programmatic in the portrayal or analysis of the captain's desire. Among other things, it is presented as deeply intertwined with class – not as such but as a locus of power. If as has been suggested the novella is based on Conrad's entanglement with two women in Mauritius – the 26-year-old Eugénie Renouf, and the 17-year-old Alice Shaw – then their very different positions on the social scale may have contributed to the novella's insistence on Alice's scandalously unrespectable status as the daughter of an 'outcast' father and

'Gipsy' mother. 'A Smile of Fortune' certainly suggests that there may be an inverse relationship between social status and sexual attractiveness, not least through the foregrounded hints that Alice, with her repeatedly missing shoe or slipper, is a sort of Cinderella. Referring to the island's 'old French families' (to one of which Eugénie Renouf belonged), the captain scornfully reports that the girls 'are almost always pretty, ignorant of the world, kind and agreeable and generally bilingual; they prattle innocently both in French and English. The emptiness of their existence passes belief' (34–5).

During his sojourn in Mauritius it appears that Conrad proposed to Eugénie Renouf only to discover that she was engaged.[20] Such an experience can hardly have been other than humiliating, and it would not have been surprising had that humiliation resulted in an anger that sought emotional revenge or at least the refuge of a relationship in which the woman was humiliated. Such speculation is just that, but it offers a plausible biographical source for the mingled masochistic and sadistic impulses that Alice Jacobus inspires in the captain and that he finds so erotically enslaving.

Alice Shaw did not belong to one of these families, and research has uncovered the fact that her father, a shipping agent, owned the island's only rose garden.[21] The story's Alice is described as having the 'dishevelled magnificent hair of a gipsy tramp' (59), and the captain – doubtless alluding to the now-discredited belief that the Roma people are of Egyptian origin, as the etymology of 'gypsy' reveals – claims that she had found her 'long, Egyptian eyes' in the sawdust of the circus (71). If we accept the suggestion that this 'harbour story' offers a liminal setting in which established conventions can be thrown off and alternative forms of behaviour tested, then the carnivalesque associations of the circus attached to the circus-rider and to Alice, her daughter, are entirely appropriate.

In his 'psychoanalytical biography' of Conrad, Bernard C. Meyer treats the report that Conrad was romantically involved with – or attracted to – two women during the brief time that he was in Mauritius with sceptical disbelief. For Meyer, 'not only does it appear improbable that he [Conrad] could have been deeply committed to two women at once in the short space of seven weeks, it is even more unlikely that the same man who behaved like the terror-stricken schoolboy toward Eugénie Renouf was capable of the bold seduction of Alice Jacobus in her secluded garden' (74). Such a view bespeaks rather a limited view of the psychology of both sexual attraction and sexual behaviour, and if one is to indulge in biographical speculation it seems quite plausible that a man humiliated by a daughter of one of the best families of the island might seek revenge on another, relatively socially disadvantaged, daughter. A much older work – Oliver Goldsmith's *She Stoops to Conquer* (1773) – offers evidence that a woman's perceived class can affect her sexual desirability in the eyes of a man. By an odd coincidence (I think that it is that – I have found no evidence that Conrad was acquainted with Goldsmith's play, although as I have noted, Jósef

Retinger reports that Conrad liked the novels of Richardson and Smollett) the hero of Goldsmith's play is named Marlow (and his father is named Charles!). The sub-title of Goldsmith's play is 'The Mistakes of a Night', and the play indeed rests upon one central mistake. Sir Charles Marlow and Mr Hardcastle are old friends. Sir Charles's son young Marlow has been chosen by Hardcastle to marry Hardcastle's daughter Kate, and as the play opens he is awaited by Kate and her father, who have never met him before. Young Marlow arrives at his destination accompanied by his friend Hastings, without knowing where he is. He is mischievously informed by Kate's half-brother Tony Lumkin that they have actually arrived at an inn, and they settle in believing this to be the case. Kate and her father have an agreement that every morning she shall receive and pay visits and dress as she pleases, while in the evening she puts on her housewife's dress to please her father. As a result Marlow believes that the 'morning Kate' is the woman who is his Intended and who is visiting the inn, while the 'evening Kate' is a servant and her father is the inn-keeper. In the company of the Kate Marlow knows to be a lady he is reserved, tongue-tied, and incapable of finishing a sentence. In the company of the Kate he believes to be a servant he is articulate, flirtatious, and indeed explicitly sexually aggressive. Moreover, when young Marlow's friend Hastings rebukes him for his willingness to rob a woman of her virtue (meaning the woman he erroneously believes to be a servant), he responds 'I don't intend to *rob* her, take my word for it, there's nothing in this house I shan't honestly *pay* for' (Goldsmith 1966, 178). Such a mercantile attitude is explicitly contrasted with the more feudal relationships between the older Marlow and his servants.

Even such a brief account[22] as this should demonstrate that sexual desire and sexual conduct are not presented as pure biological urges in Goldsmith's play, but as forms of behaviour that are saturated with and even constituted by the social, the cultural and the historical. Young Marlow's perception of Kate as a servant leads to his becoming sexually excited by her as he assumes that he enjoys a social and economic power over her, and sees her virtue as something that is for sale. Most important: these are not separate entities but are strands in a single thread. He finds her erotically stimulating *because* he thinks that she is a servant and *because* he thinks that he has power over her. His power over her is a component in her erotic force for him. Moreover his perception of their differential placing on the axis of class is one that is historically constituted and generated.

If young Marlow believes Kate to be two people, his relationship with 'them' is oddly reminiscent of accounts of Conrad's relationship with the two women with whom he was supposedly involved romantically in Mauritius: the 26-year-old Eugénie Renouf, and the 17-year-old Alice Shaw. It should be said that accounts of Conrad's relationship with Alice Shaw have been heavily based upon the fictional relationship between the narrator-captain of 'A Smile of Fortune' and the young Alice Jacobus – a notoriously unreliable way to gain access to any sort of historical actuality, and one that in this case runs the added risk of circularity if the 'facts' of Conrad's relationship are then applied to the story from which these 'facts' have been extracted. However if one pursues the possibility that Conrad's depiction of Alice Jacobus in the tale somehow encompasses his relationship with both Eugénie Renouf and Alice Shaw, then Alice Jacobus may be understood as a figure who combines the privileged and disdainful Eugénie Renouf ('Her magnificent black eyes, narrowed, long in shape, swept over me with an indefinable expression, then in a harsh, contemptuous voice she let fall in French a sort of explanation' [45–6]) and the disempowered and terrified Alice Shaw ('Then, after a gasp, she spoke with such frightful rapidity that I could hardly make out the amazing words: "For if you were to shut me up in an empty place as smooth all round as the palm of my hand, I could always strangle myself with my hair"' [66]).

Alice's doubleness is indissolubly linked to the captain's alternation between sadistic and masochistic pleasure, in much the same way as young Marlow's perception of Kate as two different women, located at different ends of the social scale, is indissolubly linked to his own alternation between a tongue-tied nervousness and extreme, aggressive sexual predation. Moreover, like Goldsmith's young Marlow, the captain travels to the place where he meets the young woman, and – again like young Marlow – he is compelled to negotiate both with the young woman and also her father. And, finally, in both cases the rival systems of commerce and sexual desire intertwine in a manner that confuses and confounds the young man.

In spite of his scepticism regarding the possibility of Conrad's having been entangled with two women during his seven-week stay in Mauritius, Meyer is acute when he observes that 'the sensuous women in Conrad's fiction are not the monolithic Rita [from *The Arrow of Gold*] and her like, but those creatures who spring from a much lower station in the hierarchy of social organization, women like Aïssa, Winnie Verloc, and the simple hired girl, Amy Foster'. Meyer also claims that

> [T]he element of dissimilarity between the lovers appears to have been a necessary condition for the emergence of passionate love in his stories, for it is mainly in those novels in which a conspicuous element of exogamy is implied that Conrad's lovers convey a credible impression of erotic feeling: 'Amy Foster,' *An Outcast of the Islands*, *Lord Jim*, 'A Smile of Fortune,' 'Heart of Darkness,' and possibly *Almayer's Folly*. But in those stories like 'The Return,' 'The Planter of Malata,' *Chance*, *Victory*, *The Arrow of Gold*, and *The Rescue*, in which the protagonists are both white and of comparatively similar backgrounds, the lovers appear to expend most of their sexual energies by backing and filling in a morass of inhibition, all the while engaging in a ruminative chatter that at times approaches sheer double-talk. (112–13)

What this skates over is the factor of class, and especially so with regard to the last four works mentioned: 'The Planter of Malata', *Victory*, *The Arrow of Gold*, and *The Rescue* . In all of these there is a disparity in the class position of hero and heroine that introduces the axis of power, and opens for feelings of sadism and/or masochism on the part of the hero.

Heart of Darkness sets the sterile and bloodless European Intended against Kurtz's fecund, energetic and sexual African mistress. Alice Jacobus combines the characteristics of these two matched or contrasted characters. On the one hand, she is an isolated young European woman, ignorant of the world; on the other hand, she is associated with the suggestively luxuriant forces of nature within her father's walled garden. Certainly her bodily reality is set against the socially correct but unbelievably empty existences of the island's respectable women. Her clothing suggests rather than conceals her young body's contours. If her repeatedly lost shoe brings to mind her status as fairy-tale Cinderella (who had two 'respectable' sisters rather than Alice's one respectable half-sister), it is also 'not really a slipper, but a low shoe of blue, glazed kid, rubbed and shabby',[23] with 'straps to go over the instep, but the girl only thrust her feet in' (72). The toe has a 'worn point' (73), and when at the end of the story the captain puts it on her foot, he seems as much gratified fetishist as Prince Charming. The shoe's marks of its owner, its shabbiness, worn point and slovenly way of being worn apparently catch the captain's attention. At the story's close we learn that the captain's command was 'like a foot in the stirrup for a young man' (88), but in this story feet do not stay where they are supposed to – even when they belong to a circus-rider or her daughter.

The Planter of Malata

Sexual obsession also plays a crucial role in 'The Planter of Malata'. The tale's central male character, Geoffrey Renouard is, like the young narrator-captain in 'A Smile of Fortune', an isolated individual. Away from Malata (another island!) where he has started a scheme involving the experimental cultivation of silk plants, he encounters the 'pagan' Felicia Moorsom[24] with her 'magnificently red' hair (9) and becomes romantically obsessed by her. As in 'A Smile of Fortune', Conrad's male hero becomes involved in a complex game of deceptions and hidden agendas that involve not just himself and the woman by whom he has been smitten, but her father, too. The father, his sister and his daughter have travelled from Europe to the great colonial city (named as Sydney in Conrad's manuscript) in search of 'Master Arthur', who had been engaged to Felicia but who left England in disgrace after being unjustly accused of financial wrongdoing. As Renouard knows, and as most readers guess before the fact is confirmed, 'Master Arthur' is actually Renouard's assistant, Walter. And Renouard also knows that the man is dead (he buried him himself, after Walter's death following an accident), but he chooses to conceal this fact so as to stay in

Felicia's company as long as possible. Thus, as in 'A Smile of Fortune', the story presents a knot of characters each of whom is driven by publicly acknowledged as well as by secretly unacknowledged motives.

Renouard's obsession with Felicia is, like that of the narrator of 'A Smile of Fortune' with Alice Jacobus, presented as a sort of addiction or sickness:

> On board the schooner, lying on the settee on his back with the knuckles of his hands pressed over his eyes, he made up his mind that he would not return to that house for dinner – that he would never go back there any more. He made up his mind some twenty times. The knowledge that he had only to go up on the quarter deck, utter quietly the words: 'Man the windlass,' and that the schooner springing into life would run a hundred miles out to sea before sunrise, deceived his struggling will. Nothing easier! Yet, in the end, this young man, almost ill-famed for his ruthless daring, the inflexible leader of two tragically successful expeditions, shrank from that act of savage energy, and began, instead, to hunt for excuses. (43)

Renouard also shares with his literary predecessor the captain-narrator a consciousness of the disparity between the force of his desire and the worth of its object. However, whereas Alice Jacobus is a social outcast, Felicia belongs to 'the cream of our society' (13). Her father chooses a somewhat different formulation, using the word 'froth' to describe her social milieu.

> [Y]ou don't know what it is to have moved, breathed, existed, and even triumphed in the mere smother and froth of life – the brilliant froth. There thoughts, sentiments, opinions, feelings, actions too, are nothing but agitation in empty space – to amuse life – a sort of superior debauchery, exciting and fatiguing, meaning nothing, leading nowhere. She is the creature of that circle. (40–41)

Conrad plays with the word 'froth' to explore the treacherous combination of outer beauty and inner emptiness represented by Felicia, linking it to the foam associated with Venus's birth: 'he would see her dazzling and perfect, her eyes vague, staring in mournful immobility, with a drooping head that made him think of a tragic Venus arising before him, not from the foam of the sea, but from a distant, still more formless, mysterious, and potent immensity of mankind' (36). Owen Knowles has drawn attention to the substantial debt the story owes to Mérimée's 'La Vénus d'Ille' (1837), a supernatural tale in which a young man is crushed by a Roman statue of Venus to which he has been 'unfaithful'. (He carelessly places his ring on the statue's finger and is unable to remove it; after he marries, the statue exacts its revenge.) According to Knowles:

The account of the statue as combining extreme beauty with the absence of sensibility finds its echo in the description of Felicia as suffering from 'the insensibility of a great passion concentrated on itself' (34). Yet both she and the statue are obscurely felt to express the ultimate truth about life: the statue stands for '*la réalité*,' while Felicia repeatedly announces that she stands for 'truth.' Such truth in physical form appears to be so witheringly final that no man can face it squarely, and both Conrad and Mérimée describe their male figures with instantly lowered eyes before the cruelly dazzling goddess-figure. (1979, 181)

Renouard's dream of the crumbling statue relies heavily on Mérimée, and, as Knowles remarks, 'Like his counterpart in "La Vénus d'Ille," Renouard is paid a visit by a ghostly night-time version of his goddess, and feels himself crushed by the "weight of the irremediable ... laid on him suddenly in the small hours of the night" (23)' (1979, 182). As in 'A Smile of Fortune', then, male sexual desire is seen as an intoxication inspired by a woman whose perceived unworthiness does not diminish her power to entrance and entrap. But while Alice may be presented as socially unworthy, the power of her fear and contempt to trigger feelings of sadomasochistic desire in the captain is convincingly and concretely detailed, and Conrad is able to build on this evocation of Alice's sexual allure for the captain to explain how and why his passion first appears and then evaporates. Because Felicia's 'unworthiness' does not give Renouard power over her, it cannot be used to explain her erotic force for him.

Renouard, like the captain, also makes passionate physical contact with the object of his obsession. After finally admitting to her that the missing man is dead, and declaring his own love, Renouard is as unable to restrain himself as the captain:

She found herself like a feather in his grasp, helpless, unable to struggle, with her feet off the ground. But this contact with her, maddening like too much felicity, destroyed its own end. Fire ran through his veins, turned his passion to ashes, burnt him out and left him empty, without force – almost without desire. He let her go before she could cry out. (77)

If the captain's desire evaporates when Alice ceases to fear him and attempts to kiss him, this passage is curiously ambivalent about Renouard's passion and desire: the former is 'turned ... to ashes', while as for the latter, he is only *almost* 'without desire'. The ambivalence serves as a token of the story's comparative lack of focus with regard to its portrayal of male heterosexual desire. Renouard's passion turns to ashes, then, after he puts an earlier fantasy of seizing Felicia 'in his arms, carrying her off in a tumult of shrieks from all these people, a silent frightened mortal, into some profound retreat as in the age of Cavern men' (45) into diminished practice. Moreover, after he has declared his passion she responds: '*Assez! J'ai horreur de tout cela*' (78), a response implying revulsion so strong as to render her incapable of expressing her horror of sex in her own language.

In perhaps less obvious ways than the earlier story, 'The Planter of Malata' also explores what are now called gender roles. Owen Knowles has pointed out that since Felicia's unjustly disgraced fiancé was named Arthur, the story can be seen as 'a mock-Arthurian quest' (1979, 183), with the woman in search of the man rather than vice-versa. Daphna Erdinast-Vulcan offers a convincing account of the way in which Renouard 'increasingly grows to resemble [Felicia] until, at the moment when he has to make a choice between truth and lies, they are described as "a well-matched couple, animated yet statuesque in their calmness and in their pallor"' (1999, 158). Both interpretations might be cited as evidence that Renouard has been unmanned by his passion, but such unmanning is not enacted in the convincing way that the captain's loss of the conventional attributes of masculinity is conveyed in 'A Smile of Fortune'. Nothing equivalent to the darker hints about the captain's feminine side and his attraction to Alice's 'masculinity' that are dropped and explored in the earlier story is to be found in 'The Planter of Malata'. Among the things that Renouard finds 'ravishing' in Felicia is 'the unfailing brilliance of her femininity' (35). His obsession, it is true, turns him from active adventurer to a man who goes every afternoon to Felicia's house 'as passively as if in a dream' (32), but there is no sense here as in 'A Smile of Fortune' that the ostensibly active hero feels a worrying pleasure in this loss of his conventional manly attributes. (The only occurrence of the word 'manly' is its ironic and dismissive application to the 'sentimental Willie', who has 'manly tears' in his eyes in Chapter XII's opening sentence.)

It is perhaps a mark of the failure of 'The Planter of Malata' to grip the reader that critical accounts invariably link it with other Conrad works. *Victory*, from which Conrad was taking a break while he wrote the tale, is most frequently chosen for comparative comment, but *Lord Jim*, *The Secret Agent*, *Chance*, 'The Return', 'The Secret Sharer', and 'The Informer' have all been compared to it. This list does not include *Heart of Darkness*, despite the fact that, like 'The Planter of Malata', it contains a 'pagan' woman whose hair resembles a helmet. Felicia's 'ivory forehead' (35) also carries echoes of Conrad's best-known work. In terms of her *inner* qualities Felicia has more in common with Kurtz's Intended than his African mistress: she exhibits utter and self-sacrificing faithfulness to an unworthy man, even after his death. Felicia's sudden recourse to French, which Alice speaks on several occasions, may also remind us of Nathalie Haldin in *Under Western Eyes* (and of Conrad himself, when writing about Mr Jones's hatred of women – see p. 59). But there are other, more telling structural parallels between 'The Planter of Malata' and *Under Western Eyes* to which it is worth devoting some attention.

At the heart of both 'The Planter of Malata' and *Under Western Eyes* is a pattern of non-symmetrical lines of attraction that can be summarized as follows.

Man A has had some knowledge of and/or involvement in Man B's death. Man A meets and falls in love with a woman who has close ties with Man B, but Man A does not at first reveal the extent (or, in the case of 'The Planter of Malata', the fact) of his relationship with Man B. When he does so, the woman recoils in horror, and the man sacrifices himself, literally or metaphorically. (If this sacrifice is as much reminiscent of Victor Haldin as it is of Razumov, one might note that Renouard's posture at the opening of Chapter VI – 'lying on the settee on his back with the knuckles of his hands pressed over his eyes' [43] – also recalls the posture of Nathalie Haldin's brother in Razumov's room.)

Under Western Eyes is vastly superior to 'The Planter of Malata', but this repeated pattern suggests that Conrad saw unavowed knowledge as a form of power that generated male heterosexual excitement but that corrupted a personal relationship. Razumov, too, gains perverted pleasure from the power of his secret knowledge of Victor Haldin's death when in the presence of his sister. One of the best critics of 'The Planter of Malata', Joel R. Kehler, has argued that in the novella Conrad attempted 'a sort of mini-epic in twelve sections of the nature, limits, and consequences of knowledge' (1976, 149). This is well-put, and certainly takes in those claims to total knowledge made by journalists and the press, a subsidiary theme in 'The Planter of Malata', as much as the corrupting effect of unavowed knowledge in personal relations. However, one of the reasons why Conrad's earlier novel provides so much deeper and sophisticated an analysis of male heterosexual desire than does 'The Planter of Malata' is that in *Under Western Eyes* Conrad is able to look at desire as manifested in two very different characters: Razumov and the older teacher of languages. An additional and more telling reason, is that Nathalie is a far more substantial character (both in terms of literary portrayal and depicted human terms) than Alice or, especially, Felicia.[25] One basic inadequacy in 'The Planter of Malata' – set in sharper relief if one reads it alongside 'A Smile of Fortune' – is that because Felicia is so trivial, the claim that Renouard is attracted to her personality is, to use a still-useful distinction, *told* rather than *shown*. While what attracts the captain to Alice is comprehensively and concretely detailed, the power Felicia asserts over Renouard is little more than asserted.

In both 'The Planter of Malata' and *Under Western Eyes* Conrad appears concerned to investigate the extent to which personality can be expressed physically, in the body and its behaviour. After Renouard's meeting with the Editor at the opening of 'The Planter of Malata', for example, we read: 'Because of the force of the physical impression he had received from her personality (and such impressions are the real origins of the deepest movements of our soul) this conception [i.e. as 'subjugated by something common'] of her was even inconceivable' (22). The contrast between the captain's perception of Alice Jacobus's desirability and the presentation of Renouard's cataclysmically passionate enslavement by Felicia could hardly be greater. Assertions in the generalized language of melodrama replace telling concrete detail.

> [H]er hair was magnificently red and her eyes very black. It was a troubling
> effect, but it had been evanescent; [...] The light from an open window fell
> across her path, and suddenly all that mass of arranged hair appeared
> incandescent, chiselled and fluid, with the daring suggestion of a helmet of
> burnished copper and the flowing lines of molten metal. It kindled in him an
> astonished admiration. (9–10)

It is not just that Felicia's 'magnificently red' and 'arranged' hair comes off
badly when set against Alice's 'dishevelled magnificent hair of a gipsy tramp'.
Certainly, when Renouard gazes at the tip of Felicia's shoe (36), the footwear
has none of the erotic charge that Alice's slipper gathers. Most important,
though, is that the initial insistence on concreteness (the passage begins by
focussing attention on the physical) moves anti-climactically to an assertion
characterized by adjectival insistence and banal generality. Towards the story's
end, this gets even worse. Felicia's bemusement at Renouard's suggestion that
she is an aristocrat prompts him (or Conrad) into yet more embarrassing excess:

> '[...] you are merely of the topmost layer, disdainful and superior, the mere
> pure froth and bubble on the inscrutable depths which some day will toss you
> out of existence. But you are you! You are you! You are the eternal love
> itself – only, O Divinity, it isn't your body, it is your soul that is made of
> foam.' (77)

The reader can be forgiven for wondering what is happening here.

Daphna Erdinast-Vulcan has described such passages as 'pseudo-poetic
discourse, an indiscriminate outpouring of lovers' sentimentality, crude enough
to sound like a parody of itself'. She notes, too, that 'the narrative throughout the
story does not dissociate itself from the discourse of the protagonist' (1999,
163). Beyond its sentimentality, Renouard's 'outpouring' is contradictory: how
can he admit that Felicia is 'the mere pure froth and bubble' with 'a soul that is
made of foam', while acclaiming her as 'eternal love itself' and as a 'Divinity'?
The passage combines unambiguous insult with an outpouring of unbounded
love. What woman could respond positively to such a declaration? It is revealing
that 'The Planter of Malata', apart from the occasional sarcasm, lacks humour.
'A Smile of Fortune', in contrast, is possessed of a vein of droll and self-
deprecatory mockery that may well have served to shield against melodrama:
wholehearted indulgence in the melodramatic cannot long survive humour or
irony.

Conrad's late memoir 'Stephen Crane' attributes the original idea for 'The
Planter of Malata' to Crane. The essay recalls an evening during which Crane
told him of 'a subject for a story. [...] He called it "The Predecessor."' Crane
wanted Conrad to collaborate with him in turning the idea into a play, but the
collaboration never took place: 'The general subject consisted in a man

personating his "predecessor" (who had died) in the hope of winning a girl's heart.' Conrad concedes that 'the action, I fear, would have been frankly melodramatic' (*Last Essays*, 115). One wonders to what extent Conrad is here half-consciously attempting to shift blame on to the now-deceased Crane for the melodramatic elements in 'The Planter of Malata'.

If 'A Smile of Fortune' casts Alice as Cinderella and the captain as a Prince Charming *manqué*, 'The Planter of Malata' seems unsure with which fairy tale it wishes to associate itself.[26] In Chapter 3, Renouard dismisses the idea that the missing Master Arthur might be worthy of Felicia: 'But no Prince Charming has ever lived out of a fairy tale. He doesn't walk the worlds of Fashion and Finance – and with a stumbling gait at that' (22). Professor Moorsom, though, on learning that Arthur is not on Malata, comments: 'How vexingly elusive the poor fellow has become! I'll begin to think that some wicked fairy is favouring this love tale with unpleasant attentions' (64).

The novella does, however, contain a dark, indirect reference to the fairy tale 'Blue Beard'. The fairy tale is attributed to Charles Perrault but the Grimm brothers also published a version of it and Conrad's epigraph to *Youth – A Narrative; And Two other Stories* (1902) is taken from the Grimm story 'Rumpelstiltskin'.[27]

In 'The Planter of Malata', after upsetting Renouard with his suggestion that they investigate the belief in ghosts among the plantation 'boys', Felicia's father attempts to placate him: 'We are all of us a little strung up', he said. 'For my part I have been like sister Anne in the story. But I cannot see anything coming. Anything that would be the least good for anybody – I mean' (70). In Perrault's tale, sister Anne waits at the window looking out for the arrival of the two brothers who will save the heroine from Blue Beard, who is calling for her to come to him. Eventually, the brothers burst in, just preventing Blue Beard from adding the heroine's body to those of his other murdered wives. Blue Beard is killed, and the heroine marries 'a very worthy man, who banished from her mind all memory of the evil days she had spent with Blue Beard'. If Professor Moorsom is Sister Anne, he must be hinting that Master Arthur is Blue Beard, and perhaps, too, that Renouard might be the 'very worthy man' who will banish from his daughter's mind the evil days spent with and in pursuit of Arthur. But Arthur is a poor Blue Beard and can be assigned the rôle only by virtue of his threat to destroy the life of the woman searching for him. Moreover, Renouard will not marry Felicia. Thus, if 'A Smile of Fortune' is an anti-Cinderella, 'The Planter of Malata' is an anti-Blue Beard.[28]

Even though when he first meets her Renouard detects something 'pagan' (9) in Felicia's appearance, the attribution is unjustified by anything revealed about her. Indeed, the association seems at odds with the repeated insistence on her membership of a mindless, upper-class set. Conrad's sense of the erotic does not seem capable of depicting the attraction that active men feel for upper-class, 'society' women without lurching into the melodramatic. (Lingard's romantic involvement with Mrs Travers in *The Rescue* offers another example of such an unconvincing depiction.)

Daphna Erdinast-Vulcan argues that 'the genre of romance, which Conrad had apparently relegated to the realm of women, unleashed the writer's own pathological fear of losing his "masculine" self and his deeply rooted misogyny, which is nowhere more conspicuous than when he sets out to "write for women"' (1999, 170). As far as 'The Planter of Malata' is concerned this is plausible; as Erdinast-Vulcan notes, the face that Renouard sees in the mirror is not that of the '"true Renouard" because, in his desire to replace the missing lover, he has exchanged his old self for the dead man, the creature of [Felicia's] romantic discourse' (1999, 159). 'A Smile of Fortune' is another matter. Although the *captain* may indeed be afraid of losing his conventionally masculine self, Conrad displays no aesthetic fear of this topic, no unwillingness to explore the fact that a considerable part of the erotic excitement that Alice stirs in the captain can be enjoyed by him only when, taking advantage of the opportunities offered by the liminal space of the harbour, he escapes from his respectable masculine self into opposed but linked erotic experiences in which he enjoys the drugged pleasure generated by Alice's fear and contempt. In 'The Planter of Malata', Renouard finds 'ravishing' Felicia's 'quietness' and 'the unfailing brilliance of her femininity' (35), things unlikely to challenge conventional gender roles.

Is 'A Smile of Fortune' better than 'The Planter of Malata' because the former recognizes that elements of sadism and masochism are integral to contemporary male sexual desire while the latter doesn't? In part, yes. Sexuality does not lead a peaceful existence untouched by history and culture. Sexualization is always deeply implicated in issues of class, race, power, and culture, and the Ripper and Crippen cases – their occurrence and sensationalized depiction in the press – must be seen as extreme manifestations of the fact that significant veins of power and violence ran through male sexuality at the time Conrad was writing and about which he was writing. His awareness of these cases while composing 'A Smile of Fortune' may well have helped him trace significant veins of power and violence in his experience of the erotic and in his depiction of it.

In both these historical periods, European male sexuality had its public, acknowledged, face and its secret, unacknowledged one. In a world in which men 'enjoyed' (in both senses of the word) legal and social power over women, such enjoyment entered into forming sexual identity and patterns of arousal. 'A Smile of Fortune' confronts the residue of social and gender inequality in contemporary male sexuality by exploring the captain-narrator's contradictorily sadistic and masochistic desire for Alice in the (appropriately) no-man's land of the harbour. He eats of the fruit of knowledge springing from the roots of his sexual desire and reaches the honest and damning conclusion that his desire leaves a smell of corruption.

Whatever lies behind or constitutes Conrad's 'decline' in the years following his completion of *Under Western Eyes* – if one believes that such a decline occurred – the evidence of these novellas suggests that it is not a concern to depict and explore sexuality and the erotic. At the heart of the disturbing power of 'A Smile of Fortune' is precisely the evocation of and investigation into the sources of heterosexual erotic desire and experience, while the inert and lifeless quality of 'The Planter of Malata' cannot be separated from its laying claim to erotic experience on the part of Renouard that it is unable to present in a convincingly enacted form because its social and cultural roots remain untraced.

The Secret Agent: power and sexuality

Because sadism and masochism are concerned with the exercise of power they offer clear symbolic possibilities with regard to the more general exercise of power within a given community or culture. The individual who is erotically stimulated by having another person at their mercy, or by being at the mercy of another person, can without too much difficulty be used to model the situation of a class or group that is socially or economically dominant or subservient, along with the ideology that supports such a social or economic arrangement. But the relationship between sexual economy and socio-political economy extends beyond such symbolic parallels. On the one hand sexual desire is thoroughly saturated with images of class. A culture's stereotypical images of sexual desirability are never class-neutral. In the cultures to which Conrad belonged and with which he was familiar – not least those of late-Victorian and Edwardian England – familiar linguistic and legal collocations would associate women, children and the poor: all had been disenfranchized for much of the nineteenth century, and although the male poor had the vote by the turn of the century, women did not. If we think of two novelists writing at the same time as Conrad – Henry James and E.M. Forster – it is hard to think of their (shared) homosexual impulses without being almost immediately impelled to consider the varied ways in which these impulses lock in in very different ways to complex social and political attitudes and engagements. Forster's desire for working-class young men exemplifies the way in which class structure seeps into sexual economy (and, presumably, vice-versa). The sexual desirability of the character Leonard Bast that the text of *Howards End* displays does not merely involve the use of class-signifiers to depict that which triggers sexual desire, it *is* a class attitude in addition to being a depiction of sexual desirability. You can no more remove class from sex than you can remove corporeality from it. Forster's Leonard Bast and James's Hyacinth Robinson (from *The Princess Casamassima*) are not just figures of the homoerotically desirable, they are also exemplars of socio-political attitudes and reflections of their authors' differential placements in the economies of their interlocking cultures. In his *The Eighteenth*

Brumaire of Louis Bonaparte Karl Marx famously commented that men (by which he means human beings) make their own history, but they do not make it in conditions of their own choosing. In like manner our sexual histories and identities are formed both in and by conditions that are not of our own choosing, and they contain and reflect these conditions.

Conrad's 'A Smile of Fortune' foregrounds the opposition between sexual desire and socio-economic interest. The captain-narrator is unable to decide whether Alfred Jacobus is using his daughter Alice as bait to entrap him into an ill-advised trade-bargain, or whether Jacobus is using the inducement of his business connections (he has the sacks that the captain needs) to entrap him into a marriage with the otherwise hard to marry-off Alice. The captain is not alone in his uncertainty; by the end of the story the reader remains in the same doubt. This inability to distinguish the economic from the erotic serves as token of the necessary interpenetration of the two. Human beings do not desire, or fall in love with, a core of personhood that is clearly distinguishable from its social, cultural, and even economic connections and manifestations. Although Alice clearly remains the same person throughout the story, an alteration in the power-nexus between her and the captain (one which can well be said to model or mimic a change in their class relation) is sufficient to fuel or to destroy the captain's desire for her. It is not Alice who is desired by the captain, but Alice-in-a-particular-relationship-to-the-captain.

This is something that Conrad appears to have understood right from the start of his career as a novelist. In *Almayer's Folly* Dain's marriage to Nina (and, the text suggests, their mutual desire) seems destined to survive because the marriage cements each in precisely that relationship to the other that evokes desire. In Conrad's next novel *An Outcast of the Islands*, Willems's desire for Aïssa does not survive because that which he desires in her is destroyed by his conquest of her.

From the opening page of *The Secret Agent* Conrad goes out of his way to draw the reader's attention not just to the interpenetration of sexuality and the socio-political, but to their overlapping, their shared elements, their partial identity.

> The window contained photographs of more or less undressed dancing girls; nondescript packages in wrappers like patent medicines; closed yellow paper envelopes, very flimsy, and marked two and six in heavy black figures; a few numbers of ancient French comic publications hung across a string as if to dry; a dingy blue china bowl, a casket of black wood, bottles of marking ink, and rubber stamps; a few books, with titles hinting at impropriety; a few apparently old copies of obscure newspapers, badly printed, with titles like *The Torch, The Gong* – rousing titles. (9)

That word 'rousing' marks the point at which the sexual and the political are one. The implication is not just that the excitement generated by the reading of the radical journals is *like* sexual arousal – it *is* in part sexual in nature, just as the purchase of the 'more or less undressed dancing girls' is in its turn a political act. That slogan from the 1970s – 'the personal is political' – is implicit on every page of this novel. (And those who coined the phrase would doubtless have understood what lies behind the narrative's ironic observation that 'Mr Verloc loved his wife as a wife should be loved – that is, maritally, with the regard one has for one's chief possession' [137].) When the Assistant Commissioner tells the 'Great Man' that 'From a certain point of view we are here in the presence of a domestic drama' (168) the utterance does not just isolate an odd twist of the plot, it pinpoints a powerful insight into the way in which patterns in the social, legal and economic relations by means of which a society is constructed reproduce themselves in the private lives and relationships of that society's members. The insight is duplicated in Ossipon's unwittingly profound train of thought: he 'even began to wonder whether the hidden causes of that Greenwich Park affair did not lie deep in the unhappy circumstances of the Verlocs' married life' (208).

If 'A Smile of Fortune' is a story in which the erotic is forged out of a sexual desire inseparable from sadistic and masochistic impulses, *The Secret Agent* presents the reader with a world rather than a relationship in which sexuality and cruelty flourish. But in the earlier work the connection between the two becomes visible only for short periods of time in brief (and highly charged) episodes. At the same time, these two elements are important constituents of what we can term the economy of desire in the novel, and even when they are not directly related each is affected by the circulation of the other.

Thus behind Stevie's love for his sister and hers for him lies the fact of their father's cruel treatment of the retarded boy. It is Winnie's love for her brother that causes her in turn to reject the young man with whom she is in love – a young man who is also threatened by his father – and to enter in to a loveless marriage with the deceived Adolf Verloc. The desire to ensure Verloc's continued support of her son and daughter leads their mother to abandon them, although 'it was hard, hard, cruelly hard' (126). Winnie's love for her brother also leads her to instil in her brother's mind the conviction that Mr Verloc is 'good', a belief that enables Verloc to use Stevie in his attempt to bomb the Greenwich Observatory. Stevie, as a result of his own treatment, 'can't stand the notion of any cruelty' (51), but his disintegrated remains affect Chief Inspector Heat's feelings 'with a sense of ruthless cruelty' (71) and suggest only 'atrocious cruelty' (72). Cruelty is passed from character to character and from generation to generation, and the vehicle in which it is conveyed is love.

Winnie's loveless marriage (she gets 'into bed in a calm business-like manner' which makes her husband 'feel hopelessly lonely in the world' [48]) may be one reason why she, like so many other Conradian married women, is childless. The love that she enjoys in bed has been received from and bestowed upon her brother, not her husband. The experience of his sister's love has had a lasting effect on Stevie: faced with the impossibility of stopping the cabman whipping his horse, he

> could say nothing; for the tenderness to all pain and all misery, the desire to make the horse happy and the cabman happy, had reached the point of a bizarre longing to take them to bed with him. And that, he knew, was impossible. For Stevie was not mad. It was, as it were, a symbolic longing; and at the same time it was very distinct, because springing from experience, the mother of wisdom. Thus when as a child he cowered in a dark corner scared, wretched, sore, and miserable with the black, black misery of the soul, his sister Winnie used to come along, and carry him off to bed with her, as into a heaven of consoling peace. Stevie, though apt to forget mere facts, such as his name and address for instance, had a faithful memory of sensations. To be taken into a bed of compassion was the supreme remedy, with the only one disadvantage of being difficult of application on a large scale. (129)

The narrative irony of the final quoted sentence bespeaks not contempt but sorrowful regret; while pointing out the inapplicability of Stevie's values and remedies for hurt it simultaneously underlines their moral superiority to those in force.

Winnie's childlessness does not indicate a marriage without sex; as the text makes clear she knows how to seduce her husband. But it does link up to a motif of sterility in the novel. The text of the serial edition of the novel makes it absolutely clear that Verloc's shop sells contraceptives in addition to pornography, both of which are associated with forms of sex that do not produce children. Moreover, early on in the novel the words 'hygiene' and 'protection' – both standard contemporary euphemisms for contraception – are linked decisively with Verloc.

> He surveyed through the park railings the evidences of the town's opulence and luxury with an approving eye. All these people had to be protected. Protection is the first necessity of opulence and luxury. They had to be protected; and their horses, carriages, houses, servants had to be protected; and the source of their wealth had to be protected in the heart of the city and the heart of the country; the whole social order favourable to their hygienic idleness had to be protected against the shallow enviousness of unhygienic labour. It had to – and Mr Verloc would have rubbed his hands with satisfaction had he not been constitutionally averse from every superfluous exertion. His idleness was not hygienic, but it suited him very well. (15–16)

What is striking about this passage – especially on a second reading of the novel, and with the various associations that have accrued to the words 'protection' and 'hygiene' in mind – is the way in which it links the socio-political control of a community by means of the police protection of a stratified class structure, with the control of fertility by means of contraception. Verloc sells contraceptives to protect his customers from unwanted pregnancies and infections, and he sells information to protect his employers in the embassy and the police from unwanted infections of a more political nature.

As I noted in my Introduction, Thomas Jackson Rice has gone so far as to claim that Conrad effectively depicts his secret agent Adolf Verloc 'as a kind of human condom, a "mortal envelope" for protection who "exercise[s] his vocation as a protector of society" by acting as a spy amongst revolutionaries, a man who has prophylactically "prevented" terrorist plots from reaching their fulfillment and thus thwarted the contagion of the pestilential anarchists' (2004, 222). Ironically, though, Mr Verloc is himself depicted as an infection; he 'generally arrived in London (like the influenza) from the Continent, only he arrived unheralded by the Press; and his visitations set in with great severity' (11). A further part of the irony here is that this equates him with the Professor who, in the closing words of the novel, is described as 'unsuspected and deadly, like a pest in the street full of men' (231).

After Winnie has killed her husband and left the shop, Ossipon mistakes her for a prostitute. In a sense this is what she has been: she has bought protection for her mother and, especially, her brother, by means of sex. Not only does this exchange turn out badly, but love once again engenders a repetition of the cruelty that originally inspired the love as counter-impulse. Winnie tells her mother: 'That poor boy will miss you something cruel' (126), and even Verloc finds himself 'thinking also how cruelly she [Winnie] would miss Stevie at first' (179). While he has been 'hurt cruelly in his vanity' (192), his wife recalls the newspaper report of an execution 'with a cruel burning pain into her head, as if the words "The drop given was fourteen feet" had been scratched on her brain with a hot needle' (201). Having used the pretence of love to gain Verloc's protection of her brother, she finds that she is treated the same way by Ossipon, who also promises love and then cruelly abandons her once he has his hands on her money.

In *The Secret Agent*, then, cruelty produces love and love produces cruelty, in a grotesque succession of monstrous spawnings that are in sharp contrast to the literal sterility of the mainly childless characters and to the metaphorical sterility of what, in his 'Author's Note' to the novel, Conrad terms 'a monstrous town more populous than some continents and in its man-made might as if indifferent to heaven's frowns and smiles, a cruel devourer of the world's light' (6). Only at this level, it would seem, is cruelty unproductive of love.

Winnie – 'capable of a bargain the mere suspicion of which would have been infinitely shocking to Mr Verloc's idea of love' (195) – has engaged in a transaction which has split sex off from love. Sex with her husband, love with her brother. This is not how Mr Verloc understands it of course: he believes that he is loved for himself. In another of the more telling ironies of the novel, the secret agent cannot believe that his wife is also a form of secret agent, even though his personal history involves, in his unfinished phrase, 'a fatal infatuation for an unworthy —' (22), the dash standing for the woman who shopped him to the French police when he stole the design of the improved breech-block of the new French field-gun. No-one in this novel can quite believe that anyone else is as calculating and self-interested as they are themselves.

There are, however, a couple of occasions on which sexuality and cruelty come together in the novel – when instead of succeeding each other they combine in full sado-masochistic force. When the Professor by chance encounters Inspector Heat in the streets of London he is described in typically ironic fashion as 'More fortunate than Caligula, who wished that the Roman Senate had only one head for the better satisfaction of his cruel lust, he beheld in that one man all the forces he had set at defiance: the force of law, property, oppression, and injustice' (68). The phrase 'cruel lust', bestowed on the Professor by proxy as it were, invites the reader to detect a sexual element in the bomb-maker's socio-political pretensions and ambitions.

The Professor is himself rigged up to explode if arrested, the device being triggered in a manner that also invites a metaphorical or symbolic reading. As he himself explains to Ossipon:

> 'I walk always with my right hand closed round the indiarubber ball which I have in my trouser pocket. The pressing of this ball actuates a detonator inside the flask I carry in my pocket. It's the principle of the pneumatic instantaneous shutter for a camera lens. The tube leads up –'
>   With a swift disclosing gesture he gave Ossipon a glimpse of an india-rubber tube, resembling a slender brown worm, issuing from the armhole of his waistcoat and plunging into the inner breast pocket of his jacket. (55)

In the serial edition of the novel the 'small cardboard box with apparently nothing inside' that is one of the things sold by Verloc – and that is mentioned at intervals throughout the novel – is labelled 'superfine India Rubber', making it unambiguously clear that it contains one or more condoms. (The Cambridge edition of the novel notes that in Conrad's manuscript the box is labelled 'superfine Indiarubber' [415].) Here the same substance seems to serve as artificial testicle and phallus, and if the Professor never lets go of the ball attached to the 'slender brown worm' when he is in public, this masturbatory grip evokes another image of sterile sexuality linked to cruelty and destruction. For him destruction is orgasmic, self-induced and futile, as well as sterile. Sexuality here has been perverted into the sadistic desire to inflict hurt – and especially on the weak. Although the Professor is described as a 'stunted, weakly figure' who speaks 'with a weak, self-confident voice' (75), he is vitriolic about Michaelis's concern for the weak, telling Ossipon:

'He [Michaelis] is elaborating now the idea of a world planned out like an immense and nice hospital, with gardens and flowers, in which the strong are to devote themselves to the nursing of the weak.'

The Professor paused.

'Conceive you this folly, Ossipon? The weak! The source of all evil on this earth!' he continued with his grim assurance. 'I told him that I dreamt of a world like shambles, where the weak would be taken in hand for utter extermination.'

'Do you understand, Ossipon? The source of all evil! They are our sinister masters – the weak, the flabby, the silly, the cowardly, the faint of heart, and the slavish of mind. They have power. They are the multitude. Theirs is the kingdom of the earth. Exterminate, exterminate! That is the only way of progress. It is! Follow me, Ossipon. First the great multitude of the weak must go, then the only relatively strong. You see? First the blind, then the deaf and the dumb, then the halt and the lame – and so on. Every taint, every vice, every prejudice, every convention must meet its doom.'

'And what remains?' asked Ossipon in a stifled voice.

'I remain – if I am strong enough,' asserted the sallow little Professor, whose large ears, thin like membranes, and standing far out from the sides of his frail skull, took on suddenly a deep red tint.

'Haven't I suffered enough from this oppression of the weak?' he continued forcibly. (225–6)

History has rendered these words even more chilling to us than they must have been to Conrad's first readers, and they provide powerful testimony to the psychosexual element embedded in fascist thinking – not least when taken in conjunction with what has a fair claim to be the most famous phrase in all of Conrad's work: Kurtz's scrawled words 'Exterminate all the brutes!' It is worth remembering that the first mass extermination carried out by the Nazis was that of the German disabled. In both cases the ostensible desire to improve the world turns rapidly into a mad, lust-fuelled desire to purge it of those who are, or who are deemed to be, weaker. Part of the chilling far-sightedness of *Heart of Darkness* is precisely that it is the person who believes that he has the power to do 'unbounded good' who ends up wishing to exterminate those he had previously intended to help.

If the prospect of exterminating the weak excites the Professor sexually, there are signs that the sight of a strong woman has a not dissimilar effect on the male gaze elsewhere in the novel. In the opening pages of the novel Winnie's charms are listed, and in addition to 'the extremely neat and artistic arrangement of her glossy dark hair' there are her youth, her full, rounded form, her clear complexion, and 'the provocation of her unfathomable reserve' (11). To list this particular 'provocation' amongst Winnie's 'charms' is to relate a perception of an inequality of power to sexual stimulation. And it is indeed her 'unfathomable reserve' that provokes: the men in the boarding house are provoked and stimulated by the sense that part of her is outside their gaze – is no-man's land. That Winnie knows what she is doing is apparent from the description of her given a page earlier in which the word 'unfathomable' appears for the first time.

> Winnie Verloc was a young woman with a full bust, in a tight bodice, and with broad hips. Her hair was very tidy. Steady eyed like her husband, she preserved an air of unfathomable indifference behind the rampart of the counter. (10)

Later on in the novel the word 'unfathomable' is twice more associated with Winnie's eyes and glance. Ironically, the narrative reveals that Winnie herself is never able to 'fathom' the twofold character of her brother's excitement (130). It is worth remembering that for a sailor such as Conrad the verb 'to fathom' is unlikely to have been a dead metaphor. It is also worth recalling that the narrator-captain of 'A Smile of Fortune' says of Alice Jacobus that 'Even her indifference was seductive' (59) – a comment that may lead the reader to suspect that it is in fact *especially* her indifference that sexually excites the captain.

'Indifference', then, is structured into the public and private life of *The Secret Agent*. I have already made reference to Conrad's comment, in his 'Author's Note' to the novel, of his 'vision of an enormous town more populous than some continents and in its man-made might as if indifferent to heaven's frowns and smiles' (6). In the final paragraph of the novel's fourth chapter there is an arresting description of the 'dismal row of newspaper sellers' who are 'dealing out their wares from the gutter'. The narrator comments that although the trade in afternoon papers was brisk, 'in comparison with the swift, constant march of foot traffic, the effect was of indifference, of a disregarded distribution' (65). If this indifference is so comprehensive that it even extends to the air preserved by Winnie Verloc behind the counter of the shop, it has to be added that such an air does not inspire a matching indifference in the men who encounter her. To these men, indeed, it serves as as much a provocation as does her associated 'unfathomable reserve'.

In this novel then there is not just one secret agent: there are, it seems, no characters who are not either willing or (as in Stevie's case) unwilling or unwitting secret agents. If secrecy is power, and if so many of Conrad's male characters are excited by being confronted with powerful, dominant or cruel women, then secrecy when possessed by a woman stimulates male sexual excitement. The most striking, and shocking, yoking together of violence and the erotic in *The Secret Agent* represents the culminating expression of an affinity between the Verlocs that has been hinted at throughout the text. After Winnie has learned of Stevie's death she is left alone with her husband – the man she blames for her brother's death – by the departure of Chief Inspector Heat. Verloc, after partaking ravenously of the roast beef, calls out her name 'in an undertone'.

> She kept her eyes fixed on his feet.
>
> She remained thus mysteriously still and suddenly collected till Mr Verloc was heard with an accent of marital authority, and moving slightly to make room for her to sit on the edge of the sofa.
>
> 'Come here,' he said in a peculiar tone, which might have been the tone of brutality, but, was intimately known to Mrs Verloc as the note of wooing.
>
> She started forward at once, as if she were still a loyal woman bound to that man by an unbroken contract. Her right hand skimmed slightly the end of the table, and when she had passed on towards the sofa the carving knife had vanished without the slightest sound from the side of the dish. (196–7)

Two different models of human relationship are appealed to in this passage. First there is the relationship of power, one involving a dominant and a subservient partner. This overlaps with a contractual relationship, something that implies the existence of two individuals who in one sense or another are free to contract themselves. (Masters and slaves do not need contracts.) These two models are reflected and refracted in the sexual and erotic relationship between Verloc and his wife. 'Brutality' implies the selfish exercise of power for personal gratification, while 'wooing' implies an attempt to involve a person in a sexual act – an attempt that presupposes the right of the other person to reject the advance. (Conrad's tale 'The Brute' offers an interesting footnote here. It opens with a discussion overheard by the first-person narrator who fails to realize that the 'she' involved, who has gone about murdering people and who has, finally, herself been murdered, is not a woman but a ship. The misunderstanding is ostensibly comic, but it allows for a momentary glimpse of a grim and murderous war of mutual brutality between the sexes the effect of which is not totally dissipated by the clearing-up of the misunderstanding.)

In *The Secret Agent*, the quoted passage implies the existence of a sexuality that mimics knowingly a power relationship while resting on an underlying sense of a 'real' equality. Put in simple terms: Verloc mimics a form of power-brutality in his sexual advance, while actually believing that beneath this game he is not obeyed as a master but loved for himself. He is sexually stimulated by pretending to be the brute that he believes himself not to be – and, the text suggests, actually is not. Winnie, meanwhile, has been prepared to play his game, but not for the reason he thinks. She plays his game to honour her part of a contract, while he plays his game believing that both partners are enjoying the charade. Verloc knows that he is rôle-playing, and knows that his wife knows this too. But while he knows that she is knowingly taking part in a sexual rôle-play, he does not know that her performance as his loving wife is also an assumed rôle.

Winnie, however, moves from game player to deadly earnest, and at the same time she shifts sides. Instead of playing pretended victim to his pretended brutality, she makes him real victim of her real brutality. As in 'A Smile of Fortune', business relations and erotic desire overlap and are impossible to distinguish. And as in *The Secret Agent* as a whole, no individual apart from Stevie is thoroughly honest or open about his or her motives, and no individual is able accurately to read the real motives of other individuals.

This is not the first time that the sexual games of the Verloc household have been hinted at in the text. When Verloc returns home after the death of Stevie, in a bad way and talking of having to go abroad, his wife – ignorant of Stevie's death – almost automatically displays herself to him in a manner that she knows will stimulate him sexually. Winnie is thinking of Stevie – who she believes to be safe.

> On this thought Mrs Verloc rose, and walking to the other end of the table, said in the fulness of her heart:
>
> 'And you are not tired of me.'
>
> Mr Verloc made no sound. Winnie leaned on his shoulder from behind, and pressed her lips to his forehead. Thus she lingered. Not a whisper reached them from the outside world. The sound of footsteps on the pavement died out in the discreet dimness of the shop. Only the gas jet above the table went on purring equably in the brooding silence of the parlour.
>
> During the contact of that unexpected and lingering kiss Mr Verloc, gripping with both hands the edges of his chair, preserved a hieratic immobility. When the pressure was removed he let go the chair, rose, and went to stand before the fireplace. He turned no longer his back to the room. With his features swollen and an air of being drugged, he followed his wife's movements with his eyes. (148)

Verloc, in spite of himself, is aroused (we assume that the swelling of his features models or mirrors that of other bodily parts): like the captain-narrator of 'A Smile of Fortune' his desire acts on him like a drug. The dying-out of the sound of footsteps on the pavement suggests that Verloc's sexual arousal as a result of his wife's kiss causes him to lose sensory contact with the quotidian world.

Winnie's concern is that it would be problematic to take Stevie abroad. Verloc has threatened to go abroad, and so there is a threat to Stevie's security. Winnie has to consolidate her seduction of Verloc to make sure that this does not happen. But things do not go quite as she has planned.

And as if excited by the sound of her uncontradicted voice, she went so far as to say in a tone almost tart:

'If you go abroad you'll have to go without me.'

'You know I wouldn't,' said Mr Verloc huskily, and the unresonant voice of his private life trembled with an enigmatical emotion.

Already Mrs Verloc was regretting her words. They had sounded more unkind than she meant them to be. They had also the unwisdom of unnecessary things. In fact, she had not meant them at all. It was a sort of phrase that is suggested by the demon of perverse inspiration. But she knew a way to make it as if it had not been.

She turned her head over her shoulder and gave that man planted heavily in front of the fireplace a glance, half arch, half cruel, out of her big eyes – a glance of which the Winnie of the Belgravian mansion days would have been incapable, because of her respectability and her ignorance. But the man was her husband now, and she was no longer ignorant. She kept it on him for a whole second, with her grave face motionless like a mask, while she said playfully:

'You couldn't. You would miss me too much.'

Mr Verloc started forward.

'Exactly,' he said in a louder tone, throwing his arms out and making a step towards her. Something wild and doubtful in his expression made it appear uncertain whether he meant to strangle or to embrace his wife. (148–9)

This same mix of the erotic and the cruel, the ludic and the violent, appears here in shadow form, playing out a scene of flirtation-seduction that later will be played out as mimicked flirtation and real murder. What is clear is that the 'half cruelty' of Winnie's glance is deliberately used for erotic effect, just as in the later scene Verloc's wooing might be taken by the uninitiated as brutality. And here, too, the expression on Verloc's face could signify either the imminence of his strangling her or of his intention to embrace her. The sex life of the Verlocs seems to be based on playing out imaginary relations of brutality, cruelty and violence that are modelled on social relations in society at large. Moreover one of the things about Winnie that is depicted as erotically stimulating (and not just for Verloc) is her unreadability, an unreadability that signals her power-denoting maintenance of a secret or private part of the self to which others do not have access. If as I have noted the narrative mentions early on 'the provocation of her unfathomable reserve' in her boarding-house days, here the combination of 'her grave face motionless like a mask' and her playful utterance suggest an invitation to Verloc to take part in a mutual game in which he is sexually stimulated by the prospect of conquering his wife's mimicked aloofness.

The OED definition of 'arch' is interesting in this context. The particular usage on which Conrad draws in the quoted passage is based on compounds such as arch-rogue and arch-knave, where the first part of the compound means chief or main. From this we get the relevant usage: 'Clever, cunning, crafty, roguish, waggish. Now usually of women and children, and esp. of their facial expression: Slily saucy, pleasantly mischievous'. The final pair of oppositions is especially interesting; both suggest exactly that form of open pretending or mimicking in which contradictions are compressed and by means of which a companion is invited to play-act.

All this takes us back to where we started. For Adolf and Winnie Verloc, sex and the erotic are accessed through and in terms of modelled presentations of larger social and economic relationships. At the same time, patterns of reference throughout the novel suggest that the violence and cruelty that are play-acted through such presentations have their origins in structures of real oppression in society at large. This is of course intimated, in a manner that seems intended to have the force of parody behind it, in Karl Yundt's early comment about economics: 'Do you know how I would call the nature of the present economic conditions? I would call it cannibalistic. That's what it is! They are nourishing their greed on the quivering flesh and the warm blood of the people – nothing else' (44). Stevie, as unable to recognize a figure of speech as is Captain MacWhirr of 'Typhoon', does not understand that the comment is metaphorical and becomes very upset. But as a succession of studies of the novel have pointed out, images of cannibalism and references to meat and butchery occur so regularly in the novel that Yundt's claim seems to have at least a local (and metaphorical) truth. Many of these images link meat and butchery with sexuality – a connection developed most extensively in Conrad's story 'Falk', but one that is also important in *The Secret Agent*. Thus Winnie's first romantic attachment is with a young butcher, and her own corporeal identity is repeatedly alluded to. The piece of roast beef from which Verloc consumes several slices immediately prior to his death is ironically presented by the narrative as 'laid out in the likeness of funereal baked meats for Stevie's obsequies' (190). When Inspector Heat examines Stevie's fragmented remains his action is presented with grim irony by the narrative as 'peering at the table with a calm face and the slightly anxious attention of an indigent customer bending over what may be called the by-products of a butcher's shop with a view to an inexpensive Sunday dinner' (71). It is, then, almost as if Verloc is eating his brother-in-law (who is more like his stepson in the Brent Street household), a sort of reverse Oedipal revenge that is strengthened by the echo of *Hamlet* in the phrase 'funereal baked meats'. But this is a *Hamlet* in which the prince dies before his stepfather and surrogate mother, one in which the queen sleeps with the usurper not in defiance of the prince's wishes but in attempted furtherance of his interests.

Oedipus, Hamlet, and also Odysseus: on Verloc's return from his trip to 'the Continent', 'across the length of the table covered with brown oil-cloth Winnie, his wife, talked evenly at him the wifely talk, as artfully adapted, no doubt, to the circumstances of this return as the talk of Penelope to the return of the wandering

Odysseus. Mrs Verloc, however, had done no weaving during her husband's absence' (139). If Verloc is Odysseus and Winnie is the faithful Penelope, then who is Stevie? Could he represent in his one person the collective body of suitors who have to be killed by the returning hero for desiring his wife?

Victory: Everyday brutality

While *The Secret Agent* suggests that the seemingly opposed professions of thief and policeman may have more in common than their members might prefer to acknowledge, *Victory* (1915) also implies points of similarity between characters – and characteristics – that seem at first sight to be opposed in every way. About halfway through the novel Axel Heyst is asked by Lena – her query takes the form of a rhetorical question – whether he has no courage. His reply takes an unusual turn.

> 'I really don't know. Not the sort that always itches for a weapon, for I have never been anxious to use one in the quarrels that a man gets into in the most innocent way, sometimes. The differences for which men murder each other are, like everything else they do, the most contemptible, the most pitiful things to look back upon. No, I've never killed a man or loved a woman – not even in my thoughts, not even in my dreams.' (162)

He then kisses Lena's hand, and continues: 'To slay, to love – the greatest enterprises of life upon a man! And I have no experience of either'. This is one of a number of points in the novel where Conrad, like his hero, seems more interested in pursuing ideas than in constructing a realistic interaction between characters. But they are odd ideas: Heyst's reply involves an unexpected yoking together of two actions that are normally distinguished both in terms of their morality and also in terms of the emotional experiences associated with them.[29] Heyst, however, is not the only character in the novel to associate these two human 'enterprises'. Early on in the novel Ricardo, talking of women to the frightened and frustrated Schomberg remarks: 'Take 'em by the throat or chuck 'em under the chin is all one to me – almost' (127). And when Ricardo first catches sight of Lena and realizes that Heyst has a woman with him, his reaction calls to mind Heyst's comment.

> With her back to the door, she was doing her hair with bare arms uplifted. One of them gleamed pearly white; the other detached its perfect form in black against the unshuttered, uncurtained square window-hole. She was there, her fingers busy with her dark hair, utterly unconscious, exposed and defenceless – and tempting.

> Ricardo drew back one foot and pressed his elbows close to his sides; his chest started heaving convulsively as if he were wrestling or running a race; his body began to sway gently back and forth. The self-restraint was at an end: his psychology must have its way. The instinct for the feral spring could no longer be denied. Ravish or kill – it was all one to him, as long as by the act he liberated the suffering soul of savagery repressed for so long. (218)

'Ravishing' is not, of course, the same as loving, and whereas Heyst's loving is reserved for a woman and killing for a man, Ricardo is prepared either to ravish or kill Lena. It is also significant that whereas Heyst himself is responsible for linking killing and loving, our knowledge that the liberating of Ricardo's repressed 'suffering soul of savagery' can be accomplished either by ravishment or murder comes not from him but from a detached narrator who presumably reads out for the reader what is purely instinctual at this point in Ricardo.

This is, nonetheless, a yoking together of apparent opposites that is familiar to the reader of both 'A Smile of Fortune' and *The Secret Agent*. It becomes even more familiar. Heyst's reaction to the unfamiliar presence of a woman seems to call out the same rapid swing of emotions in him that we have witnessed in the narrator-captain in 'A Smile of Fortune'. Towards the end of the same scene from which I have already quoted, after having heard Lena say that she is unable to believe anything bad of him, the narrative traces Heyst's violently oscillating emotional response.

> In his soul and in his body he experienced a nervous reaction from tenderness. All at once, without transition, he detested her. But only for a moment. He remembered that she was pretty, and, more, that she had a special grace in the intimacy of life. She had the secret of individuality which excites – and escapes. (164)

It is precisely Alice's ability to preserve a 'secret', and to maintain a distance from the captain – to 'escape' his control – that also 'excites' the captain-narrator in 'A Smile of Fortune', just as Winnie Verloc's unfathomableness provokes sexually excitement in the men who witness it. In *Victory*, after having jumped up and walked to and fro, Heyst's 'hidden fury' is dissipated, and we are told that his resentment is not against the girl 'but against life itself'. He then sinks down by her side and kisses her lips.

> He tasted on them the bitterness of a tear fallen there. He had never seen her cry. It was like another appeal to his tenderness – a new seduction. The girl glanced round, moved suddenly away, and averted her face. With her hand she signed imperiously to him to leave her alone – a command which Heyst did not obey. (164)

The move from tears to an 'imperious' sign is reminiscent of Alice Jacobus's behaviour, and it excites Heyst much as the captain-narrator is excited by Alice's movements between fear and contempt. At this point the scene is interrupted by a chapter break, and the opening of the following chapter signals clearly that the two have had sex.

If Heyst experiences what has to be categorized as mild and controlled sado-masochistic pleasure from Lena's power-distress, Ricardo's brutality takes an unexpected turn both in the scene in which he leaps upon the unsuspecting Lena, and also in later scenes in the novel. After Lena has repulsed him (first by squeezing his windpipe, and then with her knee), he becomes suddenly and surprisingly passive.

> Ricardo, leaning forward too, his nervous force gone, crestfallen like a beast of prey that has missed its spring, met her big grey eyes looking at him – wide open, observing, mysterious – from under the dark arches of her courageous eyebrows. Their faces were not a foot apart. He ceased feeling about his aching throat, and dropped the palms of his hands heavily on his knees. He was not looking at her bare shoulders, at her strong arms; he was looking down at the floor. He had lost one of his straw slippers. A chair with a white dress on it had been overturned. These, with splashes of water on the floor out of a brusquely misplaced sponge-bath, were the only traces of the struggle. (221)

Lena's grey eyes (the same colour as those much-mentioned eyes of Nathalie Haldin in *Under Western Eyes*) signal a range of significant qualities here: they meet Ricardo's gaze in searching observation, they are mysterious and they are capped by her 'courageous eyebrows'. Lena's strength – physical, moral, and psychological – seems instantly to project Ricardo into the assumption of a masochistic rôle, as his loss of footwear symbolically feminizes him by casting him as Cinderella in the serio-comic pantomime of their interaction. The lost slipper is hidden from Heyst's view by Lena and then returned to Ricardo after he has escaped through the window. If this detail reminds us of Alice's lost slipper in 'A Smile of Fortune', there is more to come.

As the novel approaches its climactic encounter between Heyst and Mr Jones on the one side, and Ricardo and Lena on the other, Mr Jones in his fury draws upon classical allusion to express the disgust he feels when he witnesses Ricardo and Lena together.

> 'Behold!' the skeleton of the crazy bandit jabbered thinly into his ear in spectral fellowship. 'Behold the simple Acis kissing the sandals of the nymph, on the way to her lips, all forgetful, while the menacing life of Polyphemus already sounds close at hand – if he could only hear it! Stoop a little.' (295)

The allusion draws upon Book 13 of Ovid's *Metamorphoses*, in which the Cyclops Polyphemus, in love with the sea-nymph Galatea, catches sight of her with her lover Acis. He hurls a stone at the lovers, crushing Acis, who is then transformed by Galatea into a river. The story forms the basis of Handel's opera *Acis and Galatea* (1723).

What is clearly a mis-match between the allusion and the scene in Conrad's novel, however, is that Polyphemus-Jones does not desire the nymph Lena, but Acis-Ricardo, who he is about to kill. In Ovid's tale Acis does not kiss the sandals of Galatea, so that either that detail is inserted as a metaphor of Ricardo's enslavement by Lena, or we are supposed to wonder whether Ricardo is literally kissing Lena's shoes or feet. If the second of these alternative possibilities seems unlikely, it can be supported by other elements in the text. Following Mr Jones's outburst, another strategically placed chapter break takes the narrative back in time to the conversation that unfolds between Lena and Ricardo. Ricardo attempts to persuade Lena to abandon Heyst as he, Ricardo, intends to abandon Mr Jones.

> 'For you! For you I will throw away money, lives – all the lives but mine! What you want is a man, a master that will let you put the heel of your shoe on his neck; not that skulker, who will get tired of you in a year – and you of him. And then what? You are not the one to sit still; neither am I. I live for myself, and you shall live for yourself, too – not for a Swedish baron. They make a convenience of people like you and me. A gentleman is better than an employer, but an equal partnership against all the 'ypocrits is the thing for you and me. We'll go on wandering the world over, you and I, both free and both true. You are no cage bird. We'll rove together, for we are of them that have no homes. We are born rovers!' (298)

Suddenly the allusion is not classical but Shakespearian, half-echoing Lear's words to Cordelia: 'Come, let's away to prison; we two alone will sing like birds I' the cage'. But what do we make of the phrase 'a master that will let you put the heel of your shoe on his neck'? In a manner that is once again reminiscent of 'A Smile of Fortune' it combines sadistic mastery with masochistic subservience, and the reference to Lena's shoe too reminds us of the repeated references to Alice's slipper or shoe from the novella. Conrad makes it quite clear that Ricardo's interest in Lena's foot is not merely metaphorical.

> In his intoxication he crept closer with every word she uttered, with every movement she made.
>   'Give your foot,' he begged in a timid murmur, and in the full consciousness of his power.
>   Anything! Anything to keep murder quiet and disarmed till strength had returned to her limbs and she could make up her mind what to do. Her

fortitude had been shaken by the very facility of success that had come to her. She advanced her foot forward a little from under the hem of her skirt; and he threw himself on it greedily. (300)

He is not to enjoy it for long.

> Ricardo, clasping her ankle, pressed his lips time after time to the instep, muttering gasping words that were like sobs, making little noises that resembled the sounds of grief and distress. Unheard by them both, the thunder growled distantly with angry modulations of its tremendous voice, while the world outside shuddered incessantly around the dead stillness of the room where the framed profile of Heyst's father looked severely into space.
>
> Suddenly Ricardo felt himself spurned by the foot he had been cherishing – spurned with a push of such violence into the very hollow of his throat that it swung him back instantly into an upright position on his knees. (301)

This is the second time that Ricardo has been physically repulsed by Lena – first by means of her knee, and now by her foot.

Discussing 'A Smile of Fortune' I argued that the whole novella was infused with echoes of two famous murder cases: the 'Jack the Ripper' case from 1888, the year in which Conrad was in Mauritius, and the Crippen case from 1910, the year in which the novella was written. Drawing on the research of Peter Bagnall, Robert Hampson (2001) convincingly argues the case that the alert reader is meant to recognize Ricardo as Jack the Ripper. He also suggests persuasively that the author of the 'rather summary recollections of an Assistant Commissioner of Police' that Conrad mentions in his Author's Note to *The Secret Agent* – actually Dr Robert Anderson, whose *Sidelights on the Home Rule Movement* was published in 1906 – could have provided Conrad with tantalizing information about the Ripper mystery in other writings, including an article in *Blackwood's Magazine* of March 1910, two months before Conrad's first extant reference to 'A Smile of Fortune'.

When we first meet Ricardo the narrative takes care to associate the words 'rip', and 'ripping' with him. It is ironic but revealing, though, that it is Schomberg, and not Ricardo, who first uses one of these words when the two of them are talking.

> 'Of course, I could see at once that you were two desperate characters – something like what you say. But what would you think if I told you that I am pretty near as desperate as you two gentlemen? "Here's that Schomberg has an easy time running his hotel," people think; and yet it seems to me I would just as soon let you rip me open and burn the whole show as not. There!'
>
> A low whistle was heard. It came from Ricardo, and was derisive. (89)

However it is not long before both words are clearly associated with Ricardo. In conversation again with Schomberg he remarks:

> 'Ferocity ain't good form, either – that much I've learned by this time, and more, too. I've had that schooling that you couldn't tell by my face if I meant to rip you up the next minute – as of course I could do in less than a jiffy. I have a knife up the leg of my trousers.' (105)

When Jones, Pedro and Ricardo land on Heyst's island, it is again Ricardo with whom the term is clearly associated.

> Not that the renegade seaman Ricardo knew anything of fencing. What he called 'shooting-irons,' were his weapons, or the still less aristocratic knife, such as was even then ingeniously strapped to his leg. He thought of it, at that moment. A swift stooping motion, then, on the recovery, a ripping blow, a shove off the wharf, and no noise except a splash in the water that would scarcely disturb the silence. Heyst would have no time for a cry. It would be quick and neat, and immensely in accord with Ricardo's humour. But he repressed this gust of savagery. (181)

A yet more explicit association of Ricardo with one of these words takes place immediately prior to his realization that there is a woman in Heyst's home, when his aggression is pointed in the direction of Heyst.

> 'I'll give you flowers!' he muttered threateningly. 'You wait!'
>
> Another moment, just for a glance toward the Jones bungalow, whence he expected Heyst to issue on his way to that breakfast so offensively decorated, and Ricardo began his retreat. His impulse, his desire, was for a rush into the open, face to face with the appointed victim, for what he called a 'ripping up,' visualized greedily, and always with the swift preliminary stooping movement on his part – the forerunner of certain death to his adversary. This was his impulse; and as it was, so to speak, constitutional, it was extremely difficult to resist when his blood was up. What could be more trying than to have to skulk and dodge and restrain oneself, mentally and physically, when one's blood was up? (214–5)

Beyond such a chain of association there are further hints in the text that suggest almost that Conrad is teasing his reader to make the association. Here is Ricardo talking about the secret knowledge he possesses.

> 'I would watch them and think: "You boys don't know who I am. If you did – !" With girls, too. Once I was courting a girl. I used to kiss her behind the ear and say to myself: "If you only knew who's kissing you, my dear, you

would scream and bolt!" Ha, ha! Not that I wanted to do them any harm; but I felt the power in myself. [...]' (101)

In *Victory* as in 'A Smile of Fortune' and *The Secret Agent*, however, what is significant is not the attribution of sado-masochistic impulses to a clearly evil and perverted individual, but the association of such psychosexual elements with the comparatively normal. Ricardo's admission that so far as women are concerned he would just as soon 'Take 'em by the throat or chuck 'em under the chin', comes after he has challenged Schomberg: 'Aye, you wouldn't mind taking a woman by the throat in some dark corner and nobody by, I bet!' (127). His accusation is not contested by the brutal Schomberg, who has already tried to seduce Lena by means of an offer that again echoes 'A Smile of Fortune'.

'We'll soon get rid of the old woman,' he whispered to her hurriedly, with panting ferocity. 'Hang her! I've never cared for her. The climate don't suit her; I shall tell her to go to her people in Europe. She will have to go, too! I will see to it. *Eins, zwei*, march! And then we shall sell this hotel and start another somewhere else.' (75)

What is serio-comic in 'A Smile of Fortune', however, has little about it to inspire laughter in *Victory*. Although on the realist surface of the novel the three would-be robbers are sharply distinguished from the respectable Schomberg and the self-denying Heyst, the text repeatedly hints at ways in which both of these law-abiding citizens share impulses with the murderous Ricardo.

The reader of *Victory* is required to consider the existence of what we can term structural violence in the relationship between the sexes early on in the narrative. When Heyst attends the performance of the Ladies' Orchestra that Schomberg has arranged, he is appalled by the hint of institutionalized and pitilessness prostitution.

There were perhaps thirty people having drinks at several little tables. Heyst, quite overcome by the volume of noise, dropped into a chair. In the quick time of that music, in the varied, piercing clamour of the strings, in the movements of the bare arms, in the low dresses, the coarse faces, the stony eyes of the executants, there was a suggestion of brutality – something cruel, sensual and repulsive.

'This is awful!' Heyst murmured to himself. (55)

If Ricardo represents the most extreme and psychotic marriage of sexuality and violence, here in Schomberg's respectable establishment we see the same mix in its public and acceptable variety. After Heyst has absconded with Lena, Schomberg shoots out 'an infamous word' in order to describe her to Davidson, presumably 'whore', and Lena admits much later to Heyst that 'I am not what they call a good girl' (152). But Conrad's presentation of the Ladies Orchestra makes it clear that there is a sort of sexual commerce involved in the performance that situates prostitution at the centre of the cultural exchange depicted in the novel, not on its margins. Early on in the novel we are told that Davidson feels sorry for the female musicians, and knows 'what that sort of life was like, the sordid conditions and brutal incidents of such tours led by such Zangiacomos who often were anything but musicians by profession' (32). The near-melodramatic extremes that take place on Heyst's island avoid full melodramatic falsification precisely because the reader is invited to read them as magnified pictures of the ordinary and the (semi-) respectable life that we have witnessed at the start of the novel.

Hurting the reader

Conrad's 'Author's Note' to *'Twixt Land and Sea* – the volume containing 'A Smile of Fortune', 'The Secret Sharer' and 'Freya of the Seven Isles' – contains a tantalizing set of comments concerning the third and final tale in the book.

> I was considerably abused for writing that story on the ground of its cruelty, both in public prints and in private letters. I remember one from a man in America who was quite furiously angry. He told me with curses and imprecations that I had no right to write such an abominable thing which, he said, had gratuitously and intolerably harrowed his feelings. It was a very interesting letter to read. Impressive too. I carried it for some days in my pocket. Had I the right? The sincerity of the anger impressed me. Had I the right? Had I really sinned as he said or was it only that man's madness? Yet there was a method in his fury. . . . I composed in my mind a violent reply, a reply of mild argument, a reply of lofty detachment; but they never got on paper in the end and I have forgotten their phrasing. The very letter of the angry man has got lost somehow; and nothing remains now but the pages of the story which I cannot recall and would not recall if I could. (ix–x)

I quote this passage at length because it does seem to invite analysis of the sort that is popularly termed Freudian. To start with, there is the contrast between the urbane detachment of Conrad's account, and his report that he carries the letter around with him for some days and even composes three varying replies which he never actually writes. Then there is the curious claim at the end of the quoted passage that he not only cannot remember the story that provoked such an outraged response (although he *can* remember details from the angry letter), but that he *would* not recall the pages of the story if he could .

All of this bespeaks, surely, a measure of unease on Conrad's part, or even a measure of guilt or concealment. And 'Freya of the Seven Isles' *is* a cruel story, one that engages the reader's sympathy for young lovers opposed by a jealous and vindictive rival only to force them to experience that rival's success in destroying their lives – even to the extent of the death of the two young lovers.

'Freya of the Seven Isles' contains a number of familiar elements, but in a slightly original mix. There is the character-narrator who, like the teacher of languages in *Under Western Eyes*, observes the passionate relationship between Freya and Jasper. There is the personification of Jasper's brig the *Bonito* as attractive girl – 'she was as sound as on the day she first took the water, sailed like a witch, steered like a little boat, and, like some fair women of adventurous life famous in history, seemed to have the secret of perpetual youth; so that there was nothing unnatural in Jasper Allen treating her like a lover' (157). There is the jealousy-consumed rival, Heemskirk, who is treated with cruelty and contempt by Freya and who reciprocates by cruelly destroying Jasper's brig and thus, in effect, his life. In some ways the triangle of Heemskirk, Freya and Jasper duplicates that of Falk, Hermann's niece, and the narrator-captain of 'Falk' – except that while Freya really is in love with Jasper, Falk is mistaken in believing that Hermann's nice is enamoured of the captain-narrator. Moreover Heemskirk's statement to Freya that he is 'a good friend, a gentleman ready to worship at your feet – your pretty feet – an officer, a man of family' (195) also touches some familiar Conradian chords and more than hints at a streak of masochistic pleasure at Freya's contempt on Heemskirk's part. And all these elements are woven in to a plot full of both spying, voyeurism and exhibitionism.

It is this final element in the mix of the story that is perhaps most interesting in the context of the present chapter. At a key point in the story the jealous Heemskirk observes Jasper and Freya 'carrying on' (the phrase is enclosed in quotation marks in the text) and is so affected by the sight 'that it made him stagger, with a rush of blood to his head' (184). This bit of unintended voyeurism is followed by other, more deliberate examples. Heemskirk hides in a bush and surprises Freya's maid Antonia. When Freya is told of this encounter she responds in an interesting manner.

> 'The brute!' thought Freya. 'He meant to spy on us, then.' She was enraged, but the recollection of the thick Dutchman in white trousers wide at the hips and narrow at the ankles, with his shoulder-straps and black bullet head, glaring at her in the light of the lamps, was so repulsively comical that she could not help a smiling grimace. Then she became anxious. (187)

But it is her initial enjoyment of Heemskirk's discomfiture that dominates her subsequent behaviour. And when Heemskirk forces himself on Freya physically, the pleasure that she gets from causing him pain shifts to the literal plane.

> He forgot the overturned stool, caught his foot against it, and lurched forward slightly, saying in an ingratiating tone:

'I'm not bad fun, really. You try a few kisses to begin with –'

He said no more, because his head received a terrific concussion, accompanied by an explosive sound. Freya had swung her round, strong arm with such force that the impact of her open palm on his flat cheek turned him half round. Uttering a faint, hoarse yell, the lieutenant clapped both his hands to the left side of his face, which had taken on suddenly a dusky brick-red tinge. Freya, very erect, her violet eyes darkened, her palm still tingling from the blow, a sort of restrained determined smile showing a tiny gleam of her white teeth, heard her father's rapid, heavy tread on the path below the verandah. (196)

That little smile speaks volumes. From this point on the relationship between Freya and Heemskirk – one that involves her taking pleasure from his sexual frustration and humiliation – becomes more erotically charged than that between her and Jasper (whose passion anyway has to be shared between Freya and the *Bonito*). In some ways the scene is reminiscent of the scene in 'A Smile of Fortune' when the captain-narrator is surprised by Alice Jacobus's father as he kisses Alice, as if Conrad cannot write about sexual passion between a young man and a young woman without some sort of observing father-figure stumbling into the scene. (The pattern can be related to the presence, and discovery, of the teacher of languages in the scene of Razumov's confession in *Under Western Eyes*.)

The erotic climax of the story comes before the ostensible high-point of the plot. If the 'official' culmination of the plot comes when Heemskirk destroys the *Bonito* and ruins the young lovers, the erotic explosion comes in a long scene that opens with Heemskirk spying on Freya as she watches Jasper on his brig. Against the background of this serial voyeurism an intense chain-reaction of sexual cruelty then unfolds.

He arose at daylight and started cautiously to open the door. Faint sounds in the passage alarmed him, and remaining concealed he saw Freya coming out. This unexpected sight deprived him of all power to move away from the crack of the door. It was the narrowest crack possible, but commanding the view of the end of the verandah. Freya made for that end hastily to watch the brig passing the point. She wore her dark dressing-gown; her feet were bare, because, having fallen asleep towards the morning, she ran out headlong in her fear of being too late. Heemskirk had never seen her looking like this, with her hair drawn back smoothly to the shape of her head, and hanging in one heavy, fair tress down her back, and with that air of extreme youth, intensity, and eagerness. And at first he was amazed, and then he gnashed his teeth. He could not face her at all. He muttered a curse, and kept still behind the door.

With a low, deep-breathed 'Ah!' when she first saw the brig already under way, she reached for Nelson's long glass reposing on brackets high up the wall. The wide sleeve of the dressing-gown slipped back, uncovering her white arm as far as the shoulder. Heemskirk gripping the door-handle, as if to crush it, felt like a man just risen to his feet from a drinking bout.

And Freya knew that he was watching her. She knew. She had seen the door move as she came out of the passage. She was aware of his eyes being on her, with scornful bitterness, with triumphant contempt. (203–4)

Like Ricardo's observation of Lena in the later *Victory* this scene revels in the sexual attractiveness of a women through her observation by a voyeuristic male. But unlike the scene in the later work, Freya knows that she is being observed, and starts to gain as much pleasure from the frustrated desire of Heemskirk as the narrator-captain of 'A Smile of Fortune' does from his masochistic enjoyment of Alice Jacobus's scorn and contempt.

The scene is interesting because it explores the experience of sadistic-exhibitionist sexual pleasure in a woman. To risk a half-flippant comment, I cannot help wondering whether had Freya been allowed to meet with the captain-narrator of 'A Smile of Fortune' then for once Conrad might have been able to depict an erotic relationship between a man and a woman that was equally satisfying to both partners.

If the word 'exhibitionist' seems excessive, it becomes clear as the scene continues that its use is fully justified.

Directly Freya had made out Jasper on deck, with his own long glass directed to the bungalow, she laid hers down and raised both her beautiful white arms above her head. In that attitude of supreme cry she stood still, glowing with the consciousness of Jasper's adoration going out to her figure held in the field of his glass away there, and warmed, too, by the feeling of evil passion, the burning, covetous eyes of the other, fastened on her back. In the fervour of her love, in the caprice of her mind, and with that mysterious knowledge of masculine nature women seem to be born to, she thought:

'You are looking on – you will – you must! Then you shall see something.' (204)

The scene then teeters between extreme melodrama, erotic excess and absurdity. Turning the tables on Heemskirk, Freya pretends to withdraw, but then conceals herself and secretly observes him.

Shortly after his head had sunk below the level of the floor, Freya came out from behind the curtain, with compressed, scheming lips, and no softness at all in her luminous eyes. He could not be allowed to sneak off scot free. Never – never! She was excited, she tingled all over, she had tasted blood!

> He must be made to understand that she had been aware of having been watched; he must know that he had been seen slinking off shamefully. (205)

She then sits down at the piano and plays music to taunt Heemskirk.

> She struck chords as if firing shots after that straddling, broad figure in ample white trousers and a dark uniform jacket with gold shoulder-straps, and then she pursued him with the same thing she had played the evening before – a modern, fierce piece of love music which had been tried more than once against the thunderstorms of the group. She accentuated its rhythm with triumphant malice, so absorbed in her purpose that she did not notice the presence of her father, who, wearing an old threadbare ulster of a check pattern over his sleeping suit, had run out from the back verandah to inquire the reason of this untimely performance. (205–6)

As I have suggested, the different elements in this perverse and perverted game are familiar: voyeurism, exhibitionism, sadism, masochism. The appearance (once again) of Freya's father, and the observing eyes of the narrator, also have their analogues elsewhere in Conrad's fiction. Moreover the use of music to mimic and accompany sexual desire and frustration is a technique that we have also seen Conrad make use of in 'Il Conde'.

And then there is the reader. If we return to Conrad's 'Author's Note' we must wonder to what extent those many readers who were shocked and upset by the seeming heartlessness of the story's sacrifice of the young lovers are, too, the victims of a sadistic impulse. If Freya enjoys – obtains erotic pleasure from – Heemskirk's sexual frustration and pain, and if Heemskirk enjoys destroying the *Bonito* and thus (given the way in which the brig has been identified with Freya) symbolically killing Freya and effectively (and literally) killing Jasper, is it not possible that Joseph Conrad the real-world writer is enjoying inflicting pain on his readers for once? Which of his three possible answers to the angry reader might Conrad have given to such a suggestion?

One of the reasons why the tale may have shocked and distressed readers is that for all that the narrator may remind us in some ways of the teacher of languages, he is more distanced, more unfeeling than his predecessor. He makes much of his story a joke, gently mocking all concerned. The tone of his narrative does not in any way prepare the reader for the tragedy of the plot's outcome. In this story the baton of erotically charged cruelty that is passed from character to character may, at the end, be passed from writer to reader.

4 Voyeurism in *The Shadow-Line* and *Under Western Eyes*

Proxy marriages

In their most extreme forms, sadism and masochism transform one of the partners in a sexual encounter into object rather than participant. Indeed, such an objectified individual is a 'participant' only to the extent that he or she is acted upon, and can observe, the sexual activity that is imposed upon him or her by the other, active partner. From such a position of de-activation it is only a short step to becoming an observer only – watching a sexual activity in which one is not oneself involved either as agent or as object (although retaining, perhaps, a rôle as audience). In this concluding chapter I want to trace some of the most striking examples of depicted voyeurism in Conrad's fiction, a voyeurism that, as I have suggested, can be seen as a taking to extremes of a potential implicit in masochistic pleasure. I want, moreover, to explore the ways in which Conrad, especially in *Under Western Eyes*, links such a position of emasculated voyeur to the telling, and the receiving, of narratives. The link between voyeurism and narrating is clear when the character who plays the rôle of Peeping Tom is also a narrator – as is the teacher of languages in *Under Western Eyes*. But as I will argue, the reader cannot escape complicity in the narrator's voyeuristic activities. Before turning to *Under Western Eyes*, however, I want to look at some telling scenes in two works that I have already discussed in previous chapters – *The Shadow-Line* and *Lord Jim*.

In *The Shadow-Line* the narrator-captain's 'command' – his unnamed ship – is introduced in a way that exploits to the full the metaphorical possibilities implicit in the convention that ships are female. When the fact of his command dawns on him, the captain's thoughts turn to his ship, and he thinks of the ship in a way that personifies her as a waiting bride.

A ship! My ship! She was mine, more absolutely mine for possession and care than anything in the world; an object of responsibility and devotion. She was there waiting for me, spell-bound, unable to move, to live, to get out into the world (till I came), like an enchanted princess. Her call had come to me as if from the clouds. I had never suspected her existence. I didn't know how

> she looked, I had barely heard her name, and yet we were indissolubly united
> for a certain portion of our future, to sink or swim together! (33–4)

In spite of the captain's assurance on the first page of the novella that 'This is
not a marriage story', the manner in which the captain envisages his ship makes
it seem very much like one. But it is very much an arranged marriage – one in
which the enchanted princess has no say in the matter, but must wait until her
designated husband and liberator comes and takes possession of her. Even
though the passage depicts the ship as a woman waiting for her partner, the
model is very much one taken not from the everyday world but from the
conventions and clichés of the fairy tale, and it is also one that invites the reader
to expect that the forceful, masculine narrator-captain will take and take over his
princess-ship in an act of symbolic consummation. But this is far from what
actually takes place.

In Conrad's manuscript the parallel between ships and women is drawn yet
more explicitly; the above passage is followed by the three subsequent
paragraphs, with Conrad's deletion of a word indicated by square brackets.

> A great revulsion of feeling made me tremble a little. There was some
> exultation in it and a queer feeling in my breast. It was like having been
> married by proxy to a woman one had never seen had never heard of before.
>
>   A sudden passion of anxious impatience rushed through my veins, gave
> me such a sense of the intensity of existence as I have never felt before or
> since. Every fibre of my being vibrated and it seemed to me that life had
> come to me only then, that I had been dead only a minute before.
>
>   It was then that I discovered how much of seaman (*sic*) I was, in heart, in
> mind and as it were physically – a man exclusively of sea and ships; the sea
> the only world that counted and the ships like the women in it, the test of
> [virility] manliness, of temperamen[t] of courage and fidelity – and of love.
> (xxv–xxvi)

The three deleted paragraphs present the reader with a wonderful concentration
of paradox. To start with, we have now moved from an arranged marriage to a
marriage 'by proxy', a marriage in which the captain's active involvement is
reduced yet further. He now presumably enjoys the legal status but not the
physical consummation of the union. On the one hand, the captain's Hamlet-like
inertia with which the novella opens is now seen to be the prelude to a new phase
in life, that of the abandonment of youth and irresponsibility for maturity, duty,
manhood – and marriage. But on the other hand 'a man exclusively of sea and
ships' is, presumably, a man who renounces the company of women and the
obligations of family life (as indeed so too does Hamlet). Ships are at one and
the same time *like* women and *barred* to women. The ship thus offers Conrad

(and his narrator) the magical ability to represent women while excluding their literal presence.

The third paragraph quoted presents us with two parallel universes: in the one it is women who are 'the test of [virility] manliness, of temperament of courage and fidelity – and of love', and in the other it is ships that perform this function. Where there are ships there are no women, and where there are women there are no ships. The exception to this binary divide is that found in the awful warning of the captain's predecessor, the man whose death made it possible for the narrator to advance his career. It is the previous captain who got himself, in Mr Burns's own words, '"mixed up" with some woman', a commingling of the two parallel universes that is thus exposed as fatal to both captain and ship.

Thus by means of a sort of sleight-of-hand, the captain-narrator is able to claim both that his new command takes him out of the world of women and also that it confirms his manliness. Indeed it is as if, by this device, the double meaning of 'manliness' is concealed and denied. The captain confirms his manliness by getting married, and he confirms his manliness by committing himself to a life in which actual women are not to be found, as their part is taken, symbolically, by the ship. The paradoxical semantics of 'manliness' involves a sense that the less you have to do with women the more manly you are, but if you have nothing to do with women then you raise the suspicion that you are effeminate. Conrad's sleight-of-hand allows for a manliness that magically excludes both women and effeminacy.

Even the captain's symbolic sexual consummation with his ship-bride is something that is observed, rather than experienced, by him. If he is married by proxy, his bride is initiated sexually by proxy too. The symbolic sexual initiation takes place when first the captain sets eye on the ship that has given him, and that is, his first command. The unsympathetic captain of the *Melita* – the vessel that has brought him to Bangkok to assume his command – points out the ship to the captain-narrator, and remains to interject a comment.

A voice behind me said in a nasty equivocal tone: 'I hope you are satisfied with her, Captain.' I did not even turn my head. It was the master of the steamer, and whatever he meant, whatever he thought of her, I knew that, like some rare women, she was one of those creatures whose mere existence is enough to awaken an unselfish delight. One feels that it is good to be in the world in which she has her being.

That illusion of life and character which charms one in men's finest handiwork radiated from her. An enormous baulk of teak-wood timber swung over her hatchway; lifeless matter, looking heavier and bigger than anything aboard of her. When they started lowering it the surge of the tackle sent a quiver through her from water-line to the trucks up the fine nerves of her rigging, as though she had shuddered at the weight. It seemed cruel to load her so. . . .

Half-an-hour later, putting my foot on her deck for the first time, I received the feeling of deep physical satisfaction. Nothing could equal the fullness of that moment, the ideal completeness of that emotional experience which had come to me without the preliminary toil and disenchantments of an obscure career. (41)

This passage too seems packed with paradox, but of a rather different sort. If the first of these three short paragraphs invokes an almost chaste feeling of platonic love – being in the same world as her 'is enough to awaken an unselfish delight' – the second and third paragraphs imply a satisfaction that is unambiguously physical, and sexual. So far as the middle paragraph in particular is concerned it is well-nigh certain that it contains a deliberate and relatively crude sexual sub-text. Eric Partridge's *A Dictionary of Slang and Unconventional English* confirms that 'hatchway' was naval slang for 'the female pudend', and Partridge dates the usage 'from ca. 1865'. The usage may be much older: Gordon Williams's *A Glossary of Shakespeare's Sexual Language* (1997) glosses 'hatch' as 'allusive of the vulva', and cites *The Merry Wives of Windsor* II.i.85, where Falstaff has 'boarded' 'Mrs Page in an erotic fury, drawing nautical imagery from the wives: "I'll be sure to keep him above deck," – "So will I. If he comes under my hatches, I'll never to sea again"' (1997, 153).

Partridge also glosses 'tackle' as 'the male genitals', dating this usage from the late eighteenth century (in the phrase 'wedding tackle' it is still current in British slang, although listed by Partridge only as 'wedding kit'). Williams's *A Dictionary of Sexual Language and Imagery in Shakespearian and Stuart Literature* (1994) suggests that the slang meaning is much earlier and, interestingly, records again a naval association.

In this passage, then, the loading of the 'enormous baulk of teak-wood timber' enacts a sort of symbolic defloration that causes the rigging of the ship-woman to 'quiver' and 'shudder' such that the captain-narrator finds the process 'cruel', itself a word that, as I have suggested in my previous chapter, has strong associations with sexuality in Conrad's fiction. Even the word 'rigging' here may carry a double load: both 'rig' and 'rigging' are slang terms for clothing, and in her second memoir of her husband, *Joseph Conrad and his Circle*, Conrad's widow Jessie remarks casually in an account of a journey that 'I had been busy putting my young son into a fresh rig to leave the train' (1935, 122).

Geoffrey Galt Harpham has observed (without reference to this particular extract), that although '[u]nable to handle sex when people are involved, Conrad is unable to avoid it when he boards a ship' (116). Although I am not in agreement with his initial assertion here, the claim that ships and the life that they contain seem to hold a particular sexual significance or erotic charge in Conrad's fiction, is one with which I can concur.

In the three paragraphs quoted, then, we move through unselfish and chaste adoration, through physical consummation, to a culminating 'deep physical satisfaction' that follows the symbolic mastery signalled by the placing of the captain's foot on his 'command'. There are however some oddities in this sequence. Most notable perhaps is the fact that the scene of defloration is one that is observed, rather than carried out, by the captain-narrator. It is 'they' who lower the 'enormous baulk of teak-wood timber' into 'her' hatchway; the captain's bride is sexually initiated – deflowered – by others: not just the marriage but also the wedding-night is carried out 'by proxy'. It is only half an hour later that the captain himself puts his foot symbolically on his ship's deck. The final quoted sentence is thus possessed of a sort of double meaning too, for if the ostensible meaning is that the captain's *command* has come to him 'without the preliminary toil and disenchantments of an obscure career', there is also the suggestion that the consummation of his symbolic marriage with his ship has been accomplished for him by others.

In this brief sequence of three short paragraphs we have a mixture of different elements that we will find elsewhere in Conrad's fiction: voyeurism, impotence and cruelty – with the final symbolic placing of a foot on the subdued 'bride' introducing a hint of the sado-masochistic foot-fetishism that is clearly present elsewhere in Conrad's fiction.

If this seems to be a strained reading of the passage in question it can be noted that a comparable symbolic sexual consummation that is displaced into the non-human can be found elsewhere in Conrad's fiction. John Stape has drawn my attention to a passage in Chapter 35 of *Lord Jim* in which Jim and Marlow are preparing to part.

I felt a gratitude, an affection, for that straggler whose eyes had singled me out, keeping my place in the ranks of an insignificant multitude. How little that was to boast of, after all! I turned my burning face away; under the low sun, glowing, darkened and crimson, like an ember snatched from the fire, the sea lay outspread, offering all its immense stillness to the approach of the fiery orb. (243)

Yves Hervouet was the first to point out that the phrasing of the final quoted sentence appears to be indebted to a passage from the third chapter of Guy de Maupassant's novel *Une Vie* (1883).

Le soleil, plus bas, semblait saigner; et une large traînée lumineuse, une route éblouissante courait sur l'eau depuis la limite de l'Océan jusqu'au sillage de la barque.

Les derniers souffles de vent tombèrent; toute ride s'aplanit; et la voile immobile était rouge. *Une accalmie illimitée* semblait engourdir l'espace, faire le silence autour de cette rencontre d'éléments; tandis que, *cambrant* sous le ciel *son ventre* luisant et liquide, *la mer*, fiancée monstrueuse, *attendait l'amant de feu qui descendait vers elle*. Il précipitait sa chute, *empourpré* comme par le désir de leur embrassement. Il la joignit; et, peu à peu, elle le dévora. (Hervouet 1990, 74; Hervouet's emphases)

[The setting sun appeared to be bleeding, and a wide and dazzling pathway of light ran from the horizon to the boat's wake.

The wind fell; no ripple appeared on the waters; the sun's rays reddened the motionless sail. Endless calm seemed to settle upon space, and silenced everything about that conjunction of the elements. Meanwhile, the sea, monstrous fiancée, lay with her shining, liquid bosom to the sky, awaiting the fiery lover that was descending towards her. He hastened his descent, empurpled as if with the desire for their consummation. He joined her, and, gradually, she enveloped him.]

The passage in Maupassant's *Une Vie* is undeniably far more overt in its sexual meaning than is the echo of the passage in *Lord Jim*. Even so, Conrad's apparent recollection and adaptation of Maupassant's graphic description suggests that it impressed him strongly enough to stick in his memory. It is also worth noting that although the passage from *Lord Jim* is less overtly sexual than the one in *Une Vie*, it does link the phallic sun to Marlow's burning face. In this example the violation by proxy involves not a female ship but the female sea. On a realistic level Marlow's face is burning partly because of the heat of the sun and partly because of the emotions (gratitude, affection) stirred up by Jim's having singled him out. If on a symbolic level Marlow's burning face has phallic power through its association with the sun and the sun's sexual union with the feminine sea, on a realistic level Marlow is feminized as a result of being singled out by the active Jim and by displaying that most conventionally female of responses – a blush. In 'A Smile of Fortune', when Jacobus brings flowers to his ship the captain-narrator 'assured him jocularly, as I took my place at the table, that he made me feel as if I were a pretty girl, and that he mustn't be surprised if I blushed' (22–3). In *Lord Jim* Egström tells Marlow that visiting skippers would report of Jim that he would 'blush like a girl when he came on board' (140). Conrad's adaptation of Maupassant's image, then, manages simultaneously both to masculinize and to feminize Marlow. It is striking that here the *parting* of Marlow and Jim is accompanied by a symbolic sexual *consummation* on the part of the natural world, and that the homoerotic implications of Marlow's blushing in Jim's presence are at least partially neutralized by a symbolic displacement of this emotion into the sexual consummation enjoyed by male sun and female sea.

   Although I have suggested that Marlow's burning face may suggest an affinity between him and the phallic sun, the affianced pair in the chapter from which the quoted scene is taken are – at least ostensibly – not Jim and Marlow, but Jim and his 'opportunity'. As in the passage from *The Shadow-Line* there is a marriage between male and female, but not between two flesh-and-blood individuals. In the final paragraph of this chapter Marlow notes that:

> He was white from head to foot, and remained persistently visible with the stronghold of the night at his back, the sea at his feet, the opportunity by his side – still veiled. What do you say? Was it still veiled? I don't know. For me that white figure in the stillness of coast and sea seemed to stand at the heart of a vast enigma. The twilight was ebbing fast from the sky above his head, the strip of sand had sunk already under his feet, he himself appeared no bigger than a child – then only a speck, a tiny white speck, that seemed to catch all the light left in a darkened world. ... And, suddenly, I lost him. ... (244)

The reference here to the 'veiled opportunity' picks up an image introduced earlier in *Lord Jim* in Chapter 24, where Marlow comments of Jim that 'his opportunity sat veiled by his side like an Eastern bride waiting to be uncovered by the hand of the master', a comment that among other things serves to remind us that the word 'master' can mean both 'captain' and patriarchal husband in Conrad's writing. If convention has it that it is the bride who should wear white, here it is the groom whose totally white apparel suggests an existential virginity that will be sacrificed only in death – if then.

The most memorable occurrence of the image of the opportunity-bride is to be found in the antepenultimate and penultimate paragraphs of *Lord Jim*, after Jim has been shot dead, when Marlow comments:

> For it may very well be that in the short moment of his last proud and unflinching glance, he had beheld the face of that opportunity which, like an Eastern bride, had come veiled to his side.
>
> 'But we can see him, an obscure conqueror of fame, tearing himself out of the arms of a jealous love at the sign, at the call of his exalted egoism. He goes away from a living woman to celebrate his pitiless wedding with a shadowy ideal of conduct. Is he satisfied – quite, now, I wonder? We ought to know. He is one of us – and have I not stood up once, like an evoked ghost, to answer for his eternal constancy? (303)

This final passage seems to establish that – on the symbolic level at least – Jim's 'wedding' is consummated only by means of a death with his veiled 'opportunity' that abandons the 'living woman' Jewel. If Jim is wed to a shadowy ideal of conduct then he cannot have married the living Jewel. Moreover, if the captain-narrator of *The Shadow-Line* experiences a 'deep physical satisfaction' when he sets foot on the deck of his symbolically deflowered ship, Marlow is unsure as to whether Jim is 'satisfied – quite, now'. Jim's eternal constancy ensures that he, as Marlow remarks of Kurtz's Intended, is 'one of those creatures that are not the playthings of Time' (183) – although while his constancy is signalled by his constant whiteness, hers is signalled by the black of mourning.

In both *Lord Jim* and *The Shadow-Line*, then, an act of symbolic heterosexual consummation is observed rather than experienced. In *Lord Jim* the consummation is displaced into the natural world and represented by the setting sun and the ocean, and while it is clearly implied that the relationship between Jim and Jewel is sexually consummated, a different form of consummation between Jim and his 'veiled opportunity' is deferred and, finally, experienced only in a death than may not have been accompanied by any 'satisfaction'. In *The Shadow-Line* the captain is married 'by proxy' to his ship and observes her symbolic sexual violation by others. It seems hardly accidental than in both works the most profound and emotionally charged relationships depicted are those that involve only men: Jim and Marlow, the narrator-captain and Ransome. That reliable sign of emotional or erotic arousal in Conrad's work – blushing – occurs (as in the mention of Marlow's 'burning face' quoted above) when two men are together, and often when they are about to part. Thus when the captain returns to the Officers' Sailors' Home after having received his first command, he encounters the benevolent Captain Giles.

> I extended my hand to him warmly and he seemed surprised, but did respond heartily enough in the end, with a faint smile of superior knowledge which cut my thanks short as if with a knife. I don't think that more than one word came out. And even for that one, judging by the temperature of my face, I had blushed as if for a bad action. (31)

The scene is mirrored when Ransome bids farewell to the captain at the end of *The Shadow-Line*. In the final paragraph of the work Ransome, upon being asked to shake hands by the captain, 'exclaimed, flushed up dusky red, gave my hand a hard wrench' and then leaves the captain alone.[30]

In *Lord Jim* Jim's habit of 'stubborn blushing' is commented upon by Marlow, but Marlow himself blushes too when in the presence of men. Recounting his discussion with the French Lieutenant, Marlow reports that his 'face burned as though I had been young enough to be embarrassed and blushing', and his blushing in Jim's presence has already been noted. But in the presence of women he does not blush – although he recalls of Jewel that her 'movements were free, assured, and she blushed a dusky red'.

Venuses in fur

At the start of the second chapter of *The Secret Agent* there is a brief reference that has echoes elsewhere in Conrad's fiction.

> Through the park railings these glances beheld men and women riding in the Row, couples cantering past harmoniously, others advancing sedately at a walk, loitering groups of three or four, solitary horsemen looking unsociable, and solitary women followed at a long distance by a groom with a cockade to his hat and a leather belt over his tight fitting coat. Carriages went bowling by, mostly two horse broughams, with here and there a victoria with the skin of some wild beast inside and a woman's face and hat emerging above the folded hood. And a peculiarly London sun – against which nothing could be said except that it looked bloodshot – glorified all this by its stare. (15)

It is revealing to compare this passage to two other passages from, respectively, *Under Western Eyes* and *The Arrow of Gold*.

> Inwardly he wept and trembled already. But to the casual eyes that were cast upon him he was aware that he appeared as a tranquil student in a cloak, out for a leisurely stroll. He noted, too, the sidelong, brilliant glance of a pretty woman – with a delicate head, and covered in the hairy skins of wild beasts down to her feet, like a frail and beautiful savage – which rested for a moment with a sort of mocking tenderness on the deep abstraction of that good-looking young man. (30)

> In the wide fireplace on a pile of white ashes the logs had a deep crimson glow; and turned towards them Doña Rita reclined on her side enveloped in the skins of wild beasts like a charming and savage young chieftain before a camp fire. She never even raised her eyes, giving me the opportunity to contemplate mutely that adolescent, delicately masculine head, so mysteriously feminine in the power of instant seduction, so infinitely suave in its firm design, almost childlike in the freshness of detail: altogether ravishing in the inspired strength of the modelling. That precious head reposed in the palm of her hand; the face was slightly flushed (with anger perhaps). She kept her eyes obstinately fixed on the pages of a book which she was holding with her other hand. I had the time to lay my infinite adoration at her feet whose white insteps gleamed below the dark edge of the fur out of quilted blue silk bedroom slippers, embroidered with small pearls. (288)

In his *Joseph Conrad: A Psychoanalytic Biography*, Bernard C. Meyer devotes some attention to a number of drawings by Conrad. One depicts a young man and woman seated on a sofa. The woman is leaning towards the man, who is jammed in the corner of the sofa, leaning away from the woman and holding one arm up as if to ward her off. She in contrast has her arm stretched out behind him. In front of the two is a tiger-skin, flat except for the head that is baring its fangs.

As Meyer puts it: 'As if retreating from both beast and lady, the man sits retracting his pigeon-toed feet, his knees pressed firmly together like a well-behaved girl, with his left forearm guarding the vicinity of his genitals' (329). The combination of powerful and aggressive woman, the skin of a wild animal, and a passive, retreating, but possibly excited man (or perhaps excited observer) can be traced through these three quotations and the drawing.

Meyer was the first commentator to deduce that Conrad had almost certainly read Leopold Sacher-Masoch's *Venus in Furs*, and his argument is generally convincing. He concentrates upon resemblances between Sacher-Masoch's novel and, especially, 'The Planter of Malata' and *The Arrow of Gold*, drawing attention to similarities between Sacher-Masoch's heroine Wanda von Dunajew and the heroines of these two works of Conrad, Felicia Moorsom and Doña Rita. He also points out that some of the fetishistic references to Wanda's feet in *Venus in Furs* have their parallels in Conrad's fiction, and although he does not mention 'A Smile of Fortune' in this context, the obsessive references to Alice Jacobus's feet and slippers in this tale can plausibly also be linked to Sacher-Masoch's novel.

If anything Meyer understates the presence of *Venus in Furs* in Conrad's work. One striking echo that he does not cite is that while the main character of *Venus in Furs* is named Severin, the double-agent and eponymous hero of Conrad's tale 'The Informer' is named Comrade Sevrin – although the wearer of fur in this work is the anarchist Mr X. In this tale Sevrin is exposed as a double-agent because of his love for the naïve upper-class woman who supports the anarchist group, and he commits suicide when his true sympathies are revealed. In a broad sense, then, his destruction by the strong, female, upper-class enthusiast of the tale is consonant with the pattern of masochistic male and powerful, destructive female that is presented in *Venus in Furs*. I have also pointed out earlier that during the seven weeks that Conrad spent in Mauritius in 1888 – a stay that provided experiences that form the basis of the story 'A Smile of Fortune' – one of the local newspapers was serializing another novel by Sacher-Masoch.

The following passage from the English translation of *Venus in Furs* may well have constituted part of the inspiration of the three passages quoted above from Conrad's works – although it is likely that Conrad read the novel, if he did read it, in French. Sacher-Masoch's novel opens with what the reader subsequently discovers is a dream, one in which the narrator is engaged in a discussion with 'Venus', a woman who 'had wrapped her marble-like body in a huge fur, and rolled herself up trembling like a cat'. The narrator recounts this dream to his friend Severin, in whose rooms he espies 'a large oil painting'.

A beautiful woman with a radiant smile upon her face, her abundant hair tied into a classical knot, was resting on an ottoman, supported on her left arm. She was nude in her dark furs. Her right hand played with a lash, while her bare foot rested carelessly on a man, lying before her like a slave, like a dog. In the sharply outlined, but well-formed lineaments of this man lay brooding melancholy and passionate devotion; he looked up to her with the ecstatic burning eye of a martyr. This man, the footstool for her feet, was Severin, but beardless and, it seemed, some ten years younger.

'*Venus in Furs*,' I cried, pointing to the picture. 'That is the way I saw her in my dream.'

'I, too,' said Severin, 'only I dreamed my dream with open eyes.' (12)

We may recall that in 'A Smile of Fortune' the circus-rider 'soon ceased to care for him [Alfred Jacobus], and treated him worse than a dog' (36). He in his turn is 'enslaved by an unholy love-spell' (36), and the captain-narrator recalls of Alfred Jacobus 'the depth of passion under that placid surface, which even cuts with a riding-whip (so the legend had it) could never ruffle into the semblance of a storm' (56). Moreover, if Wanda rolls herself up 'trembling like a cat', Alice Jacobus rises from her chair with 'an easy, indolent, and in its indolence supple, feline movement' (68). The narrator-captain, meanwhile, finds that his obsession with Alice Jacobus 'was like being the slave of some depraved habit' (59). Dog – slave – whip – cat; the mix seems strikingly similar.

Alice's hair is, too, described in ways that seem to echo the description of Wanda von Dunajew's. To the captain-narrator, it 'looked as though it had not been touched again since that distant time of first putting up; it was a mass of black, lustrous locks, twisted anyhow high on her head, with long, untidy wisps hanging down on each side of the clear sallow face; a mass so thick and strong and abundant that, nothing but to look at, it gave you a sensation of heavy pressure on the top of your head and an impression of magnificently cynical untidiness' (43–4).

Set alongside the passage quoted from *Venus in Furs* the three passages quoted above do seem to gather together a shared complex of associations: the pretty woman observed by a man (in two cases a young man, whose look is returned by the woman), the skin of a wild beast or beasts, a general sense of a powerful or dominant woman, and some form of masculine subservience (the groom following the ladies at a long distance, the inwardly weeping and trembling Razumov glanced at with 'mocking tenderness' by the pretty woman, and Doña Rita reclining like a 'young chieftain' [the noun has a masculine ring to it] and ignoring the 'infinite adoration' that M. George lays at her feet). The description of Doña Rita in particular manages to make her a veritable unity of opposites. Her 'adolescent, delicately masculine head, so mysteriously feminine in the power of instant seduction, so infinitely suave in its firm design, almost childlike in the freshness of detail' seems to freeze in stasis a succession of binary opposites (although the 'mysteriously feminine' may be introduced to hold back some of the worrying implications of her 'delicately masculine head').

The mention of Doña Rita's feet and 'quilted blue silk bedroom slippers' also calls to mind the captain's fixation on Alice's feet and slippers in 'A Smile of Fortune'. It seems hardly accidental that the pretty woman who observes Razumov is covered in the hairy skins of wild beasts *down to her feet*.

Whether this particular complex of associations is or is not drawn primarily from *Venus in Furs* is probably, as Meyer admits, impossible to establish definitively – although it does seem hard to deny the likelihood that it owes some of its masochistic implications to Conrad's memory of that text. If we home in on the 'skins of wild beasts' it seems possible to identify some of the elements that provide this repetitive transtextual motif with its power quite independently of their inclusion in Sacher-Masoch's text. To start with, furs and skins denote class privilege; they are worn by the rich. In each of the quoted passages there is a perceived imbalance in class-power status, with the man the junior partner in each case (women followed by groom; pretty woman clad in 'hairy skins [...] down to her feet' observing poor student; royal mistress adored by poor sailor-adventurer). In the second and third passages the attractiveness of the young woman is stressed.

Fur and skins also denote the taming of the wild, the reduction of that which is powerful, dangerous and alien – and probably by implication masculine – to servitude. (Here the drawing by Conrad provides a telling parallel: the tiger is tamed just as the man on the sofa is tamed and emasculated.) Fur also enjoys associations with the genital region – an association made most apparent in the phrase from *Under Western Eyes* – 'the hairy skins of wild beasts'. In the passage from *The Secret Agent* the word 'cockade' seems carefully chosen to introduce a hint of phallic presence, especially as each of the grooms is wearing 'a leather belt over his tight-fitting coat'. There is also a further hint of phallic reference in the mention of the 'folded hood' of the coach.[31] All three quotations use the references to fur and skins as a component in a deliberate contrast between a delicate femininity and the wild, aggressive masculinity implied by the hairy skins. At the same time, all three passages associate women with power and men with subservience or weakness; the wild beasts are tamed, reduced to empty skins. Another recurrent element is that of redness: the 'bloodshot' London sun, the crimson glow in the fireplace and Doña Rita's 'slightly flushed' face.

Doña Rita's 'adolescent, delicately masculine head' associates her with a number of Conradian heroines who combine a certain 'masculinity' with the power to evoke a heterosexual desire in the men who observe them. Most notable among these 'masculine' heroines is Nathalie Haldin in *Under Western Eyes*. I have already quoted Richard J. Ruppel's claim that

In *Under Western Eyes* (1911), the language-teacher narrator can be seen as a rather bitter, closeted homosexual, sexually attracted to Razumov. In Natalia Haldin, the narrator has found a 'virile' young woman whom he can admire, even sexually, and the somber, disappointed tone of the novel might be attributed to his knowledge that a union between them is impossible. (2003, 152)

This seems excessive: the disappointed tone of the teacher of languages can be explained more convincingly by reference to his age, and the text contains little if anything to confirm any sexual attraction to Razumov on his part. Katherine V. Snyder suggests, more persuasively I think, that when Conrad changed the title of this novel from *Razumov* (Conrad's working title) to *Under Western Eyes*, the change marked a shift of focus from Razumov to the point of view of the English narrator, so that the novel in its final form 'focuses less on Razumov than on the female object of his desire, the Russian expatriate, Natalia Haldin' (1999, 141). I am however less convinced that Snyder is right that the teacher of languages' conception of Natalia 'as "unfeminine" or even "masculine" signals her status as a fetish' and as 'a "phallic woman"' (166). What a number of Conradian males find sexually stimulating in 'masculine' women is not so much the opportunity to indulge a closeted homosexuality, but rather the masochistic potentialities implicit in the power that is codified in the heroines' masculine characteristics. 'Masculinity', when associated with a young and attractive woman, becomes a way of encoding power, and this perceived power is productive of sexual excitement in the masochistic male observer. But discussion of this issue requires a separate section.

Hypocrite lecteur

Literary fiction is, arguably, a voyeuristic genre. As readers we witness the lives, public and active, private and contemplative, of characters who cannot look back at us. Were we to position ourselves in something like the same relationship to real people as we position ourselves in relation to the fictional characters of a novel, we would probably be breaking the law (if we were not employed by the prison or security services). The writer of literary fiction can choose to treat this characteristic of the genre as an unacknowledged formal necessity to which it would be inappropriate the draw the reader's attention, or alternatively he or she may challenge the reader by foregrounding his or her one-way observations of characters' lives and privacies.

In his late (1935) essay 'Techniques', Conrad's former friend and collaborator Ford Madox Ford (Hueffer) claimed that in their collaboration 'our eyes were forever on the reader' (McShane 1964, 69). However it is worth asking to what extent the two authors wanted the reader's eyes to be on his or her own activities as reader. So far as Conrad is concerned, there is evidence within his fictional work that frequently he did wish the reader's engagement with the text to be a self-conscious one. Apart from the fact that those characters of his who are readers of fiction (Singleton, Jim, Carlier and Kayerts), or readers of 'the lighter sort of historical works in the French language' (Pedrito Montero), do not seem to profit from the activity, there are also some striking moments in the fiction when Conrad seems concerned to jerk the reader out of a comfortably passive process of judging the behaviour of the depicted characters that he or she encounters while avoiding any possibility that they may return the favour. In the early (1898) tale 'Karain', a work focussed upon – among other things – the perceptions that different cultures have of each other, Conrad's narrator suddenly breaks into the narrative flow with a question that doubtless his creator was simultaneously asking himself: 'We cheered again; and the Malays in the boats stared – very much puzzled and impressed. I wonder what they thought; what he thought; ... what the reader thinks?' (64–5). It is a turning of the tables: instead of the reader contemplating what is going on inside the heads of the characters in the story, the personified narrator wonders what is going on inside the head of the reader. I have elsewhere associated this moment with what I have called 'the returned gaze' in Conrad: moments at which characters who have been the passive recipients of the narrative gaze stare back at the narrator – and the reader (Hawthorn 2001). Thus early on in *Heart of Darkness* when the narrating Marlow, on his way to his command in Africa, sees a 'boat from the shore' that is 'paddled by black fellows', he notes that 'They were a great comfort to look at' (114). But Marlow is less happy when he is receiving the gaze of others rather than looking at them. When the older of the two 'knitting women' in the Company's office glances at Marlow above her glasses, 'The swift and indifferent placidity of that look troubled me' (111). When Marlow's helmsman is dying from a spear thrust, 'He looked at me anxiously, gripping the spear like something precious, with an air of being afraid I would try to take it away from him. I had to make an effort to free my eyes from his gaze and attend to the steering' (150–51). The look stays in Marlow's memory as a challenge, requiring him to allow the helmsman a humanity he has previously denied: 'the intimate profundity of that look he gave me when he received his hurt remains to this day in my memory – like a claim of distant kinship affirmed in a supreme moment' (156). Moreover, because as readers of the work we see things through Marlow's eyes, the helmsman's look also makes demands upon us.

Conrad is not the first novelist to attempt to render the reader uneasy about his or her voyeuristic activity. The reader of Nathaniel Hawthorne's *The Scarlet Letter* (1850) is for example forced to confront the fact that their desire to know certain things from an extradiegetic perspective is shared from an intradiegetic perspective by the morally degenerate character Chillingworth, who is guilty of invading the sacred territory of the human privacy, of violating the closed territory of a fellow human being's heart – which is surely just what we too want to do as we read *The Scarlet Letter*.

In reading a novel we share the privacies and secrecies of depicted characters and derive pleasure (and other things) from being a sort of ghost in their lives –

unperceived by them, unable to interact with them, incapable of influencing what happens to them, but knowing their lives perhaps better than they are depicted as doing themselves. Of course, having had such experiences we may then share them with other readers in discussion, and expose *our* private reactions and responses to *them*. Nonetheless, however demanding and painful the reading of fiction may be, however much a novel interrogates the reader and forces him or her to face unpleasant truths, including unpleasant truths about him- or herself, there remains this strongly voyeuristic element in the reading of fiction. We take pleasure in watching the lives of others who are unable to return our gaze, who are (postmodernist exceptions aside) unaware of our existence. Such a perspective gives us a sort of power, but it also carries with it the stigma of impotence. Like Peeping Tom in the myth of Lady Godiva we enjoy the power of secret knowledge, of intrusion into other privacies, while remaining incapable of extending this power beyond the gaze. The punishment of Peeping Tom was blindness – symbolic castration. He saw, but the knowledge he thus gained rendered him symbolically impotent. A paradox about the activity of the voyeur is that it empowers as it disempowers: the voyeur obtains that knowledge-which-is-power while simultaneously conceding his or her own impotence, his inability to do anything other than look.

One of the ways in which fiction can be argued to have a moral force is precisely that the reader's frustration at his or her inability to act on the course of events or to interact with characters results in a renewed desire to act in the lives lived outside the fictional world. A literary work can also – as in the case of *The Scarlet Letter* – enact and expose the disempowerment of the voyeur. One of the questions that I wish to pose in what follows, concerns the extent to which Conrad does something similar with regard to the intradiegetic character-narrator of *Under Western Eyes* – the teacher of languages.

Unlike Charles Marlow, who appears in four of Conrad's fictions, the teacher of languages (he is never named – something that exaggerates our sense of his anonymous semi-participation in life) appears in only this one work. Moreover while in each of the Marlow narratives ('Youth', *Heart of Darkness*, *Lord Jim* and *Chance*) Marlow's narrative is nested within the comments of a frame narrator, in *Under Western Eyes* the whole of the telling is the responsibility of the teacher of languages, although he does claim that much of his information comes from a diary kept by Razumov, given to him by Nathalie Haldin, and subsequently lent by him to Sophia Antonovna. While in the Marlow narratives Marlow's spoken account is reported to the reader by the frame narrator, in *Under Western Eyes* the teacher of languages's account itself frames the report of Razumov's diary, is given directly to the reader in unmediated form, and is not specified as either spoken or written.

In the first two 'Marlow' narratives the 'inner narrator', Marlow himself, is essentially recounting a story about events in which he was a central and active participant. The centrality and the activity are undiluted in 'Youth' but somewhat diminished in *Heart of Darkness* by virtue of the fact that while in 'Youth' Marlow is the primary actor in the narrated events, in *Heart of Darkness* that rôle has to be allotted to (or shared with) Kurtz. By the time of *Lord Jim* Marlow's rôle has become largely that of facilitator and reporter of Jim's life-actions, along of course with the rôle of chronicler of his own responses to Jim. In *Chance* Marlow's single status and his grumpy eccentricity are stressed in a way that place him closer to the teacher of languages than are his earlier incarnations. It is arguable, then, that in each successive work in which he appears Marlow is less the active participant in life and more the passive observer of the lives of others. His passivity-voyeurism thus makes the teacher of languages resemble the Marlow of *Chance* (a novel the composition of which Conrad interrupted to write *Under Western Eyes*) much more than the Marlow of 'Youth'. In very general terms the ageing process seems to have been accompanied by a steady shift toward an interest in the complexities of contemplation rather than action for Conrad.

We must ask: to what extent are the passive and contemplative perspective and rôle of the teacher of languages in *Under Western Eyes* exaggerated to the point that his voyeurism goes beyond what is technically necessary for him to function as mere narrator, becoming so extreme as to become part of the thematics of the novel? Even without the contribution of the teacher of languages, this is a novel in which what in recent theory has become known as 'the gaze' is clearly of central thematic importance.[32] Russia is a country full of spies, with both the authorities and the revolutionaries spying on each other – and not just in Russia but also in Switzerland. References to eyes abound in the novel (and its title prepares us for this emphasis); Razumov's secret meetings at an oculist's shop, Peter Ivanovitch's dark glasses, the constant mention of Nathalie Haldin's grey eyes, the repeated attention to eye-contact between characters (or its avoidance) – all of these elements help to make this a novel that is saturated with references to looking and being looked at. Moreover Razumov, like Verloc in Conrad's previous novel, is a secret agent, a person whose job is to look without revealing that he is looking. As I have observed elsewhere, it is striking how well an authorial comment from *The Secret Agent* describing Verloc fits the teacher of languages: 'The part of Mr Verloc in revolutionary politics having been to observe, he could not all at once, either in his own home or in larger assemblies, take the initiative of action' (44–5).

A secret agent is not, however, a voyeur. Voyeurism is inescapably associated with the sexual; primarily with the obtaining of sexual stimulation and pleasure from looking at rather than from engaging in sexual activity, but also with a concomitant inability to engage in physical sexual activity – in other words, with impotence. The voyeur is by convention understood to be a man who derives sexual stimulation or gratification from looking rather than from shared sexual activity either because he will not, or can not, engage in such shared sexual activity. There is thus a clearly implied element of voyeurism in the captain-narrator's observation of the symbolic violation of his bride-ship in *The Shadow-Line*: he watches because either he enjoys watching more than doing, or because he cannot do but can only watch.

What of the teacher of languages? One point worth stressing is that while in the story-world of *Under Western Eyes* the teacher of languages is unregarded almost to the point of invisibility (although not by Nathalie Haldin), for the reader this retreat from active engagement in life is itself foregrounded. We could say that for the reader the teacher of languages retreats into the limelight: he insists so much upon his marginal or uninvolved rôle that he draws attention to his marginality and social disengagement. And he insists in particular upon what we can term his lack of sexual currency. Consider the following passage from early on in the first chapter of Part Second of the novel, where the teacher of languages recounts the details of his first meeting with Nathalie Haldin and her mother.

> I addressed Miss Haldin, asking her what authors she wished to read. She directed upon me her grey eyes shaded by black eyelashes, and I became aware, notwithstanding my years, how attractive physically her personality could be to a man capable of appreciating in a woman something else than the mere grace of femininity. Her glance was as direct and trustful as that of a young man yet unspoiled by the world's wise lessons. And it was intrepid, but in this intrepidity there was nothing aggressive. A naive yet thoughtful assurance is a better definition. She had reflected already (in Russia the young begin to think early), but she had never known deception as yet because obviously she had never yet fallen under the sway of passion. She was – to look at her was enough – very capable of being roused by an idea or simply by a person. At least, so I judged with I believe an unbiassed mind; for clearly my person could not be the person – and as to my ideas! ...
>
> We became excellent friends in the course of our reading. It was very pleasant. Without fear of provoking a smile, I shall confess that I became very much attached to that young girl. At the end of four months I told her that now she could very well go on reading English by herself. It was time for the teacher to depart. My pupil looked unpleasantly surprised.
>
> Mrs. Haldin, with her immobility of feature and kindly expression of the eyes, uttered from her armchair in her uncertain French, '*Mais l'ami reviendra.*' And so it was settled. (76–7)

There is much in this brief passage that is worthy of note. First there is the manner in which the teacher of languages' description of Miss Haldin steers a tortuous line between insisting upon her attractiveness and denying that he is sexually attracted by her. The tension is clearer in Conrad's manuscript, in which the passage reads as follows (Conrad's deletions are enclosed in square brackets): 'shaded by black eyelashes and I became aware [how attractive her personality was] notwithstanding my years how attractive physically her personality [was] could be to a man [looking for] capable of appreciating something else in a woman than the mere grace of femininity' (293). The manuscript bears witness to how desperately hard Conrad worked to produce words that would convey a perception on the part of the teacher of languages that Nathalie's human profundity involves the intermingling of an attractive and complex personality with an expressive and desirable body – while simultaneously attempting to efface any suggestion that the English narrator is *sexually* attracted to her. I use the word 'intermingling' because Conrad seems concerned to stress that Nathalie's personality finds – among other things – *bodily* expression. Even in the published version we may pause to marvel at the contortions involved in the phrase 'how attractive physically her personality could be'. The proviso 'notwithstanding my years' seems also duplicitous (on the teacher of languages' part – and perhaps on Conrad's part too), suggesting as it does that the older a man gets the less able he is to recognize or respond to female attractiveness.

There is also the first of many striking allusions to Miss Haldin's masculine qualities: her glance (revealingly) is compared to 'that of a young man yet unspoiled by the world's wise lessons'. As with the description of Doña Rita discussed above, the description of Miss Haldin manages simultaneously to invoke both femininity (albeit ambiguously, it is not clear that Miss Haldin is possessed of femininity's 'mere grace'), and masculinity. The allusion goes along with the teacher of languages' reference to Nathalie's voice, 'slightly harsh, but fascinating with its masculine and bird-like quality' (105), and to the 'grip of her strong, shapely hand' with its 'seductive frankness, a sort of exquisite virility' (88). Such a 'masculinization' of Nathalie has convinced some critics, including Richard J. Ruppel, of the teacher of languages' homosexual inclinations, and it is indeed possible to argue that he represses his attraction to Razumov and displaces it on to Nathalie and her masculine qualities. But at the point at which the quoted passage occurs in the novel the teacher of languages has not yet met Razumov, and it seems more straightforward to read his masculinization of Nathalie as a half-suppressed admission of the fact that he is semi-masochistically attracted by her strength and power, qualities that it is easy symbolically to encode as 'masculine' and 'virile'. In 'A Smile of Fortune' the narrator-captain makes reference to Alice's 'generous, fine, somewhat masculine hand' (63) and no critic has suggested that he is a closet homosexual. (He also extends Alice's masculinity further: 'Her attitude, like certain tones of her voice, had in it something masculine: the knees apart in the ample wrapper, the clasped hands hanging between them, her body leaning forward, with drooping head' [65] – the description seems to hint at the male genitals in a state of detumescence.)

What is perhaps most interesting in the passage from *Under Western Eyes*, however, is the way in which it repeatedly suggests that the teacher of languages finds Nathalie sexually attractive, only to deflect the suggestion and further to insist upon his own sexual nullity: 'for clearly my person could not be the person'. In the course of this passage, indeed, it is as if the teacher of languages is symbolically emasculated – indeed, as if he insists on emasculating himself in front of the reader. His job as a teacher ended, he is allowed to return – but as 'l'ami' – the friend, and the friend of both Nathalie and her mother. One is reminded of the classic apologetic turnoff: 'But we can still be friends'.

By defining himself as asexual 'friend', as observer rather than sexual player, and as demasculinized man in the company of a masculinized young woman, the teacher of languages is, paradoxically, able to resexualize himself. For the more he stresses his sexual nullity the more he fulfils the rôle of masochistic man in the presence of dominant woman, and the more he stresses his inability to be more than sexual onlooker, the more he draws attention to the possibility of voyeuristic pleasure. These suggestions come to a climax (the term is not inappropriate) in the final scene between Razumov and Nathalie at which the teacher of languages's metaphorical sexual invisibility becomes astonishingly literal: *Razumov and Nathalie become totally unaware of his presence.*

> He had lowered at last his fascinated glance; she too was looking down, and standing thus between each other in the glaring light, between the four bare walls, they seemed brought out from the confused immensity of the Eastern borders to be exposed cruelly to the observation of my Western eyes. And I observed them. There was nothing else to do. (254)

We should remember that in the story-world of the novel the last quoted sentence is not true, and it suggests that what the teacher of languages actually means (or feels) is that there is nothing else that he is able, or willing, to do. As the scene unfolds it is only after Razumov has confessed his responsibility for the betrayal of Nathalie's brother Victor Haldin and has triggered a protest from the teacher of languages that Razumov suddenly becomes aware of the older man.

> Then I turned on him, whispering from very rage –
> 'This is monstrous. What are you staying for? Don't let her catch sight of you again. Go away! ...' He did not budge. 'Don't you understand that your presence is intolerable – even to me? If there's any sense of shame in you. ...'
> Slowly his sullen eyes moved in my direction. 'How did this old man come here?' he muttered, astounded. (260)

Having ceased to be the invisible man, the teacher of languages now wishes to force Razumov to fill this rôle: 'Don't let her catch sight of you again'. But his intervention 'astounds' Razumov, for whom (as too, we assume, for Nathalie) the 'old man' has suddenly materialized from nowhere.

This astonishing scene represents the culmination of the teacher of languages's reduction to a pair of observing eyes. It is, however, only the latest example of the sense that he has of his own nullity. Talking to Miss Haldin, the teacher of languages feels 'like a traveller in a strange country' (125), an impression confirmed a page later.

> I perceived that she was not listening. There was no mistaking her expression; and once more I had the sense of being out of it – not because of my age, which at any rate could draw inferences – but altogether out of it, on another plane whence I could only watch her from afar. (126)

In this context the fact that the eyes of impotence are Western eyes is extremely important. *Under Western Eyes* represents, amongst other things, a recognition of the human sterility of the look of power, the panoptical view that sees everything but is not itself seen, the look of the West. At the same time, however, the teacher of languages's allusion to his age links the exclusion of the westerner to the sexual exclusion of the old man – and the gaze of the culturally and politically excluded is thereby linked to the gaze of the sexually excluded.

It is very revealing, I think, that this sterility is not associated with the teacher of languages' interactive exchange of looks with Nathalie.

> 'I think very highly of you.'
> 'Don't suppose I do not know it,' she began hurriedly. 'Your friendship has been very valuable.'
> 'I have done little else but look on.'
> She was a little flushed under the eyes.
> 'There is a way of looking on which is valuable. I have felt less lonely because of it. It's difficult to explain.'
> 'Really? Well I, too, have felt less lonely. [...]' (100)

At first sight Nathalie's admission that she likes the teacher of languages' 'looking' may remind us of Leggatt's response to the narrator-captain in 'The Secret Sharer': 'When I saw a man's head looking over I thought I would swim away presently and leave him shouting – in whatever language it was. I didn't mind being looked at. I – I liked it' (110). But while Leggatt's admission invites the captain and the reader to detect a narcissistic-exhibitionist pleasure in being observed, Nathalie Haldin's comments seem clearly designed to exclude the sexual: her 'hurried' response seems deliberately designed to head off any intimacy that the teacher of languages might offer her, and the flush under her eyes too bespeaks an awareness of and embarrassment at an unspoken and presumably sexual element in his attitude towards her. Interestingly, as in the older Mrs Haldin's comment much earlier in the narrative that having completed his job as teacher he may return as friend, here the 'hurried' (presumably in order to pre-empt any further intimacy from the teacher of languages) mention of 'friendship' by Nathalie diplomatically but firmly excludes any link beyond such friendship.

To the extent that the teacher of languages represents the reader's eyes in the novel, his own declared impotence and exclusion from reciprocity is both the impotence of a West that observes with power but without intimacy, and also perhaps Conrad's own fear of the impotence of the writer and reader of novels, for both of whom looking without full reciprocal human involvement – voyeurism – is a function of their respective rôles.

***

Under Western Eyes is a novel that is packed full with strong women and weak men. On the one side we have Nathalie Haldin, Sophia Antonovna, and – in their very different ways – Tekla and Madame de S—. On the other hand we have the teacher of languages and Razumov. There are also the effete Prince K—, and Councillor Mikulin, the enlightened patron of the art of female dancing with his 'broad, soft physiognomy' (64). When Sophia Antonovna tells Razumov that 'What you want is to be taken in hand by some woman' (179) one feels that he is not the only one. One also feels that in this case 'want' means both 'need' and 'desire'. If Peter Ivanovitch might seem to represent an exception to my division of the cast of the novel into strong men and weak women, we should recall that the end of the work, when the teacher of languages learns that the Russian has 'united himself to a peasant girl' who he 'simply adores', the teacher of languages blurts out: 'Does he? Well, then, I hope that she won't hesitate to beat him' (280). On the realist plane it is an extremely odd response; after having witnessed Peter Ivanovitch's treatment of Tekla one might have expected that were any beating to have taken place then Peter Ivanovitch would have been the beater rather than the beaten. But on another level the comment chimes in with what the men of this novel seem to want for their sex – to be 'taken in hand' by a woman: Tekla takes first her 'poor' Andrei in hand, then she takes over from Sophia Antonovna in taking Razumov in hand. We may wonder: is the teacher of languages' blurted-out wish that Peter Ivanovitch be beaten by his peasant wife an expression of spitefulness – or of envy?

The reader of the novel too has been taken in hand throughout his or her journey through the pages of the work, not by a woman but by an emasculated male narrator. We have shared his impotence, we have shared his invisibility, we have shared his feeling of existing on another plane from the more vital characters whose urgent lives he reports on for us. And if we are left with a feeling of dissatisfaction with the voyeuristic rôle that our reading has forced us to share with the novel's narrator, then perhaps this is just what Conrad wishes us to feel.

Conclusion – and?

The son of good friends of mine had, at the age of eight, the disconcerting habit of asking, once I had delivered the punch line of a joke: 'And?' The reader may well wish that I now attempt an answer to this useful all-purpose question.

To start with, I hope that I have demonstrated that in spite of Jósef Retinger's report of Conrad's nodded assent to his assertion that in the novelist's writings 'the love motif played no fundamental part' (1941, 65), the evidence in the literary works is that Conrad's fiction is very far from being sexless, loveless, or free from the erotic. On the most basic level, if one were to remove from Conrad's plots all those actions and events that are driven by the love or sexual desire of one person for another, then there would not be so very much left. There are works in which sexual desire appears to play no part at all – 'An Outpost of Progress' is one such – but they are very few in number. One marker of the omnipresence of sexual desire and erotic arousal in Conrad's work is that there are so many more relevant examples in the fiction that I have not touched upon. Much could be added, for example, to what has already been written about the triangles of desire linking Dain Maroola, Nina and Taminah in *Almayer's Folly*, and Nostromo, Linda, and Giselle in *Nostromo*. Much too could be said about the involvement of the two father figures – Almayer and Georgio Viola – in these triangles. In spite of the enormous number of critical words that have been devoted to *Heart of Darkness* there remains more to be said, I am convinced, about the erotic links joining Kurtz, his Intended, the African woman, the Russian Harlequin – and Marlow.

Beyond this, I believe that I have demonstrated that 'love', 'sex' and 'the erotic' are by no means limited to a conventional, clichéd, or melodramatic presentation in Conrad's fiction. There are of course examples of the melodramatic in Conrad's novels and short stories, and I concur with those who have argued that the melodramatic was antithetical to Conrad's creative genius and had a negative impact on his fiction in general and on the presentation of love and sex in particular. By contrasting the treatment of sexual and erotic forces in 'A Smile of Fortune' and 'The Planter of Malata' I have attempted to demonstrate that although Conrad was capable of writing badly about sexual desire and erotic attraction, as in 'The Planter of Malata', his portrayal of the narrator-captain's sexual enslavement to Alice Jacobus in 'A Smile of Fortune' establishes that he was also capable of exploring some of the deeper, darker and certainly (in his time) publicly unacknowledged aspects of male heterosexual desire. Moreover in spite of claims that there is no evidence in the fiction that Conrad was aware of homosexuality, the evidence is clear that he was so aware, and that the lack of awareness has to be attributed not to the author, but to his readers.

This leads me to the third, and perhaps the most important justification for the present study. My case is that with a few, recent exceptions, Conrad's fiction has been read in too innocent a manner. Readers and critics have expected to find Conrad's fiction free from any deep or analytical interest in the sexual or the erotic, and this expectation has produced readings that have confirmed that this is the case. As I commented in my first chapter, had 'Il Conde' been published as a short story by Henry James then it is unlikely that its homosexual covert plot would have remained undiscussed by critics until 1975. I have referred to Thomas Jackson Rice's argument that in *The Secret Agent* Adolf Verloc is presented 'as a kind of human condom' (2004, 222). In James Joyce's 'Two Gallants' (from *Dubliners*), when we read of the character Corley that he 'walked with his hands by his sides, holding himself erect and swaying his head from side to side. His head was large, globular, and oily; it sweated in all weathers; and his large round hat, set upon it sideways, looked like a bulb which had grown out of another' (Joyce 2000, 45) we recognize, as have countless readers before us, that Corley is presented as a sort of human phallus. Corley's companion, Lenehan has already been introduced wearing a 'light waterproof' and is wearing 'rubber shoes', and this generally prophylactic appearance contrasts strongly with Corley's aggressively penile and fleshly appearance. This is the sort of sexual innuendo that readers have for many years expected from Joyce – and because they have expected it, they have not failed to recognize it and other examples in Joyce's fiction. But readers have generally *not* expected such things from Conrad.[33] It is my case that rather more expectation of this sort is needed when reading Conrad's fiction. If there is one thing that I hope the present study will achieve, it is this recognition that Conrad's fiction repays those who read it in a more knowing and less innocent manner.

It is however possible to be a knowing reader while retaining the assumption that Conrad is not a knowing writer. Geoffrey Galt Harpham, as I have noted, recognizes the significant presence of the sexual in Conrad's fiction, but sees it as present almost against the will of the author, emerging on the margins of the text like a succession of Freudian slips that have succeeded in evading the author's censor. I do not argue that there are no examples of 'fugitive sexual energy' as Harpham calls it, in Conrad's work. But most of the examples that I have discussed in this book are not of this nature: they represent a knowing and deliberate analytical concern with the nature of human sexuality and erotic stimulation on the level of Conrad's creative intelligence. The call for a more knowing reading of Conrad's work should not be seen as a case made by a critic against the overt or conscious wishes of Conrad himself and against the artistic needs of the works themselves: it is surely undeniable that a tale such as 'Il Conde' requires a knowing reading for it to be fully appreciated.

Harpham also provides me with a convenient way in to my final justification for this book. His claim that the 'fugitive sexual energy' in Conrad's fiction 'gains [...] in gravitas by being confused with public and political themes that seem remote from it' (1996, 183) is half very right and half very wrong. It is very right because the sexual energy in Conrad's texts is inseparable from those public and political themes with which it is intertwined. But it is very wrong in claiming that Conrad's fiction somehow 'confuses' sexual energy with public and political themes, as if this were a yoking together of two unrelated areas of human experience that endows sexual energy with an undeserved 'gravitas'. What Conrad succeeds in doing in his finest works is revealing the extent of interpenetration between 'private' sexuality and 'public and political' life. The public world provides many of the models and materials from which we construct and express the private life. Sexuality is of course in origin a biological force, but the erotic is sexuality clothed in the vestments provided by a particular cultural configuration. It is, above all, in *The Secret Agent* that Conrad most clearly depicts this interpenetration of sexuality and the erotic on the one hand, and the public world of politics and law on the other. When Conrad shows the Professor experiencing sexual excitement at the thought of a mass extermination of the weak, when Winnie seduces Verloc by mimicking 'cruel' relations of power and oppression, when Verloc plays the rôle of a sort of human condom, protecting society from anarchists – none of these elements merely uses the public as metaphor for the private, or vice-versa; all reveal interconnections between the public and the private in the extra-textual world in and about which Conrad is writing.

If I am correct that in Conrad's fiction the erotic is 'sexuality clothed in the vestments provided by a particular cultural configuration', and the cultural configurations which were available as models to Conrad all involved significant structural divisions between the empowered and the disempowered, then it follows that the erotic in Conrad's fiction models, or mimics, larger social relationships characterized by inequalities of power. Male sexual excitement, sexual desire, lust – all of these are associated in Conrad's fiction with the sense of being in someone's power or of having power over another person. With Conrad's female characters sometimes it seems to be different: Alice Jacobus is portrayed as appearing to start desiring the captain-narrator of 'A Smile of Fortune' at precisely the point at which he loses sexual interest in her – when suddenly they confront each other as equals. But if in the world of Conrad's fiction power excites male desire, it also destroys relationships. No relationship in which sexual desire is based upon an excitement generated by control or subservience survives long in the fiction – although it should be added that few relationships survive long in the fiction whatever they are based on. In one sense sexuality is the arena in which the exercise of power is subjected to most rigorous critique in Conrad's work.

And here, I contend, can be found one answer to a question that I posed in Chapter 1: why is it that there is hardly any sense in Conrad's work that passionate, loving relationships of a sexual nature are able to offer a way out of the existential solitary confinement that his characters fear so much? Why is there no long-term, happy marriage in Conrad's fiction comparable to the long-term and, I have argued, happy marriage that Conrad and his wife Jessie had? There is certainly more than one answer to this question, but one important reason, it seems to me, is because in the fiction, passionate, loving relationships of a sexual nature model relations found in society at large. I also suggested earlier in this book that an Englishman might believe that his home was his castle, but Conrad the Pole knew that castles are not immune to being occupied by forces from outside. In like manner, work after work in Conrad's oeuvre demonstrates that relationships between men and women are not so much an escape from the harsh world outside them as a reconstitution on a different scale of more public, social relationships. When Adolf Verloc 'loved his wife as a wife should be loved – that is, maritally, with the regard one has for one's chief possession', when neither the narrator-captain of 'A Smile of Fortune' nor the novella's reader can be sure where the realm of courtship begins and the realm of business ends, when Willems's infatuation with Aïssa oscillates between forms of surrender and domination that mirror forms of relationship between the colonisers and the colonized, then the same point is being emphasized. We cannot use the private sphere to compensate for the inequalities and inhumanities of the public sphere if the private sphere is constructed on the basis of models and materials imported from the public sphere.

Conrad of course knew that just as there were oppositional elements in society that contended with dominant systems of value, so too could there be personal relationships that also attempted to found themselves on more human values than those that dominated the larger worlds of politics and economics. In *Nostromo*, when Mrs Gould asks Dr Monygham whether there will ever be peace, he responds 'There is no peace and no rest in the development of material interests. They have their law, and their justice. But it is founded on expediency, and is inhuman; it is without rectitude, without the continuity and the force that can be found only in a moral principle' (511). Peace, rest and continuity in intimate human relationships also require a humanity, a rectitude and a morality different from those that ran the affairs of the world in Conrad's day and continue to run them today. But attempts to structure a relationship on such alternative values are necessarily oppositional.

The picture is, however, more complicated that these generalizing comments might suggest (of course!). For if in Conrad's fiction confronting the other as an equal seems to be inimical to male desire when the other is female, when the other is male the story seems to be different. In the emotionally charged relationship between the captain and Ransome that is depicted in *The Shadow-Line* the fact of their inequality of rank is lost in the democracy of their shared respect. There are few if any lasting heterosexual relationships in Conrad's fiction of which the same can be said. I think that one key reason for this can be indicated by reference to one word: work. Where men work together the conditions of their labour produce this democracy of shared respect. Men and women do not, generally, work together in Conrad's fiction. Moreover when men stop working together in the fiction, they too generally drift apart.

***

It is a cliché that great works of literature read their readers. To put it another way: a full reading of works as different as *The Secret Agent*, 'A Smile of Fortune' and *The Shadow-Line* forces the reader to confront and deconstruct his or her own sexuality. 'His or her' is perhaps too evasive a phrase in this context as it is clear that Conrad's fiction is far more concerned with male sexuality and a male experience of the erotic than with its female counterparts. However although in some cases female characters are portrayed as the unknowing stimulation of a male erotic experience in which they do not share (as in the case of Alice Jacobus in 'A Smile of Fortune'), there are counter-examples. Conrad's exploration of the way in which sexual desire, sibling affection and a frustrated maternal love are intermixed in the character of Winnie Verloc would be one such counter-example, Freya Nelson's sadistic inflicting of pain on the frustrated Heemskirk another.

I cannot speak for the female reader, but as a male reader there is much in Conrad's fiction that disturbs me by forcing me to analyse my own responses to its depiction of sexuality and the erotic. When the narrator of 'Karain' reports: 'We cheered again; and the Malays in the boats stared – very much puzzled and impressed. I wonder what they thought; what he thought; ... what the reader thinks?' (64–5), the reader of 'Karain' is indeed forced to wonder this him- or herself. It disturbs me that I find the portrayal of Alice Jacobus – generally seen either afraid or contemptuous of the captain-narrator – to be erotically charged, especially given the links between Conrad's composition of this story and the Jack the Ripper and Crippen murder cases. If in *Under Western Eyes* the teacher of languages is depicted as emasculated voyeur, then where does this leave the reader who enjoys following his depiction of the passionate relationship between the young Nathalie Haldin and Razumov, and witnessing it through his western eyes? If the extradiegetic narrator of *An Outcast of the Islands* suggests at different times that Willems is to be either despised and pitied, or admired, for losing himself in a passionate erotic enslavement – then where do we position ourselves with regard to such alternatives?

We should not, in short, approach Conrad's fiction from the smug perspective that as representatives of a culture and an age that are more knowing about sex, more liberated in our relationship to the erotic, there is little that we can learn about sex and the erotic from these works. There is actually much that we can learn about such subjects, including much about ourselves that we may not have known before and that we may resist knowing even now.

Notes

1. See the discussion of 'The Secret Sharer' in my *Multiple Personality and the Disintegration of Literary Character* (1983).

2. The first, and classic argument for this position is that advanced by Shlomith Rimmon in her *The Concept of Ambiguity – the Example of James* (1977), and I discuss her case in a chapter on *The Turn of the Screw* in my book *Cunning Passages* (1996).

3. Jane Ford has traced the influence of Conrad's work on that of James Joyce, and she reports that Joyce's Trieste library contained copies of a number of Conrad's books, including *A Set of Six*, in which 'Il Conde' was first published in book form (Ford 1985, 15 n16). It is tempting to wonder whether Joyce spotted the use of musical register to mimic the sexual act in 'Il Conde' a century before Keith Carabine did. If he did, then his use of the firework display and the celebration of the Mass as counterpoints to the sexual-encounter-at-a-distance of Bloom and Gerty MacDowell in *Ulysses* may owe a debt to Conrad.

4. The title is not Goddard's own. His essay is reprinted in the Norton Edition of *The Turn of the Screw* (second edition, edited by Deborah Esch and Jonathan Warren, New York: W.W. Norton, 1998).

5. It is worth reminding the modern reader that 'gay', used as either noun or adjective, only acquires a specifically homosexual force in the second half of the twentieth century. Eric Partridge's *A Dictionary of Slang and Unconventional English* (1984), for example, reports that the sexual meaning of the word in Conrad's lifetime was associated with female prostitution rather than male homosexuality. Partridge dates the homosexual meaning of the term to about 1945 in the United States, and ten years later in Britain. It is however often very hard to fix such dates, and terms of sexual slang typically lead a hidden life, sometimes for many years, prior to being registered in written usage.

6. Probably anachronistic: Eric Partridge's *A Dictionary of Slang and Unconventional English* dates the modern sexual meaning of the term to the post Second World War period, but according to the same source the word had homosexual or lesbian connotations as early as 1920.

7. Had the rank mentioned been different, it might have suggested an echo from the sixth chapter of the first volume of Jane Austen's *Mansfield Park*. Addressing Mary Crawford, Edmund Ferrars inquires:

> 'You have a large acquaintance in the navy, I conclude?'
>   'Among Admirals, large enough; but,' with an air of grandeur; 'we know very little of the inferior ranks. Post captains may be very good sort of men, but they do not belong to *us*. Of various admirals, I could tell you a great deal; of them and their flags, and the gradation of their pay, and their bickerings and jealousies. But in general, I can assure you that they are all passed over, and all very ill used. Certainly, my home at my uncle's brought me acquainted with a circle of admirals. Of *Rears*, and *Vices*, I saw enough. Now, do not be suspecting me of a pun, I entreat.'
>   Edmund again felt grave, and only replied, 'It is a noble profession.' (60)

If however there is no mention of Rears or Vices in Conrad's text, the discussion among the sailors about the characteristics of a gentleman does focus on the thinness of the seats of their trousers. More seriously, Austen's text confirms – if it needed confirming – that jokes about homosexual activity and the navy had wide circulation. Even the priggish Edmund's gravity suggests that he gets the point instantly.

8. This is part of one of a number of erotic or sexually suggestive passages censored from the text in the first American edition of the novel, and detailed in Belcher (1981). Both Belcher and the World's Classics edition of the novel use the first English edition of the novel as copy text, but while the World's Classics edition includes only twenty-six minor textual amendments, Belcher's edition incorporates many more substantial amendments (including deletions) that Conrad himself made to the first English edition.

9. Critical responses to 'A Smile of Fortune' are generally more positive than those to 'The Planter of Malata', but both works have prompted wildly varying judgements. These range, in the case of the earlier work, from David Thorburn's view that in *'Twixt Land and Sea* 'so fine a story as "The Secret Sharer" is framed by the embarrassing operatics of "A Smile of Fortune" and "Freya of the Seven Isles"' (1974, 22) to Cedric Watts's view that 'A Smile of Fortune' is 'one of Conrad's most brilliant yet most neglected and under-rated works' (1985, 131). Edward Said describes 'The Planter' (with considerable reservations, it is true) as 'Conrad's most pessimistic story, and a masterpiece nevertheless' (1966, 162), while Owen Knowles praises it as 'one of the most interesting and problematic failures among Conrad's novellas' (1979, 177). Daphna Erdinast-Vulcan argues that the 'artistic failure of ["The Planter"] is due to a large extent to the failure of the initial framing strategy' (1999, 162), a suggestion taken up

later in this chapter.

10. See the entries in Knowles and Moore (2000) on 'A Smile of Fortune', 'The Planter of Malata', 'Australia', and 'Mauritius'.

11. Summarized in Ray, ed., 1990, 64–5, the story is from Archibald Marshall's *Out and About: Random Reminiscences* (London: Murray, 1933, 145). In Ray's report, Crippen was arrested in Canada, and Marshall was sent a list of the books that he had read on the voyage. He invited Conrad to write an article about Crippen's 'sea library', but 'poor dear Conrad exploded in epistolary fury at being asked to do such a thing and severed his connection with our journal' (Ray 1990, 65).

12. Stephen Donovan has drawn my attention to a comparable passage in *The Arrow of Gold* in which the narrator is surprised by Therese's nervousness but explains that 'there had been [...] a case of atrocious murder', and that even though Therese did not read the papers she could not avoid hearing of it. The passage goes on to detail the narrator's chaffing of Therese about the many murderers in the house – to which teasing she responds in kind, rather as Alice's *gouvernante* does (138–9).

13. Stephen Donovan has suggested to me that the captain's 'daily' dose of 'sensation' can be compared to Alice's reading of the sensational stories in the dailies. In such a reading, sexuality is no longer an unchanging biological force but a biological impulse mediated through culturally distinct institutions, experiences and expectations.

14. For interesting discussion of the phrase 'irrealizable desire' see two articles by Yael Levin (Levin 2004 and 2005).

15. Stephen Donovan has pointed out to me that in November 1909, Winston Churchill was sensationally 'horsewhipped' by a Suffragette ('cut with a whip' is probably more accurate). A letter from Conrad to John Galsworthy of the 15 November 1909, comments at length on a story in the issue of the *Standard* that discusses the incident (CL4, 288–90). The link between the whipping of a man by a woman and the Suffrage Movement is thought-provoking, given that *Chance* is occupied with the wider issue of women's rights.

16. The allusion is to the saw 'Don't care didn't care: don't care was hanged', a standard adult response to a child's utterance of 'I don't care', still current in my own childhood. In her first memoir of her husband Jessie Conrad reports that when a maid was admonished for putting one of their boys in danger, her 'only

answer to our agitated questions was a silly giggle and an impudent "Don't care"' (1926, xvii).

17. In a letter to John Galsworthy of 5 August 1910, Conrad reported that he had written 14,000 words of 'A Smile of Fortune' and expected that another 6,000 would finish it. (The story in Dent's Collected Edition is 25,655 words long). A letter to E.L. Sanderson of 2 September 1910 states that the story is 'just finished' (CL4, 364). The arrest warrant for Crippen was issued on 16 July, and he and his mistress were arrested in Quebec at the end of July, when Conrad was asked to review Crippen's library for the *Daily Mail* (see note above). Crippen's trial began on 18 October 1910; he was executed on 23 November. Thus while Conrad was writing the second half of 'A Smile of Fortune' (including his comment about what is done to 'objectionable old women' in Europe) the newspapers were full of the discovery of a body in Crippen's house and of Crippen's flight and arrest. Even had Conrad not read these, his attention would have been drawn to the murder and arrest by the request to write on Crippen's 'library'. Thus both in 1888 and in 1910 the newspapers would have brought to his attention the link between sexuality and male violence to women.

18. Roberts's *Conrad and Masculinity* (2000) and *Conrad and Gender* (1993) contain valuable material on the work of a writer who once was comfortably believed to be concerned with a straightforward and unproblematic masculinity.

19. For 'mincing', see p. 50.

20. For a summary of Conrad's contact with Eugénie Renouf, see Najder 1983, 107–109.

21. Najder, citing an article by P. J. Barnwell about Conrad in the *Dictionary of Mauritian Biography*, describes Alice Shaw's father as a shipping agent (1983, 522 n. 76). Jocelyn Baines calls him 'a stevedore' (1971, 128).

22. I discuss these issues at greater length in my chapter on *She Stoops to Conquer* in *Multiple Personality and the Disintegration of Literary Character* (1983).

23. The information that Alice's shoe is of kid may reflect Conrad's awareness that it has been suggested that Cinderella's 'glass slipper' is the result of a confusion between two French words: *vair*, a leather made from *petit-gris* (otherwise Siberian squirrel), and *verre* (glass).

24. The name Moorsom is unusual, and Conrad may well have known that Robert Moorsom captained *HMS Revenge* at the Battle of Trafalgar. 'Renouard' carries with it suggestions of Reynard the fox, and in French of 'reknotting', or the need to undo one's ties to begin a new life. But it cannot be said that such suggestions contribute much to the tale.

25. My comments in the following chapter on the significance of Conrad's manuscript amendments to a passage in which the teacher of languages reports the power of Nathalie's physical presence (see p. 148) are relevant here.

26. Both works are packed with intertextual allusions. Cedric Watts (1985) mentions a number in 'A Smile of Fortune', including 'The Sleeping Beauty', which also boasts an imprisoned heroine in a walled garden. Erdinast-Vulcan (1999) draws a parallel to the plot of *The Tempest* (although with a different outcome) and relates Alfred Jacobus to the biblical Jacob, who impersonates his brother Esau. Kirschner (1966) and Hervouet (1990) have traced Conrad's heavy reliance on Maupassant's 'Les Soeurs Rondoli' (1884) for the portrayal of the alluring Alice, and they as well as Knowles (1979) have shown how Anatole France, Maupassant and Mérimée have, as Hervouet puts it, left 'tangible marks' on 'The Planter of Malata'. If phrases and short sequences in 'A Smile of Fortune' seem to stem from 'Les Soeurs Rondoli', 'The Planter of Malata' owes a comparable debt to Mérimée's 'La Vénus d'Ille' (1837), but this similarity is also a difference: the allusions and intertextual links in 'A Smile of Fortune' combine to achieve a subtextual symphonic force, but in 'The Planter of Malata' the associations produce discord rather than harmony.

27. In this and other cases Conrad seems to have chosen his epigraph on the basis of the words alone, and not on the basis of their meaning in their original context. In 'Rumpelstiltskin' a Dwarf grants a miller's daughter the power to spin straw into gold against the promise that her first-born child will become his. When eventually the dwarf returns to collect his prize he is offered all the wealth of the world. In the words chosen by Conrad, 'but the Dwarf answered: "No, something human is dearer to me than the wealth of the world"'. Jessie Conrad uses (almost) the same words as epigraph to her second (1935) memoir of her husband.

28. The story of Bluebeard seems to have been well-known in Conrad's household. In her 1935 memoir of her husband Jessie reports that in early 1906 the Conrads 'discovered a charming French woman who readily undertook the boy's French lessons. Mademoiselle Sée was lively and very amusing. Her pet name was "Madame Barb-à-Bleu"; she boasted of a fictitious husband whenever her business took her out of her native town' (1935, 111).

29. However in the late 'The Tale' Conrad draws on the saying 'All's fair in love and war' to allow the character-narrator to comment 'Everything should be open in love and war' (67). Given the way in which this short fiction draws parallels between the subterfuges of love and those of war the association is possibly better thematically motivated than it is in *Victory*.

30. In my Introduction to the new World's Classics edition of *The Shadow-Line* (2003) I comment on the captain-narrator's reference to 'the green sickness of late youth' that descends upon him and carries him off. The 'green sickness' in question is otherwise known as chlorosis and is typically associated with adolescent girls. In her book *The Disease of Virgins: Green Sickness, Chlorosis and the Problems of Puberty* (2004), Helen King notes, interestingly, that blushing was seen as a typical feature of both adolescence and chlorosis (King 2004, 90). King's book also includes a whole section entitled 'Green sickness as a liver disorder' – perhaps it is not accidental that the Chief Engineer tells the unsettled narrator of *The Shadow-Line* that his problem 'is nothing but deranged liver'.

31. The passage from *The Secret Agent* does not specify a single sighting, but refers to 'solitary women followed at a long distance by a groom with a cockade to his hat and a leather belt over his tight fitting coat' and 'here and there a victoria with the skin of some wild beast inside and a woman's face and hat emerging above the folded hood'. The repeated nature of these apparently identical sightings has the effect of underlining their social representativeness. At the same time the somewhat unlikely claim that they all share precisely the same details is reminiscent of what Gérard Genette has dubbed the pseudo-iterative – a narrative form in which 'scenes presented, particularly by their wording in the imperfect, as iterative' are possessed of a 'richness and precision of detail [that] ensure that no reader can seriously believe they occur and reoccur in that manner, several times, without any variation'(Genette 1980, 121).

32. I discuss this at greater length in my Introduction to the new World's Classics edition of the work (2003). See too Katherine V. Snyder's interesting discussion 'Masculine Affiliation, Male Feminism, and the Bachelor's "Way of Looking On"' in her *Bachelors, Manhood and the Novel 1850–1925* (1999, 156–71).

33. One reader who did perhaps pick up some of the sexual hints in Conrad's fiction is James Joyce. Jane Ford's 1985 article 'James Joyce and the Conrad Connection: The Anxiety of Influence' argues that 'Conrad's influence can be detected throughout Joyce's work' (1985, 5), and she suggests that the Odyssean references added to *The Secret Agent* by Conrad as he revised and expanded the serial version of the novel for book publication between January and June 1907

may have encouraged Joyce to construct a more overtly Homeric novel himself. Conrad's use of the motif of contraception in *The Secret Agent* may well have inspired Joyce to follow his example. I have myself argued a connection between Conrad's tale 'To-morrow' and Joyce's 'Eveline' (see Hawthorn, 2003).

Bibliography

Many of Conrad's works included in the standard Dent Collected Edition have been superseded by editions offering more reliable texts. Where available I quote from the Cambridge Edition of the Works of Joseph Conrad and, where there is no Cambridge Edition of the work in question, from the World's Classics Edition published by Oxford University Press. For *The Nigger of the 'Narcissus'* I have chosen to use the Everyman Centennial Edition edited by Allan Simmons. For all remaining texts I have used the Dent Collected Edition.

This use of volumes from different editions means that some shorter works are contained in more than one edition listed below. I have accordingly indicated which edition I have used for the works in question.

Joseph Conrad's works excluding letters

Conrad, Joseph (1994), *Almayer's Folly. A Story of an Eastern River*, David Leon Higdon and Floyd Eugene Eddleman (eds), in The Cambridge Edition of the Works of Joseph Conrad. Cambridge: Cambridge University Press. All quotations from *Almayer's Folly* are taken from this edition.

Conrad, Joseph (1947), *Almayer's Folly* and *Tales of Unrest*. Dent Collected Edition. London: Dent. See note to previous entry. Each work is separately paginated in this double volume. All quotations from 'An Outpost of Progress', 'The Lagoon' and 'The Return' are taken from *Tales of Unrest* in this volume.

Conrad, Joseph (2002), *An Outcast of the Islands*, J.H. Stape (ed.), in Oxford World's Classics Edition. Oxford: Oxford University Press.

Conrad, Joseph (1954), *A Set of Six*. Dent Collected Edition. London: Dent. All quotations from 'Il Conde', 'The Brute' and 'An Anarchist' are taken from this edition.

Conrad, Joseph (1988), *Chance: A Tale in Two Parts*, Martin Ray (ed.), in Oxford World's Classics Edition. Oxford: Oxford University Press.

Conrad, Joseph (2002), *Heart of Darkness and Other Tales*, Cedric Watts (ed.), in Oxford World's Classics Edition. Oxford: Oxford University Press. All quotations from *Heart of Darkness* and 'Karain' are taken from this edition.

Conrad, Joseph (2002), *Lord Jim: A Tale*, Jacques Berthoud (ed.), in Oxford World's Classics Edition. Oxford: Oxford University Press.

Conrad, Joseph (1984), *Nostromo: A Tale of the Seaboard*, Keith Carabine (ed.), in Oxford World's Classics Edition. Oxford: Oxford University Press.

Conrad, Joseph (1955), *Tales of Hearsay* and *Last Essays*. Dent Collected Edition. London: Dent. Each work is separately paginated in this double volume. All quotations from 'The Tale' are taken from *Tales of Hearsay* in this volume.

Conrad, Joseph (1947), *The Arrow of Gold. A Story Between Two Notes*. Dent Collected Edition. London: Dent.

Conrad, Joseph (1946), *The Mirror of the Sea* and *A Personal Record*. Dent Collected Edition. London: Dent. Each work is separately paginated in this double volume.

Conrad, Joseph (1997), *The Nigger of the 'Narcissus': A Tale of the Forecastle*, Allan Simmons (ed.), in Everyman Centennial Edition. London: Dent. All quotations from this work are taken from this edition.

Conrad, Joseph (1950), *The Nigger of the 'Narcissus', Typhoon, Falk, and Other Stories*. Dent Collected Edition. London: Dent. See previous entry. All quotations from 'Falk' and 'To-morrow' are taken from this edition.

Conrad, Joseph (1949), *The Rescue: A Romance of the Shallows*. Dent Collected Edition. London: Dent.

Conrad, Joseph (1990), *The Secret Agent. A Simple Tale*, Bruce Harkness and S.W. Reid (eds), in The Cambridge Edition of the Works of Joseph Conrad. Cambridge: Cambridge University Press.

Conrad, Joseph (2003), *The Shadow-Line. A Confession*, Jeremy Hawthorn (ed.), in Oxford World's Classics Edition. Oxford: Oxford University Press.

Conrad, Joseph (1947), *'Twixt Land and Sea*. Dent Collected Edition. London: Dent. All quotations from 'A Smile of Fortune', 'The Secret Sharer', and 'Freya of the Seven Isles' are taken from this edition.

Conrad, Joseph (2003), *Under Western Eyes*, Jeremy Hawthorn (ed.), in Oxford World's Classics Edition. Oxford: Oxford University Press.

Conrad, Joseph (2004), *Victory: An Island Tale*, Mara Kalnins (ed.), in Oxford World's Classics Edition. Oxford: Oxford University Press.

Conrad, Joseph (1950), *Within the Tides: Tales*. Dent Collected Edition. London: Dent. All quotations from 'The Planter of Malata' are taken from this edition.

Conrad, Joseph (1984), *Youth, Heart of Darkness, The End of the Tether*, Robert Kimbrough (ed.), in Oxford World's Classics Edition. Oxford: Oxford University Press. See also entry for *Heart of Darkness and Other Tales* above. All quotations from 'The End of the Tether' are taken from this edition.

Letters written by Joseph Conrad

Karl, Frederick R. and Davies, Laurence (eds), (1986), *The Collected Letters of Joseph Conrad*. Vol. 2. 1898–1902. Cambridge: Cambridge University Press.

Karl, Frederick R. and Davies, Laurence (eds), (1988), *The Collected Letters of Joseph Conrad*. Vol. 3, 1903–1907. Cambridge: Cambridge University Press.

Karl, Frederick R. and Davies, Laurence (eds), (1990), *The Collected Letters of Joseph Conrad*. Vol. 4, 1908–1911. Cambridge: Cambridge University Press.

Karl, Frederick R. and Davies, Laurence (eds), (1996), *The Collected Letters of Joseph Conrad*. Vol. 5, 1912–1916. Cambridge: Cambridge University Press.

Davies, Laurence, Karl, Frederick R., and Knowles, Owen (eds), (2002), *The Collected Letters of Joseph Conrad*. Vol. 6, 1917–1919. Cambridge: Cambridge University Press.

Davies, Laurence and Stape, J.H. (eds), (2005), *The Collected Letters of Joseph Conrad*. Vol. 7, 1920–1922. Cambridge: Cambridge University Press.

Newspapers

I have looked at newspapers from two periods and two places. First, I have consulted microfilms supplied by the British Library of local newspapers available to Conrad during his stay in Mauritius from 7 August to 30 September 1888. These include the following newspapers: *Journal de Maurice*; *République Française*; *The Commercial Gazette*; *Le Progrès Colonial*. Some of the text of these papers is hard to read – the effect of smudged printing being compounded by effects of age and reproduction. I have referenced issues but not pagination, as the latter is not always unambiguous.

Second, I have looked at the London *Daily Mail* during the period in which the drama of the Crippen case was reported, a period during which Conrad wrote some articles for the paper.

Critical and other works

Austen, Jane (1934), *Mansfield Park: A Novel*, in R.W. Chapman (ed.), *The Novels of Jane Austen*, vol. III. Third edition. London: Oxford University Press.

Bagnall, Peter (1999), 'Joseph Conrad and Jack the Ripper'. PhD Thesis, University of Oxford.

Baines, Jocelyn (1971), *Joseph Conrad: A Critical Biography*. First published, 1960. London: Penguin.

Belcher, Mary Gifford (1981), 'A Critical Edition of Joseph Conrad's "An Outcast of the Islands"'. PhD thesis. Lubbock: Texas Tech University.

Billy, Ted (1997), *A Wilderness of Words: Closure and Disclosure in Conrad's Short Fiction*. Lubbock: Texas Tech University Press.

Bock, Martin (2002), *Joseph Conrad and Psychological Medicine*. Lubbock: Texas Tech University Press.

Bristow, Joseph (1997), *Sexuality*. London: Routledge.

Carabine, Keith (2005), '"A very charming old gentleman": Conrad, Count Szembek, and "Il Conde"'. *Conradiana* 37 (1–2), 57–77.

Christie, Agatha (1960), *Murder is Easy*. First published, 1939. Glasgow: Fontana/Collins.

Collits, Terry (2005), *Postcolonial Conrad: Paradoxes of Empire*. London and New York: Routledge.

Conrad, Jessie (1926), *Joseph Conrad as I Knew Him*. London: William Heinemann.

Conrad, Jessie (1935), *Joseph Conrad and his Circle*. New York: E.P. Dutton.

Dickens, Charles (1971), *Bleak House*. Norman Page (ed.). Harmondsworth: Penguin.

Dolan, Paul J. (1969), '"Il Conde:" Conrad's Little Miss Muffett'. *Conradiana* 1(3), 107–11.

Dryden, Linda (2000), *Joseph Conrad and the Imperial Romance*. Houndmills: Palgrave.

Elbert, Monika (2001), 'The Ligeia syndrome, or, many "happy returns," in Conrad's gothic'. *Conradiana* 33(2), 129–52.

Erdinast-Vulcan, Daphna (1999), *The Strange Short Fiction of Joseph Conrad: Writing, Culture, and Subjectivity*. Oxford: Oxford University Press.

Ford, Jane (1995), 'An African encounter, a British traitor and *Heart of Darkness*'. *Conradiana* 27(2), 123–34.

Ford, Jane (1985), 'James Joyce and the Conrad connection: the anxiety of influence'. *Conradiana* XVII(1), 3–17.

Genette, Gérard (1980), *Narrative Discourse: An Essay in Method*. Jane E. Lewin (trans.). Ithaca NY: Cornell University Press.

Goldsmith, Oliver (1966), *She Stoops to Conquer: Or, The Mistakes of a Night*, in Arthur Friedman (ed.), *Collected Works of Oliver Goldsmith*, vol 5. Oxford: Clarendon Press, 102–217.

Graver, Lawrence (1969), *Conrad's Short Fiction*. Berkeley and Los Angeles: University of California Press.

Greene, Graham (1969), 'The domestic background'. (Review of Jessie Conrad [1935].) In Graham Greene, *Collected Essays*. London: The Bodley Head, 185–7.

Hagopian, John V. (1965), 'The pathos of "Il Conde"'. *Studies in Short Fiction* 3, 31–8.

Halvorson, John and Watt, Ian (1991), 'Notes on Jane Anderson: 1955–1999'. *Conradiana* 23(1), 59–87.

Hampson, Robert (2001), 'Silence and secrets in Joseph Conrad's *Victory*'. *Chia Journal of Humanities and Social Sciences* 3, 225–46.

Harpham, Geoffrey Galt (1996), *One of Us: The Mastery of Joseph Conrad*. Chicago and London: University of Chicago Press.

Hawthorn, Jeremy (1996), *Cunning Passages: New Historicism, Cultural Materialism and Marxism in the Contemporary Literary Debate*. London: Arnold.

Hawthorn, Jeremy (1983), *Multiple Personality and the Disintegration of Literary Character*. London: Edward Arnold.

Hawthorn, Jeremy (2001), 'Power and perspective in Joseph Conrad's political fiction: the gaze and the other', in Gail Fincham and Attie de Lange (eds), *Conrad at the Millennium: Modernism, Postmodernism, Postcolonialism*. New York: Columbia University Press, 275–307.

Hawthorn, Jeremy (2003), 'The richness of meanness: Joseph Conrad's "Tomorrow" and James Joyce's "Eveline"', in Jakob Lothe, Juan Christian Pellicer and Tore Rem (eds), *Literary Sinews: Essays in Honour of Bjørn Tysdahl*. Oslo: Novus Press, 107–20.

Hervouet, Yves (1990), *The French Face of Joseph Conrad*. Cambridge: Cambridge University Press.

Hughes, Douglas A. (1975), 'Conrad's "Il Conde:" "A deucedly queer story"'. *Conradiana* 7(1), 17–25.

James, Henry (1999), *The Turn of the Screw*. Norton Critical Edition. Second Edition. Deborah Esch and Jonathan Warren (eds). New York: W.W. Norton.

Jones, Susan (1999), *Conrad and Women*. Oxford: Clarendon Press.

Joyce, James (2000), *Dubliners*. Introduction and notes by Terence Brown. London: Penguin.

Kaplan, Carola M (2005), 'Beyond gender: deconstructions of masculinity and femininity from "Karain" to *Under Western Eyes*'. In Carola M. Kaplan, Peter Mallios and Andrea White (eds), *Conrad in the Twenty-First Century: Contemporary Approaches and Perspectives*. New York: Routledge, 267–79.

Kehler, Joel R. (1976), '"The Planter of Malata": Renouard's sinking star of knowledge'. *Conradiana* VIII(2), 148–62.

King, Helen (2004), *The Disease of Virgins: Green Sickness, Chlorosis and the Problems of Puberty*. London: Routledge.

Kirschner, Paul (1966), 'Conrad and Maupassant: moral solitude and "A Smile of Fortune"'. *Review of English Literature* 7, 62–77.

Knowles, Owen (1979), 'Conrad and Mérimée: The legend of Venus in "The Planter of Malata"'. *Conradiana* 11, 177–84.

Knowles, Owen, and Moore, Gene M. (2000), *Oxford Reader's Companion to Conrad*. Oxford: Oxford University Press.

Lange, Robert (1992), 'The eyes have it. Homoeroticism in *Lord Jim*'. *Philological Papers* 38, 59–68.

Levin, Yael (2004), 'A haunting heroine: the dictates of an "irrealizable desire"'. *The Conradian* 29(1), 127–38.

Levin, Yael (2005), 'Conrad, Freud, and Derrida on Pompeii: a paradigm of disappearance'. *Partial Answers* 3(1), 81–99.

McShane, Frank (ed.) (1964), *Critical Writings of Ford Madox Ford*. Lincoln: University of Nebraska Press.

Mégroz, R. L. (1931), *Joseph Conrad's Mind and Method*. London: Faber and Faber.

Meyer, Bernard C. (1967), *Joseph Conrad: A Psychoanalytic Biography*. Princeton NJ: Princeton University Press.

Moser, Thomas C. (1957), *Joseph Conrad: Achievement and Decline*. Cambridge, Mass.: Harvard University Press.

Najder, Zdzisław (1983), *Joseph Conrad: A Chronicle*. Halina Carroll-Najder (trans.). Cambridge: Cambridge University Press.

Partridge, Eric (1984), *A Dictionary of Slang and Unconventional English*. Eighth edition. Paul Beale (ed.). London: Routledge & Kegan Paul.

Ray, Martin, (ed.) (1990), *Joseph Conrad: Interviews and Recollections*. London: Macmillan.

Retinger, J.H. (1941), *Conrad and his Contemporaries*. London: Minerva Publishing Company.

Rice, Thomas Jackson (2004), 'Condoms, Conrad, and Joyce', in Ellen Carol Jones and Morris Beja (eds), *Twenty-First Joyce*. Gainesville: University Press of Florida, 219–38.

Rimmon, Shlomith (1977), *The Concept of Ambiguity – The Example of James*. Chicago: University of Chicago Press.

Roberts, Andrew Michael (ed.) (1993), *Conrad and Gender*. Amsterdam and Atlanta: Rodopi.

Roberts, Andrew Michael (2000), *Conrad and Masculinity*. Houndmills: Macmillan Press.

Ruppel, Richard J. (2003), '"Girl! what? Did I mention a girl?" The economy of desire in *Heart of Darkness*'. In Philip Holden and Richard J. Ruppel (eds), *Imperial Desire: Dissident Sexualities and Colonial Literature*. Minneapolis and London: University of Minnesota Press, 152–71.

Ruppel, Richard (1998), 'Joseph Conrad and the ghost of Oscar Wilde'. *The Conradian* 23(1), 19–36.

Sacher-Masoch, Leopold (1997), *Venus in Furs*. Ware: Wordsworth.

Said, Edward W. (1996), *Joseph Conrad and the Fiction of Autobiography*. Cambridge, Mass.: Harvard University Press.

Said, Edward W. (1995), *Orientalism*. Reprinted with a new Afterword. London: Penguin Books.

Séaghdha, Barra Ó. (2005), 'Re-viewing Casement'. *The Irish Review* 33, 85–95.

Smollett, Tobias (1999), *The Adventures of Roderick Random*, Paul-Gabriel Boucé (ed.). This edition first published 1979. Oxford World's Classics Edition. Oxford: Oxford University Press.

Snyder, Katherine V. (1999), *Bachelors, Manhood, and the Novel 1850–1925*. Cambridge: Cambridge University Press.

Steinmann, Theo (1975), 'Il Conde's uncensored story'. *Conradiana* VII(1), 83–6.

Stott, Rebecca (1992), *The Fabrication of the Late-Victorian Femme Fatale*. Houndmills: Macmillan.

Thorburn, David (1974), *Conrad's Romanticism*. New Haven: Yale University Press.

Vicinus, Martha (1996), 'Turn-of-the-century male impersonation: rewriting the romance plot', in Andrew H. Miller and James Eli Adams (eds), *Sexualities in Victorian Britain*. Bloomington and Indianapolis: Indiana University Press, 187–213.

Watts, C.T. (ed.) (1969), *Joseph Conrad's Letters to R.B. Cunninghame Graham*. Cambridge: Cambridge University Press.

Watts, Cedric (1984), *The Deceptive Text: An Introduction to Covert Plots*. Brighton: Harvester.

Watts, Cedric (1985), 'The narrative enigma of Conrad's "A smile of fortune"'. *Conradiana* 17(2), 131–6.

White, Andrea (1993), *Joseph Conrad and the Adventure Tradition: Constructing and Deconstructing the Imperial Subject*. Cambridge: Cambridge University Press.

Williams, Gordon (1994), *A Dictionary of Sexual Language and Imagery in Shakespearian and Stuart Literature*. London: Athlone.

Williams, Gordon (1997), *A Glossary of Shakespeare's Sexual Language*. London: Athlone.

Wills, John Howard (1955), 'Adam, Axel, and "Il Conde"'. *Modern Fiction Studies* 1, 22–4.

Woolf, Virginia (1966), *Collected Essays*. Vol. 1. London: The Hogarth Press. Contains 'Mr Conrad' (1924), 302–8, and 'Mr Conrad: a conversation' (1923), 309–13

Woolf, Virginia. (1971), *Night and Day*. London: The Hogarth Press..

Zuckerman, Jerome (1964), '"A smile of fortune": Conrad's interesting failure'. *Studies in Short Fiction* 2, 99–102.

Index

Marshall, Archibald 161 n11
Marx, Karl and Marxism 78, 108
masculinity ii, 10, 13, 30, 43, 49,
    51, 62, 67, 72, 74, 76, 93, 94,
    102, 106, 129, 132, 136, 139,
    141–3, 148, 149
masks 43, 44, 117
masochism 9, 11, 14, 16, 61, 66,
    78, 79, 85–92, 95, 96, 98, 99,
    106, 107, 109, 112, 121, 122,
    125, 127, 129–31, 135, 140,
    142, 143, 148, 149
masquerade 93
Maupassant, Guy de 135, 136
    'Les Soeurs Rondoli' 163 n6
Mauritius 12, 15, 78, 80, 84, 85,
    87, 88, 95–8, 123, 140, 168
Mégroz, R.L. 17–19
melodrama 7, 79, 80, 103–105,
    126, 129, 153
Mérimée, Prosper 100, 101, 163
    n26
Meyer, Bernard C. 3, 11–13, 20,
    57, 58, 87, 96, 98, 139, 140,
    142, 171
Milton, John 6
mimicry 23, 108, 115, 117, 118,
    130, 155
mincing 50, 51
miscegenation 75
misogyny 3, 75, 93, 106
modernism 8, 26, 37, 38, 79
modernity 79
Moorsom, Robert 163 n24
Moser, Thomas C. 6, 7, 11, 13, 64,
    79, 91, 93, 171
murder 18, 50, 54, 80–5, 92, 93,
    105, 115, 117, 119, 120, 122,
    123, 125, 157
Mycielski, Zygmunt 22
Najder, Zdzisław 1, 2, 5, 8, 15, 22,
    96
narcissism 150

Nazism 113
Neve, Ethel le 85, 94
Nevinson, H.W. 57
obsession 12, 14, 58, 86, 79, 80,
    88–91, 93, 95, 99–102, 140, 141
Odysseus 118, 119, 154
onlookers 85, 89, 149
Ovid
    The Metamorphoses 57, 122
paedophilia and pederasty 21, 22
panopticism 150
pantomime 121
Partridge, Eric 47, 134, 159 n5, 159
    n6
Peeping Tom 131, 145
Perrault, Charles 105
phallicism and the phallus 22, 62,
    72, 112, 136, 142, 154
Pinker, J.B. 85
Polyphemus: see *Acis and
    Polyphemus*
Pompeii 20, 22, 32, 171
pornography 110
postcolonialism vi
postmodernism 145
power 7, 10, 12, 14, 15, 34, 35,
    37–9, 47, 51, 52, 54, 55, 61, 78,
    79, 81, 86, 87, 91, 92, 95, 97,
    99, 101, 103, 105–109, 113–15,
    117, 121, 122, 125, 128, 136,
    139, 140–45, 148, 150, 151,
    155, 156
privacy 5, 8–11, 14, 25, 36, 54, 57,
    109, 114, 117, 126, 143, 145,
    155, 156
prostitution 9, 27, 47, 111, 125, 126
psychoanalysis 3, 11, 20, 139
psychology 5, 6, 11, 64, 67, 78, 79,
    96, 113, 120, 121, 125
psychosis 125
puberty 138
Quinn, John 57
race 5, 14–16, 49, 75, 106, 120